D0225398

THE PUBLIC INTEREST

THE
PUBLIC
INTEREST

**A CRITIQUE
OF THE THEORY OF A POLITICAL CONCEPT**

By Glendon Schubert

GREENWOOD PRESS, PUBLISHERS
WESTPORT, CONNECTICUT

Library of Congress Cataloging in Publication Data

Schubert, Glendon A.
  The public interest.

  Reprint. Originally published: Glencoe, Ill. : Free
Press, 1961.
  Bibliography: p.
  Includes index.
  1. Public interest. I. Title.
[JC507.S35 1982]   320'.01'1   82-15509
ISBN 0-313-22364-5 (lib. bdg.)

320.011
S384

Copyright © 1960 by The Free Press, a Corporation

Designed by Sidney Solomon

Reprinted with the permission of The Free Press, a division of
Macmillan Publishing Co., Inc.

Reprinted in 1982 by Greenwood Press
A division of Congressional Information Service, Inc.
88 Post Road West, Westport, Connecticut 06881

Printed in the United States of America

10 9 8 7 6 5 4 3 2 1

To
Susan, Kathleen, and Robin

preface

It is impossible to say when a book begins in terms of its wellsprings; the catalyst for this work occurred in a dialogue during the initial two weeks of the 1955 fall term, when Norton E. Long became both my colleague and my office-mate for a while. During this long, but by no means lost, academic weekend, Professor Long played a role in which he excels—that of Socrates, of course; and I—there was really no choice—I was cast as a Sophist. It was, for me anyway, an immensely exhilarating, if somewhat debilitating, intellectual experience. It had to end, or at least diminish, when the normal pressures of academic life brought about an enforced preoccupation with realities closer at hand than the ultimate questions of political responsibility in the Athenian democracy, or in Utopia, or even in the United States.

The matter doubtless would have rested thus as an episode, a fleeting moment of euphoria in the midst of ennui, were it not for the fact the Professor Long had agreed to lead a panel discussion on the general theme of responsibility in political decision-making, to be held at the annual meeting of the Midwest Conference of Political Scientists, in Milwaukee, the following May. I was delighted to accept his invitation to prepare a panel paper discussing political responsibility in administrative and judicial decision-making; not least so because the other panel papers were to be read by such distinguished political scientists as Professors Hans Morgenthau and Leo Strauss, of the University of Chicago, and Philip Monypenny, of the University of Illinois. Under such circumstances, I felt bound to undertake a careful and systematic examination of the literature in the fields which were to be my responsibility.

The resulting paper subsequently was published in the form of two articles, one [1957b] in the *American Political Science Review* and the other [1958a] in the *Midwest Journal of Political Science*. I should like to record my gratitude to the editors of these journals, and to Evron M. Kirkpatrick of the American Political Science Association and to Harold A. Basilius of Wayne State University Press, for their permission to rework the articles into the revised and extended form in which they appear. I am indebted to Alexander J. Morin for having first suggested the desirability of expanding the articles into a longer essay which would consider the theory of the public interest in more general terms. Similar encouragement and advice were provided by Dean Wayne A. R. Leys, of Roosevelt University, Co-chairman (with Charner M. Perry) of the Committee to Advance Original Work in Philosophy, of the Western Division of the American Philosophical Association.

The research and the writing of the extended essay which constitutes this book were made possible by a grant from the Legal and Political Philosophy Program of the Rockefeller Foundation; in particular, through the sympathetic interest of Dr. Kenneth W. Thompson. I should also like to acknowledge my appreciation for the interest in this work (and in the related activities of Dean Ley's committee) evinced by Alfred de Grazia, Managing Editor of that budding journal of applied political theory, *The American Behavioral Scientist* [formerly *PROD*]. I have profited from an exchange of correspondence with Professor Arthur S. Miller, of the Lamar School of Law of Emory University, who shares my interest in the theory and practice of responsible political behavior.

During the summer of 1958, I presented a series of lectures on public-interest theory at the Summer Institute of Executive Development for Top-Level Federal Administrators, convened under the auspices of the University College of the University of Chicago. The comments of several of the "students" attending the Institute were extremely valuable to me in reformulating my own thinking about some aspects of the subject. In particular, I am grateful to Dr. Stanley Gabis, presently my colleague but then the Director of the Institute, for having invited me to participate in the work of this program.

Heinz Eulau, of Stanford University, read and offered detailed criticisms upon the entire manuscript; his suggestions were invaluable to me in the task of revising the work for publication. I wish to give more than routine acknowledgment of my appreciation of the interest manifested by my editor, Jeremiah Kaplan, who also read an early draft of the entire manuscript.

To Mrs. Celia Lapham, I am indebted for an exceptionally accurate and competent job of typing. Finally, but not least, I must express my thanks to Alvin Dozeman, formerly graduate assistant in political science at Michigan State University, who checked the citations and prepared the index, among other tasks, and who worked with diligence and ingenuity as my research assistant and general rear echelon during an academic year that I spent abroad. His assistance and the typing of the manuscript both were made possible by successive grants from the All-University Research Fund of Michigan State University.

Particularly in a work dealing with a controversial theme, is it important to perpetuate the academic custom of relieving the persons acknowledged from any responsibility for errors that may be inferred from, or detected in, the presentation or interpretation of the data discussed below. In seeming contrast to the more elusive pin-pointing of responsibility for the political decision-making with which the book is concerned, fixing responsibility for the book itself is ridiculously easy. To this end,

I shall borrow, if it is not presuming too much, the slogan from a placard which (it is said) used to adorn the desk of President Truman: "The buck stops here."

Oslo, Norway   GLENDON SCHUBERT
November, 1959

contents

prologue: a trilogy

I. The Rational Query

A former congressman, who is now a professor of political science, asks whether it is possible to have a responsible political majority under the American system of government:

> With President, Congress, and perhaps even the Court, in deadlock, there is no referee. There is no way to determine the will of the people; there is no obtainable majority, no responsibility to anyone for anything. . . .
> In our system of separation of powers, the bitter struggle between the executive and legislature is inevitable, inexorable, and continuous. The excuse is a different interpretation of the public interest, but the stakes are power. Nor do we have any method for determining who

1

represents whom or what. I have personally sat many hours on the floor of the United States House of Representatives, watching an irresponsible and sometimes angry group of men tear to pieces a significant proposal emanating from the White House. When all or much of this opposition consisted of members of the President's party, one could not help but wonder what ought to be done. Who was right? Who did represent the members of the Democratic party? Who represented the American people? This group would often be joined by all or most of the opposition party, forming a majority in the House which could defeat the measure, or amend it into unacceptability or impotence.

The important question, then, is not who was right or who represented whom. The question is—and in a democratic society it *must* be answered—how are you going to find out? How do you determine the people's will? The public interest? [McMurray, 1958, p. 179.]

II. The Idealist Dialectic

TWO GREAT AMERICANS, each of whom had immeasurable influence upon American political institutions, and who together symbolize the antipodes of American political thought, face each other across a conference table. The occasion is probably a meeting of the cabinet, toward the close of the first term of Washington's administration. The scene was described almost half a century ago by a Columbia University historian: "Hamilton even went so far, in a political argument with Jefferson, as to bring his fist down on the table and shout, 'Your *people*, sir, is nothing but a great beast!' " [Muzzey, 1911, p. 192.]

A few years earlier, on June 18, 1787, Hamilton had attracted considerable attention among the other delegates by his speech to the Philadelphia Convention, in which he said:

[The] house of Lords is a most noble institution. Having nothing to hope for by a change, and a sufficient interest by means of their property, in being faithful to the National interest, they form a permanent barrier against every pernicious innovation, whether attempted on the part of the Crown or of the Commons. . . . All communities divide themselves into the few and the many. The first are the rich and well born, the other the mass of the people. The voice of the people has been said to be the voice of God; and however generally this maxim has been quoted and believed, it is not true in fact. The people are turbulent and changing; they seldom judge or determine right. Give therefore to the first class a distinct, permanent share in the government. They will check the unsteadiness of the second, and as they cannot receive any advantage by a change, they therefore will ever maintain good government. Can a democratic assembly who annually resolve in the mass of the people, be supposed steadily to pursue the public good? Nothing but a permanent body can check the imprudence of democracy. [Farrand, 1937, pp. 228–89, 299.]

Perhaps the most trenchant criticism of Colonel Hamilton, and of the political philosophy for which he served as spokesman, has come from an American poet of the twentieth century. Carl Sandburg, definitive biographer of Lincoln and champion of Americana, has undertaken to articulate the authentic voice of the people, in his reply to Alexander Hamilton:[1]

In the days of the cockade and the brass pistol
Fear of the people brought the debtors' jail.
The creditor said, "Pay me or go to prison,"
And men lacking property lacked ballots and citizenship.
Into the Constitution of the United States they wrote a fear
In the form of "checks and balances," "proper restraints"
On the people so whimsical and changeable,
So variable in mood and weather.

Lights of tallow candles fell on lawbooks by night.
The woolspun clothes came from sheep near by.
Men of "solid substance" wore velvet knickerbockers
And shared snuff with one another in greetings.
One of these made a name for himself with saying
You could never tell what was coming next from the people:
"Your people, sir, your people is a great beast,"
Speaking for those afraid of the people,
Afraid of sudden massed action of the people,
The people being irresponsible with torch, gun and rope,
The people being a child with fire and loose hardware,
The people listening to leather-lunged stump orators
Crying the rich get richer, the poor poorer, and why?
The people undependable as prairie rivers in floodtime,
The people uncertain as lights on the face of the sea

---

1. Carl Sandburg, *The People, Yes* (New York: Harcourt, Brace, 1936), pp. 52–54. Reprinted by permission of Harcourt, Brace and Company, Inc.

Wherefore high and first of all he would write
God, the Constitution, Property Rights, the Army and the Police,
After these the rights of the people.

  The meaning was:
The people having nothing to lose take chances.
The people having nothing to take care of are careless.
The people lacking property are slack about property.
Having no taxes to pay how can they consider taxes?
"And the poor have they not themselves to blame for their poverty?"

Those who have must take care of those who have not
Even though in the providence of events some of
Those who now have *not* once *had* and what they had *then*
Was taken away from them by those who *now have*.

  Naughts are naughts into riffraff.
  Nothing plus nothing equals nothing.
  Scum is scum and dregs are dregs.
  "This flotsam and jetsam."

There is the House of Have and the House of Have-Not.
God named the Haves as caretakers of the Have-Nots.
This shepherding is a divine decree laid on the betters.
"And surely you know when you are among your betters?"

  This and a lot else was in the meaning:
  "Your people, sir, is a great beast."
  The testament came with deliberation
  Cold as ice, warm as blood,
  Hard as a steel hand steel-gloved,
  A steel foot steel-shod
  For contact with another testament:
  "All men are born free and equal."

The cow content to give milk and calves,
The plug work-horse plowing from dawn till dark,
The mule lashed with a blacksnake when balking—
Fed and sheltered—or maybe not—all depending—
A pet monkey leaping for nuts thrown to it,
A parrot ready to prattle your words
And repeat after you your favorite oaths—
Or a nameless monster to be guarded and tended
Against temper and flashes of retaliation—
These were the background symbols:
  "Your people, sir, is a great beast."

III. The Realistic Question

ANOTHER COLUMBIA UNIVERSITY HISTORIAN, who was a political scientist as well, became famous for his economic interpretation of the Constitution and for a parody of Plato's classic dialogue, which he also called *The Republic*. In another book, published in the heyday of the New Deal, Charles Austin Beard undertook a critical examination of *The Idea of National Interest*. Beard found that, from the beginning of government under the Constitution, there had always been an intimate relationship between the claims of *special* interests and the definition of the *public* or national interest. "According to one common hypothesis," Beard wrote, "business enterprise discovers what is good for itself, and whatever is good for business enterprise is *ipso facto* good for the country." [Beard, 1934a, p. 412.][2]

Two decades later, the inauguration of President Eisenhower marked the replacement of the Fair Deal by Modern Republicanism. At the hearing on the question of confirming his nomination as Secretary of Defense, Charles Erwin Wilson[3] was being interrogated by a committee of the Senate, particularly in regard to the possibility of a conflict of interest arising out of Wilson's large holdings in General Motors stock. What would Wilson do, asked a senator, if he were Secretary of Defense and faced with a decision in which the interests of General Motors conflicted with the interests of the United States?

Mr. Wilson replied without hesitation, confidently uttering what proved to be merely the first of a series of celebrated malapropisms:[4] ". . . for years I thought what was good for the country was good for General Motors, and vice versa." He was promptly and generally misquoted, even by responsible com-

2. From C. A. Beard and G. H. E. Smith, *The Idea of National Interest* (New York: Macmillan, 1934). Reprinted by permission, as are other quotations from the same work that appear elsewhere in this volume.

3. Charles Erwin became known colloquially in Washington as "Engine Charlie" Wilson, to distinguish him from President Truman's then recently resigned Director of Defense Mobilization, Charles Edward ("Electric Charlie") Wilson. Democrat Wilson had been an executive of General Electric; Republican Wilson, an executive of General Motors.

4. *New York Times*, January 24, 1953, p. 8, col. 8.

mentators,[5] as having made the statement [cf. Blough, 1958, p. 16] which became associated with his name: "What is good for General Motors is good for the country."

Less than two years later, Secretary Wilson was being interviewed by a journalist, with special reference to an increase in unemployment among auto workers in the Detroit area. As the former president of General Motors, Wilson could speak on the subject with considerable expertise, apart from his authority as Secretary of Defense to approve an increase in defense contracts for the automotive industry in the Detroit area. Such an increase would, of course, help to alleviate unemployment; it would also help General Motors (among other auto manufacturers); but would it help national defense? Secretary Wilson now faced, in actuality, precisely the kind of decision about which he had been questioned at the time of his confirmation.

Should the Defense Department give out more contracts in order to cut down on temporary unemployment? Secretary Wilson, always the soul of candor, ventured an allegorical reply:[6] "I've always liked bird dogs better than kennel-fed dogs myself—you know, one who'll get out and hunt for food rather than sit on his fanny [haunches] and yelp [yell]." Walter Reuther, head of the UAW-CIO, promptly demanded Secretary Wilson's resignation, charging that Wilson thought that American workers should be treated like dogs.[7] The labor press thenceforth began to refer to him as "Bird Dog" Wilson. Reuther made it clear that, in his view, he (Reuther) spoke for American workingmen, and *therefore* for the common man, for the American people.

Is what is good for General Motors good for the country? Is what is in the interest of the UAW in the public interest?

---

5. Cf. *New York Times*, February 14, 1954, sec. 6, p. 11, col. 4, and February 28, 1954, sec. 6, p. 4, col. 4.

6. *New York Times*, October 12, 1954, p. 13, col. 4. On the following day, an expurgated version of Mr. Wilson's remarks, which involved essentially the substitution of the bracketed words, was printed. *New York Times*, October 13, 1954, p. 14, col. 4, 6.

7. *New York Times*, October 13, 1954, p. 1, col. 2, and p. 14, col. 3, 4–6.

the quest for responsibility

> Who shall speak for the people?
> Who has the answers?
> Where is the sure interpreter?
> Who knows what to say?
>
> Sandburg, *The People, Yes.*

The search for forms of government conducive to responsible decision-making is as old as political philosophy. Taking Western political thought as an example, we find that Plato suggested, in the *Republic* and in the *Laws,* two of the three general theories of responsible decision-making that we shall examine in this book. Fashions change, however, including fashions in the use of political concepts; and the verbal formula which denotes the idea of responsible official decision-making for Americans in the twentieth century is "the public interest." The concept of the public interest lies at the heart of democratic theories of government. Systematic and critical analysis of this concept is a means of investigating what Americans mean by governmental responsibility in a democracy.

There are various ways in which such an investigation might be made; it certainly would be possible to begin with Plato and trace the historical evolution of analogous concepts, such as Locke's theory of royal prerogative or Rousseau's *volunté géné-rale*. [Cf. Leys and Perry, 1959, p. 15.] I propose, however, to follow a different course, focusing attention upon the concepts of the public interest generally accepted by Americans today. The philosophical heritage of the past has operational significance for the behavior of officials today only to the extent to which it is reflected in the thinking of the present generation of Americans. What I will discuss, therefore, is the relationship between concepts of the public interest and concepts of official behavior. Our concern will be with the nexus between political theory and political behavior.[1]

A behavioral approach to the study of the public interest in governmental decision-making assumes that neither "the American people," nor special interest groups, nor political parties, nor the Congress, nor the presidency, nor administrative agencies, nor plural courts are capable of deciding *anything*, except in a metaphysical sense. The atom of organizational behavior remains the individual; we can understand how and why complex aggregations of persons (which we term "groups" or "organizations") act only by examining the behavior of the individual actors, who are human beings.[2] The decision of the individual, in turn, has meaning only as part of a process, being shaped by the antecedent decisions of other persons and entering as a factor in the subsequent decisions of still others. When we take into consideration such social dimensions, all decision-making by governmental officials is a factor in group (or institutional) decision-making. [Snyder *et al.*, 1954, pp. 63–64.] From this point of view,

---

1. By political "behavior," I refer to a contemporary interdisciplinary movement among social scientists, rather than to an outmoded brand of psychology.
2. As John Dewey has said, "[the public] arrives at decisions, makes terms and executes resolves only through the medium of individuals. They are officers; they represent a Public, but the Public acts only through them" [1927, p. 75].

the focus for decision-making analysis should be upon the inter-action of individuals who are confronted with the obligation of making choices as part of their official responsibility.[3]

It will be some time, however, before it will be possible to base an investigation, such as I have proposed, upon empirical studies in the social psychology of official decision-making. Except in a most fragmentary way, such research has not yet been under-taken in groups as complex as a department of the federal gov-ernment, to say nothing of the Congress or the presidency. On the other hand, a theoretical analysis, which conceivably might lead to a statement of the concept of the public interest in opera-tional terms,[4] would constitute an "island" of systematic theory[5] that could be subjected to empirical validation by behavioral scientists—assuming for present purposes that the public interest concept may have some utility for scientific investigation. In default of any systematic analysis of the concept of "the public interest" by political philosophers,[6] and in lieu of a theory based upon behavioral studies of decision-making that have not yet been made, what research strategy is open to a political scientist who seeks a better understanding of the theory of the public interest?

---

3. "Decision-making is a process which results in the selection from a socially defined, limited number of problematical, alternative projects of one project intended to bring about the particular future state of affairs envisaged by the decision-makers" [Snyder et al., 1954, p. 57].

4. For an example of the operationalization of a behavioral concept, see March [1955, pp. 431–51].

5. Guetzkow [1958, pp. 266, 281]; and Easton: "[Systematic theory] consists, first, of a set of concepts corresponding to the important political variables and, second, of statements about the relations among these con-cepts. . . . [It] corresponds at the level of thought to the concrete em-pirical political system of daily life" [1953, p. 98].

6. It should be noted, however, that the first step in this direction was taken in the spring of 1958. The Western Division of the American Phil-osophical Association established, at that time, the Committee to Advance Original Work in Philosophy, under the co-chairmanship of Dean Wayne A. R. Leys of Roosevelt University and with the assistance of a grant from the Humanities Division of the Rockefeller Foundation. The avowed objective of the committee was that of "organizing a research program based on the unsatisfactory state of the theory of the public interest." See De Grazia [1958] and Leys [1958]. For the Committee's initial published report, see Leys and Perry [1959].

Notions of the public interest not only exist, among both officials and students of politics, but they are widespread and frequently articulated. Certainly they affect both many of the actual choices that officials make and the descriptions and analyses of governmental responsibility made by scholars, journalists, and other observers. Thus conceived, the *concept* of the public interest is itself part of the data of political behavior. A possible research strategy would be to critically analyze the statements about the public interest to be found in political-science literature of the past generation and the present. It is not unreasonable to assume that a broad sampling of the political-science writings of the past thirty years is representative of the current state of American political thought on the subject of governmental responsibility; an understanding of the extant theory is necessary for any reformulation of the concept that might enable theory to better serve as the handmaiden of both practice and empirical research, assuming, as do Cassinelli [1958b, p. 61] and the Leys-Perry committee [1959, p. 5 and *passim*], that advances in public-interest theory are possible.

There is evidence to suggest that the time may be ripe for such a stocktaking.[7] Beginning in 1952, there have appeared a variety of articles and chapters which have consciously sought to focus upon the theory of the public interest: in relationship to the fields of public administration [Long, 1952 and 1954; Redford, 1954 and 1958; Macmahon, 1956; and Schubert, 1957b]; political parties [Schattschneider, 1952]; the legislative process [Huitt, 1954]; the judicial process [Schubert, 1958a]; community

7. Sorauf has suggested that "students of the domestic political process are waging a . . . debate [which] centers generally on the vadidity [sic] and applicability of concepts of the 'public interest' to the political process and policy-making. . . . [W]hile the emerging debate over the public interest has yet to develop into a first-class 'cause' in the learned journals or academic conventions, the rediscovery of Bentley's *Process of Government* and the prevalence of group interpretations of the political process have motivated a serious reexamination of the concept of the public interest" [1957, pp. 616, 617]. Within the next ten months, five other articles or comments upon public interest theory appeared in political science journals alone; my initial article on the public interest concept in administrative theory had appeared only a few months prior to Sorauf's, and at a time when his article was in the editor's hands awaiting publication.

development [Meyerson and Banfield, 1955]; and even political theory [Sorauf, 1957; Schubert, 1958b; Cassinelli, 1958a and b; and Leys, 1958]. The Western Division of the American Philosophical Association convened a symposium on public-interest theory at the society's meeting in May, 1959. A panel discussion of "The Concept of the Public Interest" was scheduled for the annual convention of the American Political Science Association in New York City early in September, 1960. The latter panel would also constitute the first session of the American Society for Political and Legal Philosophy, convening at the same time and place, which planned to make public-interest theory a major topic for discussion at their meeting.

Preceding this concentrated concern with public-interest theory in recent years, there was a period of a decade and a half, during which there was little, if any, writing on the subject of the public interest, at least by political scientists [see, however, Morstein Marx, 1949; and Dishman, 1951]. During the decade beginning with the publication of Dewey's classic volume [1927], however, there was another period in which several major contributions appeared [Dickinson, 1929 and 1930; Beard, 1934a and b; and Herring, 1936].

The Cacophony of Public Interest

MOST OF THE LITERATURE characteristically tends either to define the public interest as a universal, in terms so broad that it encompasses almost any type of specific decision, or else to particularize the concept, by identifying it with the most specific and discrete of policy norms and actions, to the extent that it has no general significance. What is conspicuously lacking is what might be called "middle-level" theory, specific enough to provide guiding norms for particular decisions and yet sufficiently general to be applicable to a wide variety of substantive questions and decision-making situations.

There is, moreover, irreconcilable conflict in the views of both the universalists and the particularists. Some of the universalists define the general will (public interest) as the widespread acceptance, among members of a society, of the legitimacy of organized political authority which mediates conflicts of interest within the society. Others hypostatize a "common good" of widely shared but quite specific values, which they view as a counterpoise in opposition to a host of "special interests." Still others conceive of a higher morality that transcends positive law and man-made political institutions; for these theorists, the public interest lies in the divination of, and obedience to, a system of norms that is perfect and absolute. Basing their arguments, either implicitly or explicitly, upon the same disparate fundamental assumptions, particularists find themselves in basic disagreement over the respective merits of the institutional arrangements and political processes by means of which government functions; the only point of consensus is that each argues that his formula is "democratic" and the only secure basis for organized political society. We are all democrats, all republicans; and in the Public Interest we place our trust.

Some argue "that the people can be unwise but cannot be wrong" [Finer, 1941, p. 339]; others share Hamilton's view that "the mass of the people . . . seldom judge or determine right," thus necessitating the enlightened ministrations of an intellectual and political aristocracy [Farrand, 1937, p. 299]; others deny the existence of "the people" as a political entity, suggesting that there is no public but that there are many publics, depending upon the time and the occasion.[8]

Some would strengthen political parties—or at least two of them—as the only potentially effective instruments for synthesizing, translating, and implementing the will of the people through governmental processes; others denounce political parties as a

---

8. Dewey: "The ramification of the issues before the public is so wide and intricate, the technical matters involved are so specialized, the details are so many and so shifting, that the public cannot for any length of time identify and hold itself. It is not that there is no public, no large body of persons having a common interest in the consequences of social transactions. There is too much public, a public too diffused and scattered and too intricate in composition. And there are too many publics, for conjoint actions which have indirect, serious and enduring consequences are multitudinous beyond comparison, and each of them crosses the others and generates its own group of persons especially affected with little to hold these different publics together in an integrated whole" [1927, p. 137].

"conspiracy against the nation." (The extremeness of the phrase should not blind us to the widespread distrust of political parties among Americans, of which there is abundant evidence; witness the popularity of "nonpartisanship" in municipal elections during the first half of the present century or, for a current example at the time of this writing, the proposal of one of the two contenders for the Democratic gubernatorial nomination in Michigan, whose platform includes a plank advocating a nonpartisan legislature for the state.)

Some argue that special-interest groups (or pressure groups) provide an essential avenue of functional representation, and that the requirements of a pluralistic society demand broad access by such groups to decision-making points in government; for these group theorists, the public interest is the resultant of the group struggle. Others consider special interests to be "selfish," and envisage a morality play in which the Common Good is placed in a never-ending conflict with selfish, private, Special Interests; but Men of Good Will must ensure the triumph of Virtue over Vice and, hence, the ultimate victory of the Public Interest over its many enemies.

Some see legislators as men who ought to carry out the instructions of either their constitutents (i.e., the people) or the political parties (i.e., the chosen instruments of the will of the people). Others (and this is the image which the legislators themselves usually propagate for public consumption) would atomize legislative assemblies, with each member cast in a role which requires him individually to study the facts, consult his own conscience, and vote for the "general interest" of all the people. And others argue that legislators do in fact, and ought in principle, to function as built-in lobbyists for special interests, consulting neither conscience nor party nor constituency (in the aggregate) as a guide to behavior.

Some would strengthen the American presidency, on the assumption that this is the only office that can serve as the instrument of a national majority and that can undertake (it should be added) a vigorous prosecution of programs which the president (as the interpreter of their will) deems to be "in the public interest." A recent example of this theory in action would be President Eisenhower's decision to land United States marines in Lebanon on July 15, 1958, and his accompanying official statement that this action would "demonstrate the concern of the United States for the independence and integrity of Lebanon, *which we deem vital to the national interest* and world peace." Presumably, the editorial "we" refers to "the American people"; so the President in effect said that it was in the public interest to dispatch troops to Lebanon. Others, who repeat (in the mid-1950's) the teachings of Wilson the academic (in the mid-1880's), and who disavow the example of Wilson the president, advocate the weakening of the presidency by subordinating it to the direction of Congress. The reformers who would substitute a modified parliamentary system for our present presidential system of national government find that it is in the public interest to minimize the personal discretion of the president; the same result is achieved by group theorists who would put the organization man in the presidency, substituting the institution for the man as decision-maker.

There are similar differences of professional opinion concerning the proper role of a responsible bureaucracy—and I specifically include within the concept of bureaucracy, for present purposes, not only administrative agencies but the so-called independent regulatory commissions and the courts as well. Some view the bureaucracy as the rational instruments of legislative and/or executive policy; public servants are thus perceived as agents of the public will. Others posit an independent role for a bureaucracy which will exercise "creative intelligence" to advance the public interest, as defined by the bureaucrats. Finally, there are those who see the bureaucracy as just another battleground for resolving the struggle for supremacy among multifarious competing groups.

In addition to those theorists who identify the public interest with particular institutional arrangements for the making of decisions, there are, of course, a large number of non-theorists who would equate with the public interest a miscellany of particular actions in a substantive sense. Thus, it is argued that it is in the public interest to have a high tariff on Swiss watches, or a low tariff on Swiss watches; it is in the public interest to have rigid price supports for selected agricultural products, and it is in the public interest to have a flexible program of parity controls; what is good for General Motors is good for the United States, and what is in the interests of the American workingman is in the interests of all of the people.[9] It is by such means that the promoters of special interests—who may be perfectly sincere in making their pleas—attempt to attract support for their positions (or to neutralize the potential opposition) by clothing a narrow and secular goal in the presumably more legitimate semantic garb of an appeal to the self-interest of Everyman.

If I have succeeded in correctly specifying the babel of many voices which characterize the meanings attributed to the public interest by both the practitioners of government and the professional students of their behavior, how can one hope to bring cosmos out of such chaos? Is it possible to speak of even a finite number of theories of the public interest, to say nothing of any single theory of the public interest? If it is possible to do this, it will probably be only within the framework of certain explicit and rigid limitations upon the scope of what is considered to be relevant to the concept and its investigation.

Two such limitations already have been stated: that the data for systematic analysis be largely limited to the writings of political scientists during the period of the three recent decades, 1927–58. A third limitation is to consider only the theorists who are concerned with how to define the concept, and to disregard substantive definitions of the concept in terms of particular public policies. In order to make this point clear, let us take, as an example, Charles A. Beard's *The Idea of National Interest* [1934a]. Beard's book is one of the few [such as Herring, 1936; and Meyerson and Banfield, 1955] that consciously have attempted to make use of "public interest" as a political concept for analytical purposes, and his is the only discussion of the historical evolution of the concept that I have encountered.

9. For other examples of substantive, secular identifications of the public interest, see Leys and Perry [1959, pp. 52–69].

National Interest and Public Interest

BEARD'S PARTICULAR CONCERN is with the concept in relationship to American foreign policy. Here, the term "national interest" is commonly employed as a synonym for what, in regard to domestic affairs, is called the public interest. Beard points out that the national interest is a modern concept, noting that, "although employed as if it were a fixed principle, somewhat like the law of gravitation, the idea of national interest is, relatively speaking, a newcomer among the formulas of diplomacy and international morality" [p. 4]. He identifies a number of "pivots of diplomacy," which are the historical antecedents of the idea of national interest. These are, in chronological sequence, the "will of the prince," "dynastic interests," the *"raison d'état,"* and "national honor." As Beard explains, the shifting from one formula to another symbolized the evolution of democratic government in the West; thus,

> With the establishment of parliamentary supremacy, the idea of state reason and state interest became largely obsolete in England, surviving longest in the language of the courts of law in dealing with high treason and other state cases. As use of the term declined, such notions as the interest of England, the public interest, and national interest took its place. [p. 16.]

Somewhat ironically, however, the newer terms quickly became vehicles for protecting the public against itself, by serving as the stereotyped verbal formulæ for the withholding of "official secrets" from both the people at large and their representatives:

> Although national interest was opposed to dynastic interest, its official interpreters might exclude the nation from knowledge of specific operations in foreign affairs on grounds of "the public interest." . . . [and now] When foreign offices, confronted by inconvenient questions from parliamentary bodies, decline to give out information, they do not appeal to any reason of state, but to the new slogan, "public interest." [pp. 25, 15.]

Beard wrote a quarter of a century ago. An observer of the Truman and Eisenhower administrations would note the considerable expansion that has taken place, in regard to domestic affairs, in the president's reliance upon his direct constitutional powers to withhold information and administrative documents from both the press and Congress, always with appropriate incantations which include the invocation of "the public interest." Beard's point is as timely as the latest headline.[10]

Beard traces the origins of the concept "national interest" to sixteenth-century Italy, and he finds that both variants of the formula—the national interest and the public interest—were commonly used in England by the end of the seventeenth century. The older variants—the will of the prince, dynastic interest, and state reasons—had no roots in the American colonies; but commonwealth or national interest became watchwords in the struggle for independence, and the "national honor" came to be frequently invoked (e.g., in the public papers and speeches of Theodore Roosevelt) [p. 17]. The term "national honor" had fallen into desuetude by the time Beard wrote, however, and now appears to have passed into oblivion. In its place, we have analogues: "the national interest," for use primarily in discussing foreign affairs; and "the public interest" for use primarily in discussing domestic affairs. Beard finds [p. 26; and cf. Chapter 2 and *passim*] that "the term, national interest, has been extensively employed by American statesmen since the establishment of the Constitution." Eisenhower's statement concerning the landing of the marines in Lebanon testifies to the continuing vitality of the phase.

Thus far, our discussion of Beard has been based upon his introductory chapter. The remainder of his book is devoted to extended analysis of the meaning of national interest in terms of substantive foreign policies (e.g., the acquisition of overseas bases and the expansion of foreign commerce versus continental territorial expansion). Beard identifies two conflicting concepts of national interest, stemming from Hamilton and Jefferson, re-

10. At the time of the 1951–52 steel seizure dispute, President Truman wrote a public letter to Charles E. ("Electric Charlie") Wilson, accepting his resignation as Director of Defense Mobilization, in which the President stated: "Since you have discussed at length in your letter certain matters relating to the current wage negotiations in the steel industry, I feel that I should make certain comments on that situation, although I fear that *no real gain for the public interest can come from airing such confidential matters* at this time." [Emphasis added; McConnell, 1960, p. 29.]

spectively. Each concept is an aggregate of specific, substantive, foreign-policy goals.[11] Writing during the honeymoon of the New Deal, Beard concluded that the two opposing concepts finally had merged in a synthesis which was "awaiting formulation at the hands of a statesman as competent and powerful as Hamilton or Jefferson" [p. 553]. It belabors the commonplace to remark that only eight years later, Beard must have deeply regretted his premature encomium for "that man" who was then entering upon his third term in the White House and who was about to lead the nation into a second world war.

A more recent example of a basically similar book, which is also concerned with a critical examination of American foreign policy, is Hans J. Morgenthau's *In Defense of the National Interest* [1951; and cf. Cook and Moos, 1953]. Morgenthau equates the national interest of the United States with a variety of substantive policy norms: *Real politik;* the balance-of-power system; anti-moralism and anti-internationalism; pro-MacArthur but anti-Truman/Acheson; anti-governmental-responsiveness to public opinion polls; etc.[12]

It happens that the Beard and Morgenthau books deal with the foreign-policy isotope of the concept, but they illustrate the insuperable problem implicit in any attempt to define the public interest in terms of substantive content, whether in regard to foreign policy or domestic policy.[13] Policies change with circumstances. Therefore, attempts to define the public interest in substantive terms necessarily build upon shifting sands.

Even if we are to confine our investigation to the process theorists, a fourth limitation is necessary in order to keep the scope of our inquiry within feasible bounds: that we shall concern ourselves with public-interest theory almost exclusively as

---

11. In a companion volume [1934b], Beard presented his own personal views on wise public policy in domestic and foreign affairs.

12. In a subsequent article, Morgenthau [1952, p. 973] defined national survival as the "irreducible minimum" of the national interest, "for it encompasses the integrity of the nation's territory, of its political institutions, and of its culture." For other contemporary substantive definitions of "national interest," see Leys and Perry [1959, p. 68].

13. For the statement of what I understand to be a contrary view, see Leys and Perry [1959, p. 45].

this relates to the *national* government. The reason for this limitation is perhaps best explained by examining the complexity of the interrelationships among the major components—which most political scientists doubtless would consider to be the functional prerequisites—of the American political system.

The Actors: Basic Decision-making Roles

1. The Public.—In a democracy, it generally is accepted that the *ultimate* source, at least, of political authority is the people. The people, yes, but which people? If we think of popular political action in terms of voting, almost half are legally disenfranchised by age, residence, and other requirements; furthermore, many of the electorate fail to exercise their franchise. The maximum level of voting participation, which occurs in presidential elections, includes little more than half of the American people who are legally qualified to vote. Active participation in the work of political parties is extremely low. Affiliation with interest groups and vicarious political participation, through group activity, represents a third alternative, the importance of which has been much emphasized by pluralists in recent decades. Contemporary empirical studies by sociologists, however, suggest that the notion that Americans are a nation of joiners is just another myth. Apart from perfunctory affiliation with churches and labor unions, which does not extend to active participation in group decision-making and the development of group policy, pilot research studies in urban communities indicate that most Americans do not belong to *any* organized group [Greer, 1958]. Interest groups are dominated by their professional bureaucracies and the supporting fractions of activists, which means that the voice of the interest group is neither *Vox Populi* nor *Vox Dei;* it is the voice of the Organization Man.

Nevertheless, orthodox theory suggests that the "public" engages in political action directly by selecting party nominees for public (and, sometimes, party) office in primary elections and by electing legislators and the chief executive.[14] (In state and local elections, popular choice extends directly to include many administrators, commissioners, and judges as well.) The public is supposed to influence the decision-making of public officials by direct personal communication with officials and, more importantly, by indirect functional representation through the agency of interest groups.

2. *Interest Groups.*—Interest groups are supposed to seek access to political parties as well as to public officials. Most groups prefer to appear to be nonpartisan (or bipartisan), but others affiliate with parties to the extent that, for instance, Michigan Republicans have charged for years that the state Democratic organization is dominated by the United Automobile Workers. In addition, it is assumed that interest groups attempt to "protect" the interests of their "members," by putting "pressure" upon legislators, the president, administrative agencies, and regulatory commissions. The recent notoriety enjoyed by the N.A.A.C.P. has provided conspicuous empirical evidence [see, e.g., Vose, 1958 and 1959] to support the argument, which group theorists have been advancing for years, that interest groups put pressure upon the courts as well.

3. *Political Parties.*—It is generally agreed that political parties do provide the candidates for elective (and many appointive) public offices, frequently under what are nominally nonpartisan as well as partisan systems of election and/or appointment. All elections to national office are nominally partisan; when the president crosses party lines to make important appointments, the event is sufficiently unusual to be newsworthy. Nominal nonpartisanship is more common in state and local elections. To use Michigan again as an example, justices of the state supreme court

14. Dewey has argued that: "We say in a country like our own that legislators and executives are elected by the public. The phrase might appear to indicate that the Public acts. But, after all, individual men and women exercise the franchise; the public is here a collective name for a multitude of persons each voting as an anonymous unit. As a citizen-voter, each one of these persons is, however, an officer of the public. He expresses his will as a representative of the public interest as much as does a senator or a sheriff" [1927, p. 75].

are nominated in open party conventions, photographed in group campaign pictures together with the other (partisan) candidates for state-wide office, and appear before the voters on a separate ballot labelled "nonpartisan."

There is some disagreement over this, but it is generally accepted that political parties are most virtuous when the majority party exercises a predominant, and perhaps determinative, influence upon the decision-making of legislators and the chief executive. The heads of at least the principal agencies—but not the regulatory commissions—are also supposed to be amenable to the control of the "majority" party; but for a political party to intervene in the decision-making of civil servants or judges is considered downright corrupt.

4. Legislators.—Our scene is becoming more complex as we proceed to add components. If we assume only one-way communication, limit our attention to only one level of government, and concern ourselves with only the first three actors, we have three types of political-action channels:

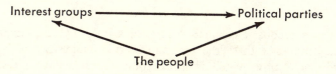

The addition of the legislature, however, *doubles* the number of channels:

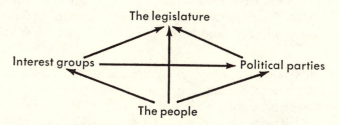

It is generally agreed that the legislature has the primary function of deciding basic issues of domestic public policy, and that legislative decision-making reflects, at least in substantial part, the complex intermixture of pressures emanating differentially from the people directly, from interest groups, and from political parties.

5. Chief Executives.—The addition of the chief executive increases the number of unilateral channels to ten, and this number is doubled if we take into consideration only one type (*inter*-variable) of "feedback" [Guetzkow, 1958, p. 272]. In the paradigm below, we portray (by loops) only the two most obvious feedbacks in presidential decision-making:

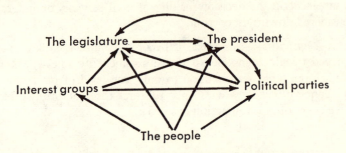

The two feedback channels portrayed signify (1) the unquestioned influence that "the program of the administration"—the yardstick against which it has become customary to measure both the success of presidential domestic leadership and the "productivity" of the Congress—has upon legislative decision-making, and (2) the influence exercised by the president within his party, as the recognized titular head (and, usually, the leader in fact) of the majority party—or, more accurately, the political party which "controls" the executive branch of government.

6. Administrative Agencies.—At this point, the limitations of a two-dimensional system of graphic representation become inadequate for portraying what is in fact a four-dimensional process. Administrative agencies are, supposedly, subject primarily to the policy norms and directive controls exercised by the president, Congress, and—by way of anticipation—the courts. There are, of course, feedback channels for all these administrative relationships; by no means of least significance are the *intra*variable feedbacks [Guetzkow, 1958, p. 272]. The feedback channel from administrative agencies to the people is certainly well recognized and important. The legitimacy of most of the remaining channels to and from administrative agencies is open to considerable question, according to the professional opinion of political scientists. But professional opinion changes; and, at least with regard to direct interest-group pressures on administrative decision-making, there appears to be growing acceptance of the pluralist view that special-interest influence is not a pernicious technique for the seduction of administrators but, rather, an essential vehicle for the full and free expression of points of view and consequences that ought to be considered in administrative decision-making.

There is an important body of theory which assumes that regulatory commissions are significantly different from other administrative agencies, in terms of functions performed, the structuring of decision-making processes, and the legitimate channels of responsibility. Adjudication is a conspicuous feature of the formalized decision-making of regulatory commissions, whose channels of responsibility are supposed to flow to Congress and the courts but not to the president. The danger of such commissions becoming the captives of their respective clienteles (i.e., the aggregates of special-interest groups most directly affected by commission decision-making) is thought to be particularly acute.

7. *Courts.*—Our seventh set of actors, judges, are supposed to have important feedback channels to most of the others, but particularly to regulatory commissions and other administrative agencies, to Congress, to the president, and to the people. On the other hand, the courts are, in orthodox theory, assumed to be independent of political influences and controls, except to the extent that the norms guiding judicial decision-making are supplied by (or logically deduced from) the Constitution (which instrumentalizes the "will of the people") and statutes (made by "the representatives of the people").

On stage thus far, we have five types of political actors, among whom free interaction is supposed to occur; and two types of bureaucratic actors (administrative agencies—including regulatory commissions—and courts), among whom interaction with the five political types is partially or almost completely inhibited—at least in theory. Two additional qualifications are necessary. The model system which we have described is essentially static, while the real political system which the model purports to describe is, of course, dynamic and in constant flux. Moreover, our model describes relationships for only one level of government, the national government, while there simultaneously coexist in the American federal system at least three other levels: international, state, and local. The latter alone consists of several thousand different "units" of government, many of which function at the same time, in the same place, in relationship to the same people. But to attempt to build dynamism and multisystems of government into our analytical system, even if this were possible, would make it so complex that it would be of little value as an aid to help us investigate public-interest theory.

Political Action: Five Factors for Analysis

WE HAVE ALREADY STATED that the fourth general limitation upon our inquiry is that we shall concern ourselves with public-interest theory as this relates to the national government only. The system of political action that we have sketched can be useful in two principal ways as we proceed with our investigation. In the first place, we should try to keep in mind the complex pattern of interaction existing among all the actors, even though we shall focus upon only one or two of these at a time. In the second place, it will be convenient to utilize these components as one of two major bases for classifying the data on public-interest theory that we shall examine. We shall modify these components only insofar as we shall group the three types of non-governmental (in the sense of public office) actors into a single aggregate component, which we shall term the constituency factor, and we shall consider each of the remaining four components to be a single factor (although pairs of these also could logically be combined to form more complex factors).[15] Thus, each of the next three chapters will be organized in terms of the following five factors:

a. Constituency (the public, political parties, and interest groups)
b. Congress
c. The Presidency
d. Administrators
e. The Judiciary

The Theorists: The Public-Interest Conceptual Triad

THE OTHER MAJOR BASIS for classifying the data borrows from a conceptual scheme suggested by philosopher Wayne A. R. Leys, in an article in which he took issue with the orthodox theory of administrative discretion that had dominated thinking in the field of administrative law for the preceding half-century—and that continues to hold sway in the writings of lawyers and political scientists alike. The godfather of orthodoxy was Ernst Freund, formerly Professor of Law at the University of Chicago, who taught that the solution to the problem of the official endowed with discretionary powers was to increase the *definiteness* of legal standards ("legal," in this context, meaning primarily statutes and administrative rules). The essence of Leys' critique is that Freund had oversimplified the problem by dealing with only one aspect of it. Leys himself would distinguish three classes of discretionary powers:

1) technical discretion, which is freedom in prescribing the rule but not the criterion or end of action;

---

15. It is possible, but inconvenient for present purposes, to combine the congressional and presidential components into a complex factor dealing with elective, "political" officials; and to combine the administrative and judicial components (which deal with appointive, "nonpolitical" offices) into a "bureaucratic" factor.

2) discretion in prescribing the rule of action *and also* in clarifying a *vague* criterion—this is the authorization of social planning;

3) discretion in prescribing the rule of action where the criterion of action is *ambiguous* because it is in dispute—this amounts to an instruction to the official to use his ingenuity in political mediation. [1943, p. 18.]

I have adapted Leys' basic system of classification in the following way. I shall divide contemporary theorists of the public interest in governmental decision-making into three groups: Rationalists, Idealists, and Realists. The Rationalists, who correspond to Leys' first category, envisage a political system in which the norms are all given, in so far as public officials are concerned, and the function of political and bureaucratic officials alike is to translate the given norms into specific rules of governmental action. The Idealists, who correspond to Leys' second category, conceive of the decision-making situation as requiring the exercise of authority in order to engage in social planning by clarifying a vague criterion. The Realists are the counterpart of Leys' third category; these theorists state that the function of public officials (both political and bureaucratic) is to engage in the political mediation of disputes; the goals of public policy are specific but in conflict. Both the Rationalists and the Realists are opposed to the Idealists, in the sense that both groups are positivists; but there are important differences in their respective theories of the public interest, and retaining Leys' classification system is of considerable help in discriminating between the differences.

In the next three chapters, we shall consider, in turn, the public-interest theories of the Rationalists, the Idealists, and the Realists, in relation to the five factor components of our model decision-making system of political action. In terms of major trends of thinking within political science, this sequence of chapters corresponds, at least roughly, to the chronology of principal shifts in emphasis among the three positions during recent decades. Generally speaking, Rationalist thought tended to dominate professional thinking at the beginning of the period that we shall examine, and the Realist position appears to be increasingly in-

fluential at the present time.[16] This generalization is subject, of
course, to the four limitations established on the scope of our
inquiry: we shall investigate the writings, by political scientists
during the past three decades, which discuss the public interest
in the decision-making of the national government, in terms of
processes of responsible decision-making rather than the substance of particular policies deemed wise or unwise.

There are, of course, various individual exceptions to what
I have described as major shifts in emphasis in the articulated
thinking of a profession consisting of more than five thousand
persons. Moreover, and speaking now in empirical terms, we
should not expect that the theoretical statements that we shall
examine will necessarily appear to be *consistent*, when they are
analyzed according to the classification schema that I have set
forth.[17] Most writers have considered only a single facet of the
public interest: with very few exceptions, professional thought
about the public interest has been segmented; writers have
focused upon specific components (such as Congress) or sub-
components (such as congressional investigating committees).
Thus, we should not be surprised to find the same writer, perhaps in the same paragraph or sentence, propounding (for example) Rationalist theory with regard to the presidency and

16. Heinz Eulau has argued, in correspondence, that I treat "the three
orientations (Rationalist, Idealist, Realist) as if they were contemporaries,
vying for the loyalty of scholars. But they are only partly so. True, contemporaries probably fall into the categories (and more so in shop-talk
than in writing), but I do feel that the bulk of polscientists today is taking
the Realist position. In other words, there has been some cumulative progress, if you wish, even if it is not apparent. Shouldn't this be acknowledged?" I am glad to acknowledge a differing opinion; but I feel obliged
to adhere to the position stated in the text; the cumulative progress of
which Professor Eulau speaks is not yet apparent to me. For an analysis
of some relevant evidence by another commentator, see Key [1958 pp. 964–68].

17. Leys and Perry have suggested that my "classifications might be regarded as ideal types rather than empirical groupings" [1959, p. 34]. Obviously, my conceptual apparatus for analyzing public interest theory, com-
bining as it does (1) an ideal refraction of the real system of political
action, and (2) an adaptation of a philosopher's typology of official decision-
making discretion, necessarily defines categories that are ideal rather than
real types. Of course, I do not claim that I derived my analytical categories
from "empirical groupings" of statements about the public interest.

Idealist theory with regard to Congress. Such inconsistencies reflect, at least in part, the general preoccupation of most of these
writers with particular institutions, and the frequent lack of any
consistent theoretical underpinnings for their work.

A concluding caveat must be given regarding my use of the
words "Rationalism," "Idealism," and "Realism." Some of the
writers we shall consider use one or another of these words in
describing their own general theoretical position as they perceive it. Most of them do not do so, however; and it is not unlikely that many of our subjects would disagree, perhaps vehe-
mently, with what they might consider to be my stigmatization
of their statements about public-interest theory.[18] As persons,
they might or might not accept classification as a "Rationalist"
or as an "Idealist." Since I am aware of, and sympathetic with,
this perfectly human kind of reaction, I wish to make it perfectly
clear that the last thing I would do is engage in the petty exercise
of pigeonholing *people* in little boxes. It is essential to my objective, however, to venture to make a consistent classification of
theoretical *statements;* whether or not my judgments have been
fairly and accurately made, the reader may determine for himself
by checking the citations.

All three of my key concepts may be considered ambiguous,
since they have been used by others who have given them definitions different from, and conflicting with, those that I have
used. A good example of this ambiguity is found in the problem
of classifying those writers who believe in natural law.[19] Various
of these persons call themselves "rationalists" and "realists";
others call themselves "idealists." As Dean Leys has pointed out:
"Among the contemporary Platonists and natural law men in
Philosophy there is a tendency to appropriate the label 'Realism'

---

18. David Truman, for instance, and with specific reference to my classification (in chap. 4, below) of his work discussing the public-interest
concept, considers that it "is somewhat inaccurate" to place him among
the followers of Arthur F. Bentley. Indeed, Truman appears to deny the
propriety of classifying *Bentley* among the Bentlians [Leys and Perry, 1959,
p. 37 n. 9], which will remind many readers of Freud's celebrated quip:
"I do not consider myself to be a Freudian."

19. Sorauf [1957, p. 627], for instance, calls Platonists "rationalist,"
while I have classified them as Idealists.

(meaning that they believe in the reality of Platonic universals)."[20] Obviously, *any* attempt to classify these writers is fraught with semantic difficulties. I have, therefore, defined and used these key concepts in a way that, in my opinion, best describes and discriminates among the central tendencies of these three theoretical positions. And although I use them freely, my intent is to eschew, not to enshrine, the tyranny of labels.

---

20. Letter to the author, dated February 27, 1956.

rationalist theory

> The people is Everyman, everybody.
> Everybody is you and me and all others.
> What everybody says is what we all say.
> And what is it we all say?
>
> Sandburg, *The People, Yes.*

The Rationalists are positivists, and many of them are logical positivists. They find both the ultimate and the proximate source of public-policy goals to repose in the people. Their assumptions, both explicit and implicit, are well summarized in the maxim, *vox populi, vox Dei*. The model of authority which they envisage is hierarchical, with the public on top and bureaucrats on the bottom. (We are reminded of Harold Laski's aphorism that the expert should be on tap, not on top.) Political parties function as a catalyst in defining the Public Will, and the job of the legislature is to translate the Public Will into law. It is the president's duty to oversee the faithful execution of the law by administrators; the duty of judges is to enforce The Law which, needless to say, is conceived of as a "seamless web."

Ideally, governmental decision-making processes become value-neutral technical processes, and the authority of public officials is the authority of expertise. Their job is to translate into specific rules of action the public-policy goals already determined by the decision of the people. It is in the public interest, therefore, to rationalize governmental decision-making processes so that they will automatically result in the carrying out of the Public Will. Human discretion is minimized or eliminated by defining it out of the decision-making situation; responsibility lies in autonomic behavior. *Vox populi* is *vox Dei*, but science is the *deus ex machina*.

According to a Realist critic:

> The will of the people . . . is regarded as a metaphysical first principle, supplying an absolute from which certain consequences can be deduced. Yet to possess meaning in political analysis, the concept must be defined in operational terms. How do you discover what the people want? . . . the will of the people . . . serves as a symbol to legitimize the acts of any group that can successfully identify itself with it in the public mind. [Long, 1952, p. 809.]

A. Constituency

THE STATEMENTS of the Rationalists abound with references to what they hypostatize as the common or general interest. The general interest is conceived of as being either those values which (it is assumed) all citizens necessarily share, or it is viewed as the lowest common denominator of values prevalent in American society. Rationalists are usually (but not always) careful to avoid defining the common interest in transcendental terms as an absolute interest of "the public." Frequently, Rationalists appear to be driven to rely upon ontological argument in their attempts to refute the Realist concept of a public interest arising out of group conflict. Professor R. M. MacIver, for instance, in a book that has been widely read by political scientists writes that:

"The public" might seem to be nothing but the amorphous residuum that lies outside the contending "pressure groups" of business large and small, of finance, of labor, of agriculture, of the organized professions, of the political bureaucracy itself, and so forth. The public interest might seem to be nothing but the diagonal of the forces that constantly struggle for advantage. Nevertheless, as we have sought to show, the whole logic of democracy is based on the conception that there is still a national unity and a common welfare. The fact that the interest in the common welfare cannot be organized after the fashion of specific interests should not conceal from us either its existence or the need to sustain it. Democracy itself is the final organization of the common interest. [1947, p. 220.]

Of course, when the public interest is identified with "common values" as broad in their scope as "the democratic way of life," we have learned nothing in particular in our quest for the meaning of "the public interest," since the concept "the democratic way of life" would undoubtedly be even more difficult to pin down and to comprehend as systematic knowledge than the object of our present investigation.

There are, however, two fairly specific notions in MacIver's argument: (1) the postulation of a metaphysical common interest, an entity which is more than the sum of its parts; and (2) opposition to the claims of any particular interest group, or any combination of interest groups, to define the common or public interest. MacIver does not, however, stop here; he seems to ally himself with the Idealists when he denies the right of majority rule, advocates what is known in constitutional law as the "preferred position" doctrine,[1] and talks about "universal good" and "universal rules" [1947, p. 221]. "Democracy," he concludes, "affirms the community." This anagram tells us little; it reads at least as well, and perhaps a little better, when it is inverted: the community affirms democracy. The phrase communicates just as much, and just as little, about the public interest in either form.

A political scientist who has attempted to describe the public interest in supramajoritarian terms is E. E. Schattschneider, who

---

1. The basic idea underlying this doctrine is that the freedoms postulated by the First Amendment to the Constitution of the United States are more fundamental than other constitutional rights and liberties; and, as a corollary, that among First Amendment freedoms, freedom of speech is perhaps most important of all.

speaks of ". . . the politics of survival, in which private and special interest conflicts are strongly subordinated to a dominant concern for the preservation of the great common interests of the nation" [1952, p. 22]. He then explains that "it is necessary only to remember that if the community is threatened, all special and private interests are equally jeopardized." This statement clearly assumes that "all special and private interests" perceive their self-interest in the continuation of the existing system of government, and that they behave rationally in terms of self-interest so perceived. This point of view should probably be interpreted as a normative proposition and as a specification of the way private and special interests *ought* to behave rationally —assuming that there really is a common interest in national survival. Obviously, the statement does not constitute a realistic description of the way many private and special interests do behave, in fact, in time of war or other national emergency. The farm bloc fights for parity (as in World War II) irrespective of the implications of such a position for general price controls; union leaders call strikes in defense industries; pacifists refuse to serve in the armed forces; Bundists provide aid and comfort for enemy spies and saboteurs; etc.[2]

Professor Schattschneider verges on the transcendental when he says that:

> The public interest may be described as the aggregate of common interests, including the common interest in seeing that there is fair play among private interests. The public interest is not the mere sum of the special interests, and it is certainly not the sum of the *organized* special interests. Nor is it an automatic consequence of the struggle of the special interests (a struggle in which everyone demands too much and feels entitled to it).

Schattschneider finds it easier to dispute the realist concept of the public interest, as in the quotation above, than to suggest a definition of his own. Having exorcised both special interests and local, particularistic interests, however, he concludes that:

> The only satisfactory political base for general policies concerning the public interest is a majority. . . . As long as majoritarian

---

2. Cf. the other-worldly comments on this point of an Idealist critic of the "common interest" notion [Cassinelli, 1958b, pp. 51–52].

politics is pursued in terms of controversies over the public interest, it may be carried on with great vigor without endangering the stability of the regime, because the public interest is best defended when competition for power is conducted on these terms. If the purpose is to exploit as fully and as effectively as possible the potentialities of general divisions about public interests, it follows that the form of political organization best adapted to this use is the political party. The parties are the only political organization established on a scale sufficiently extensive to mobilize a country-wide majority. However inadequate the traditional party structure may have been for these purposes, it is obvious that no other form of political organization can begin to compete successfully with it in a general conflict about broad policies for the control of government at its highest levels. [1952, pp. 24, 25.]

A number of specific propositions are adumbrated by Schattschneider's statement: the common interest as, basically, the majoritarian ethic; private, special, and local interests as enemies of the common interest; political parties as organizations which both synthesize and transcend the narrow demands of special interests; and the two-party system as the chosen instrument for implementing the will of the majority. V. O. Key seems to agree with at least the first three of these four propositions:

. . . from their nature political parties must seek to advance a program that will win the support of a majority of the people. . . . Political parties as a whole must attempt to gain the support of a larger constituency, and this endeavor requires a program at least ostensibly in the public interest. . . . The pressure group must appeal to the partial interest; the political party, to the common interest. [1952, p. 177.]

But the *reductio ad absurdum* of the majoritarian argument is offered by James MacGregor Burns in his book on Congress in which he states that:

In a democracy, majority rule is assumed to be the best means of discovering and satisfying the "public interest. . . ." The most democratic, stable, and effective type of majority . . . is a popular majority—namely, one-half of all the pooled votes throughout the nation, *plus one* (or more). [Emphasis added; 1949, p. 42.]

In empirical terms, a national popular majority of 50 per cent plus one voter could decide nothing; the abstraction is meaningless. No one can say, in the abstract, what kind of division such a popular majority might produce in the party composition of the House of Representatives or the Electoral College, but it could well be very one-sided. And if Professor Burns is really thinking of an Electoral-College plurality of one, the most likely result would be a national crisis (as in the Hayes-Tilden election) rather than a "stable, and effective type of majority." The American political system has not functioned, does not function, and is not likely to function in the future in response to the "will" of narrow popular majorities.[3]

The logic of the majoritarian formula implies the rejection of both the *preference* of minority to majority interests, and the *augmentation* of minority to majority interests. The public interest is identified with the interests of a majority, neither more nor less. The Rationalists' antipathy for special (i.e., minority) interests, combined with their sympathy for political parties, leads them to reject the Realist construct of a public interest which arises out of conflict among minorities, as exemplified in Schattschneider's somewhat negative definition of the public interest as an aggregate common interest. What the Rationalists object to in the Realist mechanics is that it equates the public interest with the interaction of group interests by processes *that go beyond* the accommodation provided by political party organizations; this, to the Rationalists, means the triumph of special (private, minority) interests over the public (common, general, majority) interest. The majoritarian formula also leads to the rejection of the Idealist metaphysic of absolute common good, which, to the Rationalists, suggests the inclusion of a variety of minority interests *in addition to* the majority interest. Thus, in the words of Professor Burns, "The problem arises when majority rule, in the strict sense of the term [50 per cent + 1 ?], is thrown overboard for the sake of exploiting some mystical unanimity or general will" [1949, pp. 188–89].

However this may be, substituting "popular will" for "general will" creates certain other problems. It is, I believe, generally accepted that the leading textbook on political parties and special interest groups is that of V. O. Key, and that Pendleton Herring's

---

3. For a more extended discussion of this issue, see McClosky [1949] and Kendall [1950].

The Politics of Democracy is among the most thoughtful commentaries on the American political process. Both Key and Herring are quite skeptical about the validity of the concept of "popular will." Key has written that:

> The notion of politics as the relationships between governor and governed, or as the pattern of balance or equilibrium between groups of diverse interests struggling for ascendancy, runs counter to such traditional doctrines as that of "popular self-government," the idea of the "general will," and the belief in government "of the people, by the people, and for the people." The view develops that government is identical with the mass of the population and that by some mysterious process the "will of the people" is translated into government decision and thereby the people "rule themselves." . . . Yet the assertion that people "rule themselves" does not constitute an entirely satisfactory description of the political process. . . . The problem of the politician or the statesman in a democracy is to maintain a working balance between the demands of competing interests and values. His task is not necessarily the expression of the "general will" or the "popular will." [3d ed.; 1952, pp. 9, 10.]

Herring, who is basically a group theorist, goes further. Raising doubts as to the empirical existence of popular majorities in regard to most issues most of the time, he also questions the desirability of having a public that is committed either pro or con on very many questions of public policy at any given time. Needless to say, this is rank heresy to the Rationalist position:

> The concept of the popular will can be given substance so long as a large mass of uncommitted minds can be aroused for a brief crisis of decision making. Policy is worked out by bargaining among individuals in terms of their conflicting ideals and interests. If a great mass is aligned behind each interest group leader, the bargaining process becomes all the more difficult. Thus the citizen who is not identified with a party, who does not habitually participate in politics, and whose support cannot be counted upon by any one group is the agent that keeps politicians uncertain of power and therefore responsive to the current of opinion. If all men were good citizens in the sense of being participants in all contests they would have to act in practice like declared partisans. This would bring too many political contests to a danger point of intensity. [1940a, pp. 32–33.]

Nevertheless, the Rationalists need the concept of popular will, because upon it they construct their normative theory of the American political-party system. The Rationalists require, somewhat after the fashion of God's covenant with Noah, that there be *two* political parties, both alike except for slight differences in gender.[4] These two parties, like the male and female in other species, are supposed to be pretty much alike in most respects,[5] but, like true mates, they are supposed to disagree with each other over many issues, not because they have any basic conflict in interests, but because each wants to be boss. The trouble with the existing American parties is that they are too weak, too decentralized, and they fail to disagree with each other often enough and sharply enough.

The bill of particulars, together with the specifications for party reorganization, are contained in a document entitled *Toward a More Responsible Two-Party System*, the report of the Committee on Political Parties, of the American Political Science Association [1950]. What the committee recommended was the restructuring of the major political parties along monolithic lines, with effective power lodged in the party bureaucrats (i.e., leaders) at the top of the pyramid.[6] The objective was "to create a strong and general agreement on policies" within each party and a maximum of disagreement between the two parties, so that the people would be able to choose between clear-cut alternative programs of government. Once the people had spoken, the majority party would then take over the job of running the government, in pursuance of the popular mandate given it (i.e., the will of the people), until the next election. The moralistic tone of the report, including its antagonism to minority (private, pressure, local, special) interests is suggested by the following excerpt [pp. 19–20] from the report:

By themselves, the interest groups cannot attempt to define public policy democratically. Coherent public policies do not emerge as the mathematical result of the claims of all of the pressure groups. The

---

4. Genesis 6:20, 19: ". . . of every creeping thing of the earth after his kind, two of every *sort* shall come unto thee . . . they shall be male and female."

5. One is reminded of the aphorism: "There isn't *much* of a difference, but thank God for the difference!"

6. There was no formal minority report from the committee, but see Turner [1951] and Ranney [1951].

integration of the interest groups into the political system is a function of the parties. . . .

A stronger party system is less likely to give cause for the deterioration and confusion of purposes which sometimes passes for compromise but is really an unjustifiable surrender to narrow interests. *Compromise among interests is compatible with the aims of a free society only when the terms of reference reflect an openly acknowledged concept of the public interest.* There is every reason to insist that parties be held accountable to the public for the compromises they accept.

Thus, the two major parties provide the mechanism whereby the will of the people becomes both manifest and realized in fact; political parties are the salvation of popular sovereignty.[7] The chairman of the committee which prepared the report was Professor Schattschneider.

There is a Rationalist alternative to the public-will–majoritarian-two-party-system theory that we have been examining. This is the approach that we could call today the "Madison Avenue" concept of the public interest. In a book of lectures which was the outgrowth of a short course on public relations for businessmen, Harwood L. Childs has written a chapter which he calls: "What Is the Public Interest?" After deploring the "severe setback" that the "concept 'public interest' in company with much idealism has suffered" in the 1930's, he asserts that: "The underlying motivation for public-relations study must be a desire to serve the public interest. That is obviously the inspir-

---

7. For a much more sophisticated discussion which relates to metropolitan rather than to national political parties, see Meyerson and Banfield [1955, pp. 287–94, 298–300]. The pages cited are from a chapter entitled "The Public Interest," in which the authors defend machine politics as a decentralizing device which makes government responsive to local, ethnic, minority, and other special interests. In other respects, however, the fundamental position of the authors is the same as that of the Committee on Political Parties. Meyerson and Banfield state that "Chicago was not governed, as are some cities in which strong machines do not stand between the voter and the issue, by the pull and haul of a few irresponsible pressure groups which get the voter's ear at election time; instead, there were only two important parties, both of which had to accept some responsibility for not one or a few interests but for all of the many conflicting interests that were important in the life of the city" [p. 291]. We should not be surprised to discover that Meyerson and Banfield conclude that "there was an important element of truth in the politicians' belief that *what was good for the party was in the public interest*" [pp. 299–300; emphasis added].

ing motive behind this great undertaking—the American Institute of Public Relations" [1940, pp. 22–34, esp. p. 24].

Latter-day cynics who do not inspire easily might well be tempted, at this point, to turn from Childs to *The Man in the Gray Flannel Suit*, were it not for the fact that he then proceeds to recommend the results of public-opinion polls as a reliable guide to public opinion, and therefore to the public interest. Those who recall "President" Thomas E. Dewey's brief moment of glory may have some misgivings about turning the definition of the public interest over to the pollsters, but Professor Childs does express a point of view not without adherents.

It is my thesis that the public interest, so far as the United States is concerned, is and can only be what the public, what mass opinion, says it is. By mass opinion I mean the collective opinions of the American people as a whole. [However] the degree of certainty and conviction with which public opinion supports or disapproves of public policies varies. The public conception of public interest will be clearer and more precise in some fields than others. [pp. 24–25.]

Notwithstanding his reference to the concept of the public interest as a form of "idealism," Professor Childs has no sympathy with the Idealist concept of the public interest. (He accomplishes this *tour de force* by completely ignoring the role of Elmo Ropers and Dr. Gallups as opinion leaders, to say nothing of the manipulative propensities inherent in their function. The people dance; but do they call the tune?) However, these questions do not trouble Professor Childs, who notes [p. 26] that "there still persists in some quarters the notion that somehow or other the opinions of the masses are less likely to be expressions of public interest than the pronouncements of savants."

He then asks the $64,000 question anent the public-opinion polls: "Do they indicate that mass opinion is or is not a safe guide to follow in defining the public interest?" [p. 27]. As evidence bearing upon the answer to the question, Professor Childs then presents the results of twenty-nine questions asked in public-opinion polls during the preceding three-year period. The median question [p. 28] will have to suffice as an example, which suggests, at least, the flavor of the set as a whole:

15. Are you in favor of labor unions? (July, 1937). Yes—76 per cent.

On the basis of this evidence, he asks: "can we honestly say that a domestic and political program along the lines approved by the masses would be lacking in common sense, obviously inimical to the public interest?" [p. 29]. Childs then reviews additional evidence, and concludes that it tends "to support the prophetic saying of Theodore Roosevelt that 'the majority of the plain people will day in and day out make fewer mistakes in governing themselves than any smaller body of men will make in trying to govern them'" [p. 32]. One may be pardoned, perhaps, for suggesting that T.R. is a most dubious authority upon which to rely for this kind of proposition, for reasons that will be apparent when we examine the Idealist theory of the public interest in presidential decision-making. It would have been more appropriate for Childs to have quoted P. T. Barnum, who said, after all, about the same thing.

In fairness to Professor Childs, we should note that he does enter the caveat that "in stressing the virtues of public opinion as a guide to public interest I am not unmindful of its defects" [p. 33]. He attributes the defects, however, to the "masses" rather than to the methods by which their "collective opinions" are ascertained. He concludes that "the basic problem of public relations is to adjust those aspects of our behavior which affect others in such a manner as to promote the public interest; and that the public interest is what public opinion says it is" [p. 34].

B. Congress

THERE ARE TWO contradictory Rationalist models for legislative decision-making. That of the Anglophile Rationalists is patterned after British parliamentary-party voting behavior. These Rationalists believe that members of Congress *ought* to associate together in cohesive, disciplined blocs of Republicans and Democrats, respectively, with each individual legislator bound by the authority of the caucus and the decisions on policy questions of party leaders in the two houses. Consequently, a congressman's responsiveness to the wishes of his constituents is decried as undesirable, and submission to the demands of special-interest groups is denounced as downright pernicious. The only legitimate channel of political responsibility is thought to be that provided by the two major political parties, one of which is supposed to be the majority party which runs the government, and the other of which is supposed to fulfill the role of the loyal opposition. Thus, Congress would be able to function (it is argued) as a conduit through which would flow the will of a majority of the people, expressed in elections by the manifestation of a clear preference for one of the two parties and the platform on which it stands.

The Anglophile Rationalists are driven, by the dictates of consistency, to be just as critical of a legislator who "follows his own conscience" as they are of one who succumbs to the pressures from constituents, interest groups, or even the pressures to conform to the customs and rituals which betoken membership in good standing in the legislative group. The single standard which ought to govern legislative behavior is party regularity; if a necessary consequence of disregarding constituency interests is the fall of a few legislative sparrows, the individual victims should console themselves with the thought that their self-sacrifice is, after all, for the good of the party. And what is good for the party is, of course, in the public interest.

Stephen Bailey has expressed the views of many Party Rationalists, in the conclusions that he drew from his study of the process of enactment of the Employment Act of 1946. Contrary to a consistent Anglophile position, however, Bailey links political-party leadership with the presidency rather than with the majority-party leadership in Congress:

> The individual Senators and Congressmen . . . were not representatives of national political parties based upon national programs. They were representatives of the dominant interests and culture symbols of tiny geographical areas which, even if taken in the aggregate, do not give a fair quantitative weighting to the sentiments and expectations of a national popular majority. . . . One of the most important ingredients of survival [of the American democracy] is a responsible political system which will reflect the will of the majority and which will enable the citizens to hold identifiable rulers account-

able for policy decisions. I fail to see how this can be done except by strengthening the only two instruments in our political life which have an inherent responsibility to the nation as nation: the President and the national political parties. . . . The strengthening of Presidential leadership and party cohesion *as rational instruments of majority rule* would . . . mean that . . . the public could hold an identifiable institutional leadership responsible for final decisions. [Emphasis added; 1950, pp. 238–39.]

Another recent case study of legislative policy-making has argued in behalf of both greater party cohesion and rules of procedure that would enable a majority in the House of Representatives to make decisions which, under present rules, can be blocked by leadership elites representing the interests of a minority of the House.[8] This is essentially a Rationalist argument, since it assumes the virtues of majoritarian control, and the desirability of having more cohesive congressional political-party groupings, which, in turn, would reflect more accurately than do present institutional arrangements the interests of a majority of the people.

The alternative model, which has considerable support in the writings of earlier generations of political economists, appears to have attracted very little articulate support from political scientists of the past generation, although it is mentioned in the textbooks. This theory holds that a legislator should represent the interests of the people who elect him to office, and that his primary obligations and responsibility are to his constituents rather than to the political party with which he is affiliated. The roots of this theory of representation go back over half a millenium to the origins of the English Parliament [Walker, 1948, p. 131]; and the recent absence of active defense of this theory should not be construed to mean that the idea is not widely accepted. Moreover, it is generally considered that, from the point of view of practical politics, a congressman who disregards the

---

8. "The 21 day rule was no more than a substitute for fair representation of the interests of a majority of the members of the House on the Rules Committee. Government by faction is a poor substitute for party government, however, and it makes difficult both the identification and the organization of the majority interest. In such a political milieu, the 21 day rule was a faltering step towards greater responsibility in an institutional situation fraught with irresponsibility." [Schubert, 1953a, p. 29.]

wishes of his constituents is simply committing political suicide.

These Popular Rationalists suggest, in effect, that it is both possible and desirable to short-circuit the political parties, as instrumentalities for inducing political responsibility among congressmen. Legislators should follow the public will, the "public" in this sense being defined as persons who reside in the legislator's district. Such a vague notion of constituency leaves room for a variety of interpretations; the range of meanings associated with it vary from the bedrock of "people who voted for the successful candidate"—which could well be a mere plurality of the actual voters, and hence a small minority of the people living in a district—to the other extreme, which envisages a "common interest" encompassing, for at least some issues, all of the people in a district. There is, in other words, as much lack of clarity and consistency in the Rationalist use of "public" in relation to legislative constituencies as there is when it is used to describe the American people "as a whole" [see Dahl, 1950, pp. 29–40]. Nevertheless, the position of the Popular Rationalists is that a congressman best serves the public interest when he votes according to the will of the people in his district.

This point of view is well stated by W. F. Willoughby in his textbook, *Principles of Legislative Organization and Administration* [1934]. However, Willoughby's attribution of Popular-Rationalist theory to the *British* political-party system and of the Anglophile model of strong, disciplined parties to the United States appears to be diametrically opposed to what contemporary political scientists consider to be an accurate description of the empirical facts in each case—as these facts appeared in 1934, when Willoughby wrote, as well as today. His failure to relate his models to appropriate sets of empirical data is irrelevant, however, to our present concern, since Willoughby did offer a clear statement of Popular-Rationalist theory:

> . . . all public officers, and particularly those constituting the membership of the legislative chambers, are deemed to be but servants of the people and under the obligation to exercise their functions with a view to the promotion of the latter's interests. . . . The theory underlying this doctrine [of "agency"] is that the legislative assembly is nothing more than a body with the function of putting into effect the will of the people. The relationship between the electorate under this

theory is thus one of principal and agent; and, as an agent, it is the duty of the legislator to carry out such orders as he may receive from his principal, [the] constituency electing him. [pp. 37, 39.]

Willoughby also correctly implies [p. 38] that there is conflict, not only between the Popular-Rationalist and Idealist theories, but also within the Rationalist camp. The Anglophile position, with its emphasis upon *national* political parties which line congressmen up on issues defined in terms of the interests of a majority of the *nation* as a whole, will necessarily collide with the Popular-Rationalist position, whenever the parochial interests of a congressman's district do not happen to coincide with the interests of the larger public:[9]

If he follows his own conscience, or judgment, he may fail to represent the opinion or wishes of his district or party and the latter may feel that he has been recreant to his trust; or where the interests of his particular district, or state, are in conflict with those of the country as a whole, should he favor the latter, the former might feel that he has not properly discharged his trust of looking after its welfare.

The notion that unity can be created out of diversity, greatness will arise out of mediocrity, and that a rainbow is a necessary function of each storm cloud has great popular appeal, particularly among Idealists. Their enthusiasm for such essential harmonies not infrequently leads Idealists to advance what are patently Rationalist arguments. Thus, Ernest S. Griffith, formerly Director of the Legislative Reference Service of the Library of Congress, has stated what might be termed the "*e pluribus unum*" formula for constructing, at least on a verbal level, a bridge between constituency and national interests:

Congressmen necessarily and properly reflect the attitudes and needs of their individual districts, and many, if not most, of these are economic. It is [however] the supreme task of Congress on the domestic front to create out of these individual, often very limited, local outlooks an amalgam that shall in some measure represent their fusion into the more general national interest and welfare. [1951, p. 3.]

Griffith's reference to an "amalgam" immediately evokes images of the group struggle postulated by the Bentlians, but Griffith

_____
9. Cf. Dahl [1950, pp. 40–41].

is no instrumentalist, and he relies upon neither political parties nor interest groups to bring about the synthesis which he recommends. As we shall see in the next chapter, for Griffith, congressmen become enlightened through experience, and the public interest is a by-product of the larger vision of the public good which is revealed to Good Congressmen.

There are various problems involved in relating Constituency-Rationalist theory to the real world. Precisely how, for instance, does a legislator determine the interests of his constituents, assuming that he should feel obligated to recognize them as an authoritative set of norms to guide his official behavior? A possible mechanism, at least for the Senate, was offered, for a time, by the use of specific instructions. This system functioned, however, only while United States Senators were elected by state legislatures instead of by direct popular vote; the Seventeenth Amendment formally terminated a process whose functional vitality already had become vitiated by the time the Civil War broke out.[10]

What other alternative sources and processes of instruction are recognized? None that we have not already mentioned. Individual constituents may vote; they may, as individuals, write, telephone, wire, or talk directly to their legislative representatives; they may communicate indirectly through the "lobbying" activities of organizations which they support (but rarely control); they may, as individuals, respond to various questionnaires or other interviewing devices intended to identify "public opinion" in a legislative district; and they may (in principle) act through political-party channels to instruct their representatives [Dahl, 1950, chap. ii].

Although the Rationalist literature that I have examined does not attempt to specify, other than in terms of such generalizations as I have stated above, the *processes* of constituency in-

---

10. Riker states that: "State legislatures and the parties that preferred them to the national legislature did indeed try to enforce accountability by means of the doctrine of instructions. Hence that doctrine was, next to the method of election itself, the main avenue through which state legislatures pushed themselves into national affairs. [But the] idea that senators ought always to obey their immediate constituents is now almost forgotten. Only scholars still know that it was ever acted upon" [1955, p. 455].

fluence, there is and has been for some years a sharp divergence of professional views on the question of the actual correlative influence of party and constituency pressures. By and large, the conclusions arrived at by various investigators reflect differences in the research methods employed. The political scientists who have made case studies in which they have attempted to trace, in detail, the ramifications of legislative behavior, radiating from the resolution of a single issue of public policy, conclude that political parties are weak and disorganized; legislative leadership is dispersed among bipartisan and multifactional elite groups; constituency pressures are primarily group pressures (rather than those of individuals or party); and legislators are open to the seduction (to which they frequently succumb) of nationally organized special-interest groups [Bailey, 1950, pp. 236–40; Latham, 1952a, pp. 209–10]. Congressmen are, hence, irresponsible, to *either* their constituents *or* the political party whose label they bear, in regard to the vast majority of bills, which (it is claimed) have no direct effect upon the constituency interests of most individual congressmen, and regarding which the political parties take no stand. Rationalists and Realists (and many Idealists as well) agree upon the diagnosis of the disease, but these theorists part company when it comes to prescribing a remedy.

There have appeared, within the past decade, several quantitative studies of congressional-voting behavior that tend to refute the orthodox view of legislative anarchy [Dahl, 1950; Grassmuck, 1951; Turner, 1952; Westerfield, 1955]. The most relevant to our present concern is the doctoral dissertation of the late Julius Turner, who made extensive statistical analyses of roll calls in the House of Representatives for a sample of sessions covering a twenty-five-year period. In particular, he sought to determine the extent to which congressmen voted according to the party line or according to constituency interests. Since various Rationalists accept *either* responsiveness to party *or* responsiveness to constituency as legitimate, it is useful to examine Professor Turner's conclusions respecting the voting behavior of congressmen in those roll calls where party and constituency interests coincided. Under these circumstances, those who voted contrary to the conjoint pressures of party and constituency can be said to have been independent in their voting, in the sense that their votes must be attributed to some other source of influence—conscience, nationally organized interest groups, log-rolling, etc. Turner found that less than 4 per cent of the congressmen

. . . opposed party and [constituency] group [pressures] on more than 20 per cent of the roll calls, and none opposed party and group more than 35 per cent of the time. Thus it appears that independent action on the part of a congressman when the pressures of party and group coincided was a rare event, an action which was indulged in on less than one-tenth of the votes of two-thirds of the representatives. The figures become even more impressive when it is recalled that the group pressures which we have measured make up only a part of the pressures on Congress. Those instances in which we find evidence of congressional opposition to party and other measured groups may reflect the pressure of unmeasured factors, rather than the independent judgment of the representative. . . . [The] conclusion is that the representative process as practised in twentieth-century America involves, insofar as voting behavior is concerned, the attempt of the representative to mirror the political desires of those groups which can bring about his election or defeat. [pp. 168, 178; and cf. Dahl, 1950, p. 46.]

The significance of Turner's (and related) research findings [cf. Farris, 1958, p. 335] is that Rationalist theories of legislative-voting behavior may correspond much closer with the actual behaviors of congressmen than either Rationalists, Idealists, or Realists generally have assumed. In particular, Turner's conclusions challenge the assumptions about the effectiveness of the American party system as a factor determining legislative voting, upon which rest the Schattschneider report and the recommendations, in general, of the Anglophile Rationalists. Irrespective, however, of whether the Party-Rationalist view of reality is a correct one, the normative problem of which theory of legislative decision-making *ought* to be followed by congressmen remains.

C. The Presidency

THERE ARE TWO antithetical Rationalist conceptions of the presidency. Both of them can readily be traced to the constitutional principle of separation of powers and to divergent assumptions about the responsiveness and representativeness of the executive and legislative branches of the government. According to one view, the path to more responsible government lies in strengthening the presidency; the strong-presidency proponents have generally assumed that the weakness of Congress is beyond hope of effective remedy. These Rationalists see the president as the dominant leader of the majority party and, in addition (or in the alternative), as the only national official chosen by a popular majority of the voters and hence qualified to carry out the "mandate of the people." This strand of Rationalist thought would substitute the president for Congress as the agent of the majority political party to implement the public will.

The second view, which is a logical extension of the theories of Anglophile Rationalism that we have examined, would sublimate the presidency to the control of Congress. The president should be weak and Congress should be strong; it is Congress which speaks with the authentic voice of the American people, or at least, a majority of them. It is this view that the late Mr. Chief Justice Fred Vinson once characterized as the "messenger-boy concept of the office."[11]

The issue posed by these alternative conceptions of the American presidency has constituted one of the great, continuing debates of our constitutional politics. It was raised in the first term of the first Congress, in what is known as "the decision of 1789," regarding the removal power of the president [Hart, 1948, pp. 155–214]. A century and two-thirds of constitutional practice has given us a compromise, although the balance of power seems clearly to have favored the presidency during at least the first two of the preceding three decades upon which this study focuses. As the late Mr. Justice Robert Jackson remarked, also in the Steel Seizure case:

> Just what our forefathers did envision, or would have envisioned had they foreseen modern conditions, must be divined from materials almost as enigmatic as the dreams Joseph was called upon to interpret for Pharaoh. A century and a half of partisan debate and scholarly

11. *Youngstown Sheet and Tube Co.* v. *Sawyer* (The Steel Seizure Case), 343 U.S. 579, 708–9 [1952].

speculation yields no net result but only supplies more or less apt quotations from respected sources on each side of any question. They largely cancel each other out. [343 U.S. 579, 634–35.]

He adds, in a footnote, that: "A Hamilton may be matched against a Madison. . . . Professor Taft is counterbalanced by Theodore Roosevelt. . . . It even seems that President Taft cancels out Professor Taft."

Jackson might well have added that Chief Justice Taft agreed with President Taft in cancelling out Professor Taft; or that President Wilson cancelled out Professor Wilson. The views expressed by the budding political scientist in his immensely popular *Congressional Government*, in which Wilson wrote, [1885, p. 301; and cf. Young, 1958, p. 213] that "Congress is, as it were, the corporate people, the mouthpiece of its will," already had been greatly modified as Wilson stood on the threshold of his political career. As the result of such intervening events as the Spanish-American War and the pre-eminent example of Teddy Roosevelt, Wilson the politician had come to the contradictory conclusion that "only the President represents the country as a whole" [1908, p. 203; and cf. Macmahon, 1958, p. 103]. It would have been much more descriptive of the contents of his Columbia University lectures if they had been published under the title *Presidential Government*, rather than *Constitutional Government*. We shall consider Wilson's earlier and Rationalist views in this chapter, and his later views, which certainly are in closer accord with his subsequent behavior as president, in the following chapter as an expression of Presidential Idealism.[12]

Louis Brownlow, long-time student of the presidency and friend of presidents, has also been one of the most outspoken proponents of the Popular-Rationalist theory of strong presidential leadership:

---

12. Contrast *Congressional Government* [pp. 265–66, 308, 311–16, 332–33], in which Wilson argues the position of Anglophile Rationalism and congressional supremacy, with *Constitutional Government* [pp. 59, 70, 81, 109–10, 127, 202–3, 215], in which Wilson advocates Presidential Idealism and presidential dominance over both Congress and the majority party. Cf. Wann [1958, pp. 65–66].

. . . the Presidency in its modern meaning, in its current concept, emerged under Theodore Roosevelt. The eighteenth century concept of the Chief Magistrate ended with John Quincy Adams. Andrew Jackson was both the leader and the symbol of the democratic revolt that made the President the choice of the mass of the voters at the polls and made the Presidency an instrument for the expression and enforcement of the national will. . . . The President does not obtain his executive power from an Act of Congress; nor is he responsible to the Congress or to the Supreme Court. The President holds his executive power by a direct mandate of the people as set forth in the Constitution, and it is toward the people as a whole—and not the Congress or the Supreme Court—that his lines of responsibility run. [1949, pp. 56, 21.]

And Brownlow quotes George Fort Milton, to the effect that "the President of the United States of America has become the principal representative of the will of the people of the most powerful democracy in the world" [1949, p. 14].

A more moderate statement of the Popular-Rationalist theory of the presidency, however, is that of Emmette Redford:

The chief organ of comprehensive representation is the presidency. To an extent the two-party system provides comprehensive representation, but since the national party organizations are so weak and the parties are so divided in the Congress and the nation, and the majority party is so largely under the leadership of the President, the presidency becomes the center through which the nation as a whole is represented. This function of the presidency is safeguarded to the nation through the requirement of a majority electoral vote for election of its incumbent. To win a majority the candidate must bridge the interest conflict and make his appeal on the basis of generally-shared attitudes. The function is further enforced by the high responsibility of the office. Inevitably a responsible man must try to exercise its functions for the welfare of the nation. Inevitably he will be forced to try to take a broadly-gauged view of what constitutes the general welfare. The presidency is, therefore, our most democratic and our most publicly-oriented office. And its strength and its service derive from the breadth of the constituency which it represents. [1958, pp. 129–30.]

The theories of both the Popular-Rationalists and the Administrative Rationalists (to be considered at a later point in this chapter) were combined in the *Report* of the President's Committee on Administrative Management, which Franklin Roosevelt submitted to Congress in January, 1937. The members of the

Committee included Louis Brownlow as Chairman, Charles E. Merriam, and Luther Gulick (an Administrative Rationalist). All three members of the committee are considered to be distinguished political scientists. The *Report* was highly controversial at the time it was published; today, after the passing of more than two decades, many of the Committee's specific recommendations remain the subject of scholarly [e.g., Davis, 1953, pp. 733–39], to say nothing of political, dispute. The Committee disdained for itself the Rationalist role of functioning as scientific experts. Instead, they chose the more exhilarating Idealist role of serving as policy engineers. Their *Report* [President's Committee, 1937, p. 1], which certainly represents the work of a kind of professional interest group, follows the technique employed by most special interests and is cloaked in the flags of democracy and the public interest:

> Our American Government rests on the truth that the general interest is superior to and has priority over any special or private interest, and that final decision in matters of common interest to the Nation should be made by free choice of the people of the Nation, expressed in such manner as they shall from time to time provide, and enforced by such agencies as they may from time to time set up. . . . By democracy we mean getting things done that we, the American people, want done in the general interest. . . . After the people's judgment has been expressed in due form, after the representatives of the Nation have made the necessary laws, we intend that these decisions shall be promptly, effectively, and economically put into action.

And the most appropriate instrument for carrying out the public will is none other than the president [pp. 1, 2]:

> The President is indeed the one and only national officer representative of the entire Nation. . . . As an instrument for carrying out the judgment and will of the people of a nation, the American Executive occupies an enviable position among the executives of the states of the world, combining as it does the elements of popular control and the means for vigorous action and leadership—uniting stability and flexibility. The American Executive as an institution stands across the path of those who mistakenly assert that democracy must fail because it can neither decide promptly nor act vigorously.

In recommending reorganization of the executive branch to enhance the power of the president as the general manager of the administrative functions carried out by the national government, the Committee was careful to point out [p. 4] that "economy" and "administrative efficiency," while important by-products that could be anticipated if the Committee's recommendations were accepted, were not the basic objective of executive reorganization: "There is but one grand purpose, namely, to make democracy work today in our National Government; that is, to make our Government an up-to-date, efficient, and effective instrument for carrying out the will of the Nation." In this respect, the Brownlow Committee's *Report* differs sharply from the more recent reports of the two Hoover Commissions, both of which have assumed that executive reorganization can, and should, be sold *to* "the people" just like soap. "Billions" of dollars could be saved by changing the government's procedures for purchasing and accounting for paper clips; Economy and Efficiency, like Cleanliness, are next to Godliness; etc. But on the basic question of integrating administrative services under the over-all managerial control of the president, both Hoover Commissions have stood fast in the faith proclaimed by the Brownlow Committee. This establishment, within a single generation, of what has now become the official dogma of executive reorganization, has provoked one political scientist to comment:

Value in politics and administration is most often expressed as a kind of will—be it that of political superiors, the legislature, the sovereign, or the people. The pyramidal form of most ideal organization charts, the preoccupation with the location of authority, and the structuring of a tight paper-chain of command evidence basic concern with administration as "will" organization. The concern with legitimate hierarchy is similar in nature to the legalist's devotion to sovereignty. It amounts to a search for an absolute, a first principle, from which all else may flow with the appealing logic of a deductive system. The Hoover Commission provides a useful contemporary administrative *summa theologica* on this point and a forceful tract in favor of administrative monotheism. Its evangelists have preached up and down the land the gospel, "Give the President the power to act." One might almost echo, "In his will is our peace." [Long, 1954, p. 24.]

A journalist, Sidney Hyman, has written a recent book on the presidency in which he has asked how the president is to divine the public will, and how he is to know which majority is likely to support him:

> If the President intends to follow "the will of the people," who expresses that will? His problem would be simplified if the coalition he built for an election-day victory remained stable. But it does nothing of the sort. It is torn apart when one minority gets what it wants, when a second gives up hope, and when all are suddenly lashed by the intrusion of physical events, unforeseen and unprovided for in the campaign formula. To get any kind of measure enacted, the President has to build a special coalition for the immediate object in view. Sometimes he can do this by reshuffling the forces within his party. He can also pick up support from among dissidents in the opposition party, or he can appeal directly to the nation in the hope that its groundswells will override all party lines. But whatever he does, he is never free of the nagging question of whether the real majority is not made up of the shy and silent citizens who can flare like a pillar of phosphorous when they are rubbed the wrong way. [1954, pp. 52–53.]

This is the dilemma for the Popular Rationalists. In principle, it is possible to link presidential responsibility and obligation with quadrennial electoral majorities, but this notion fits very badly the most conspicuous facts of political life. The party platform is too inspecific, the president's control over Congress too tenuous, and the environment of presidential decision-making is in such obvious flux that "the popular mandate" has little qualitative significance. At most, an overwhelming plurality of both popular and electoral votes, which is likely to carry with it the by-product of safe majorities for the president's party in both houses of Congress, is a quantitative mandate to do *something*, together with some assurance (through congressional support) of the relative capability for taking action. Such a decisive *quantitative* mandate is the exception, however, rather than the rule; even when it exists, reaction normally sets in midway during the presidential term and either narrows the margins of the administration's congressional pluralities or turns control of at least one house of Congress over to the opposition. And this discussion has ignored factional differences within a party, such as the differences over the civil rights issue which are reputed to separate northern and southern Democrats.

There is an additional difficulty with Popular Rationalist

theory, in that it places the president in the role of the leader of
direct popular majorities, who carries out "their" will. Even if
we assume, contrary to the available evidence, that such popular
mandates exist, they are formed so infrequently to be of dubious
value as a device for controlling the president in his day-to-day
decisions. Particularly would this appear to be true for a sec-
ond-term president, now that we have the Twenty-second
Amendment. Which decisions, among the many that a president makes during the first, second, and third years of his term,
will be remembered at election time? If they are remembered,
how many will relate what the president actually did to the
campaign promises of four years ago? The opportunity, at least,
is present for the president to become more than the instrument
of a majority of the voters; and there are many Idealists who,
both by practice and precept, advise him to become the leader
of all of the American people, to say nothing of the free peoples
of the world.

Party Rationalists admonish against these dangers, and suggest
that the solution to all sides of the problem may be found in linking the presidency to the leadership of a strong, hierarchically organized, disciplined, national political party. It is the party, rather
than the president personally, which commands the support of a
majority of the voters; and it is the party which will control the
president and which will make it possible to avoid "The Danger
of Overextending the Presidency," as it is called by the report of
the Schattschneider Committee (on political parties). The president, warns the Committee,

. . . is the only politically responsible organ of government that has
the whole nation as constituency. Elected by the people at large, the
President must look upon himself as its spokesman. In him alone all
Americans find a single voice in national affairs. . . . If he acts in pursuit of a broad program that has been democratically formulated in
his party, nearly all of his party is likely to put itself behind the
measures called for by the program. Then the question of political
support presents no difficulties, which is the solution suggested in this
report. [pp. 93, 94.]

If, however, American political parties are not so organized, and
do not so function, as to provide this kind of guidance and support,

what then? This, of course, is the major problem to which the Committee's report is directed, and we have seen that the Committee found that various and monumental changes would be necessary before the American party system could, in fact, provide "the solution" suggested in their report. What follows must, logically, represent the Committee's view of what tends to happen in the real world, given the unsatisfactory party system that we have in fact:

Lacking his party's support for a broad program, the President is left with only one course. He can attempt to fill the void caused by the absence of an effective party program by working up a broad political program of his own. . . . *When the President's program actually is the sole program . . . either his party becomes a flock of sheep or the party falls apart.* In effect *this concept of the presidency disposes of the party system by making the President reach directly for the support of a majority of the voters.* It favors a President who exploits skillfully the arts of demagoguery, who uses the whole country as his political backyard, and who does not mind turning [it] into the embodiment of personal government [p. 94.]

Similar views have been expressed by Professor James M. Burns, whose "50 percent plus one" majoritarianism was discussed earlier in this chapter. According to Burns,

The real problem of the Presidency is the pressure on the Chief Executive, especially in times of crisis, to forsake his function as majority leader and to assume the more exhilarating role of acting for the whole people as Chief of State. . . . If power must be delimited in a democracy, then majority rule performs that task admirably. . . . On the domestic front, at least, majority control is the great safeguard. Once a President breaks away from the majority that elected him to office, he operates virtually without political controls. He may feel responsible to the voters as a whole, but such responsibility leaves him the widest leeway. . . . By rising above "partisanship" he can find new combinations of groups in Congress to back up his policies. For the first time in his experience, perhaps, he enjoys almost solid support in the press. Presidential appeals to the patriotic feeling of an aroused citizenry tend to replace tiresome bargaining with party officials. [1949, pp. 188, 190–91, 189.]

The solution suggested by Burns is the same as that of the Schattschneider report: to take the necessary steps in order to achieve "party government" which, according to Professor Burns, "can be had" if the American people are willing to pay the necessary price. Party government would solve the problem because,

> The great task of American democrats is to bind the President to the majority will of the nation without shackling him as a source of national leadership and authority. We must institutionalize the office politically. . . . In trying to elect him the party gathers its far-flung forces every four years in a massive effort that does something to knit the party together, if only temporarily. President and party are essential to each other; because he must keep his party's support he is subject to a measure of party discipline; because the party needs his leadership it submits to a measure of national control. [pp. 191, 198.]

The Party Rationalists have no doubts but that the presidency is a more responsible political institution than Congress; they believe that this is true, in fact, now, and that the presidency offers a much more promising prospect for attaining perfection in the way of responsibility than does Congress. A characteristic statement is that of E. Allen Helms, who says that "the public looks to the President for leadership and regards him as more representative of the general interest. Congress, it believes, is more representative of special interests" [1949, p. 64].

The same view is expressed by Professor Wilfred E. Binkley: "The function of the President in our system is to discover and somehow or other to promote the public welfare amid the mosaic of conflicting interests represented in Congress" [1947, p. 297]. The Realists, of course, have criticized this widely held notion. Pendleton Herring, for instance, notes that

> The president is commonly thought of as representing the general welfare; Congress is the tool of "special interests." In fact presidential policy, however "pure" in motivation, *must* mean the promotion of certain interests at the expense of others. [Emphasis added: 1940, p. 9.]

And Carl J. Friedrich, who attacks on logical grounds the Party-Rationalist notion of presidential "representativeness," has suggested that

> The American President would seem to be "more representative" than any individual member of the House or the Senate, but the Senate and the House, when acting with large bi-partisan majorities,

would be "more representative" than the President (who is necessarily of one party). [1950, p. 463.]

Indeed, Friedrich adds, "In relation to certain functions, the Supreme Court . . . is 'more representative' than either Congress or the President because it is 'nonpartisan.' " This latter suggestion—that a "nonpartisan" group of judges who hold office for life can be more responsible to the people than their elected representatives in the "political" branches of the government—is rank heresy to the Party Rationalists, although the idea is perfectly acceptable to both Legal Rationalists and Legal Idealists.

Perhaps the most extreme statement of the strong-presidency position is to be found in Henry Hazlitt's *A New Constitution Now*. This entire book is an extended argument in favor of scrapping the Constitution of 1787, so that a thorough-going imitation of the British parliamentary system could be tried out. Hazlitt concludes with the following exhortation:

> Let us adopt responsible cabinet government. Let us *trust* somebody, and give him authority as long as he remains in power; but make him at all times strictly accountable for his use of that power, and removable the moment he shows himself unwilling or incompetent to carry out the national will. [Emphasis in the original; 1942, p. 289; and cf. Wilson, 1885, pp. 283–84.]

Since Hazlitt advocates a system of "cabinet government," in which the president would be the counterpart of both king and prime minister, with the at least nominal objective of *strengthening* the presidency, his position should be sharply distinguished from that of most other Anglophiles, who see in "cabinet government" a device for *weakening* the presidency and expanding the powers and political leadership of Congress.

The opposing Rationalist model for the presidency represents an extension of the position of those Anglophile Rationalists, who believe that responsible party leadership already exists in Congress, or at least, that it would exist if certain organizational reforms were made in Congress and the political-party system. Essentially, these proponents of a weak presidency would make the president the captive of Congress through the device of a more or less modified version of British cabinet government. Instead of the cabinet being wholly the creature of the president, responsible to him and serving at his pleasure (as at present), these Anglophiles would have a cabinet composed largely or exclusively of congressmen and responsible to Congress.

The most extreme version of this scheme is that suggested by Professor Caleb Perry Patterson. Patterson [1947, p. 258] takes his cue from Woodrow Wilson's well-known argument that a president who "lost the confidence" of both houses of Congress should resign in favor of the Leader of His Majesty's [i.e., the People's] Opposition. For Wilson, loss of confidence could occur in either of two principal ways: (1) the voters could reject the president and his party at the polls; or (2) the president could fail to command the support of majorities in both houses of Congress on a major issue. Wilson was apparently serious about the first, at least to the extent that he contemplated resignation in favor of Hughes[13] in the event that the Republicans carried the election of 1916. However, he never saw fit to act according to his second precept, although Congress provided him with numerous appropriate occasions during both of his terms. And, of course, the Senate's rejection of the League of Nations would seem to have provided Wilson with a made-to-order opportunity for establishing the initial precedent in favor of "responsible government," as he himself defined it. But Wilson was thirty-five years older in 1919 than he was when, as a graduate student, he wrote *Congressional Government*, without yet having set foot in the nation's capitol [Price, 1943, p. 317]. Furthermore, there is, as Justice Jackson pointed out, a difference in the views of presidents and professors.

Even Patterson [1947, p. 259] would stop short of "an unlimited cabinet system" which "would mean the destruction of the presidency, bicameralism, and constitutional terms of office." But he does recommend

---

13. In order to make this possible, the scheme was for both the vice president and the secretary of state to resign; Wilson then would appoint Hughes as secretary of state; Wilson himself would then resign, and Hughes would become president (or, at least, "Acting President"), in accordance with the terms of the version of the Presidential Succession Act then in effect. The Senate, of course, might have proved to be the fly in the ointment, by refusing to rise above its principles to confirm the Hughes nomination to the vacancy in the office of secretary of state.

. . . making the ministers responsible to the Congress and . . . forcing the President to act through ministers chosen from the Congress. This means that the Congress must be organized on a party basis by the creation of a body of political leaders who will be responsible to the party system and who will initiate legislative policy, and, thereby, serve as a check upon the President by means of the party system in the Congress. [p. 260.]

The president's cabinet, therefore, would consist exclusively of "ministers" who are the party leaders of the two houses of Congress; these ministers would select from among their own number a chief who is to be called, no less, the "prime minister." Patterson devotes a score of pages to the depiction of the details of his plan, but the literary model that comes irresistibly to the mind of the reader is not Walter Bagehot's *The English Constitution;* it is Charles Lewis Dodgson's *Through the Looking Glass.* For the American president, Patterson would substitute, in effect, the president of France under the Third or Fourth Republic.

Professor Charles Hyneman has demonstrated that it is possible to arrive at similar (though more moderate) conclusions, arguing from the premises of legislative Popular Rationalism. In a book [1950, p. 569] which reflects, in substantial measure, his administrative experiences during World War II, Professor Hyneman takes issue with the Party Rationalists who would strengthen the presidency at the expense of Congress:

A particular President may at a given moment enjoy a greater measure of popular confidence among the people than any majority that could possibly be created out of the membership of the two houses of Congress. But a nation cannot build its institutions on a presumption that a monopoly of authority will always be wisely exercised. There is no evidence that mankind in any generation and in any country has ever been able to devise an electoral system that will always turn up men of honor who will conscientiously seek to carry out the public will. No matter what devices we provide to enable an official to determine what the people want, we cannot be sure that he will make use of them or conform to what they reveal. We are thrown back, therefore, in our hope for accountability to the people, upon an assembly made up of a large number of men.

As a first step toward a parliamentary system—which *he* advances, however, on purely pragmatic grounds—Professor Hyneman proposes:

... the creation of a Central Council made up of *leaders of the party that has been given the job of running the government*. The Central Council would be given responsibility for formulating the program of the government-of-the-day and for directing its execution. The President, as the party's acknowledged leader and the man elected by the people to head the government, would select from among the members of his party who are to serve in Congress a small group that he recognizes to be essential to the success of his Administration. This group, with the President always taking the lead, would enlarge its own membership until it is agreed that the group includes those individuals who, collectively, can command the support of the party as a whole and give the country a program of legislation and administration that promises to return the party to power at the next election. Some members of the groups of leaders thus brought together (the Central Council) presumably would occupy official positions in the two houses of Congress; others would head important administrative establishments; some persons who hold no public office in the ordinary sense of the term might be included because they can bring to the Council advice and public support which are essential to the success of the party. [pp. 571–72.]

A proposal almost identical to that of Professor Hyneman has come from no less authoritative a source than Edward Samuel Corwin, Professor Emeritus at Princeton University, and long-time *doyen* of public-law scholars in the United States. Professor Corwin was among the original group of preceptors brought by Woodrow Wilson to Princeton and his book *The President: Office and Powers* is considered to be the authoritative work on the subject. Since Professor Corwin has retained his proposal for a "Legislative Council" through various editions of the book since its original publication in 1940, we can assume that this idea represents his mature and considered views on the question. Of course, we could also say that the idea represents, in a sense, reiteration of the original views of Professor Woodrow Wilson, modified to take into consideration the changes that the passing of sixty years had wrought in the American polity.

Professor Corwin argues [1948, pp. 353, 361] that his proposal offers an alternative to the presidency as "a potential matrix of dictatorship." The proposal?

It is simply that the President shall construct his Cabinet from a joint Legislative Council to be created by the two houses of Congress and to contain its leading members. Then to this central core of advisers may be added at times such heads of departments and chairmen of independent agencies as the business forward at the moment naturally indicates.

These variations on the same theme have not been completely ignored, although they represent the views of what appears to be a very small minority of Americans, and a small minority of political scientists. The formal cabinet-councils, recommended by Patterson, Hyneman, and Corwin, should not be confused with informal breakfast gatherings at the White House, whether the president chooses to consult with "the Administration's lieutenants" on the Hill or with a bipartisan group of legislative leaders [e.g., Dahl, 1950, chap. xiii] in order to "brief" them on the situation on, say, the moon. Such latter developments have not—at least, not yet—become institutionalized; and they leave the president free, not necessarily in terms of actual choice but in terms of formal obligation and responsibility, to consult whomever and whenever he wishes. Sidney Hyman has commented that

A presidential council formed of legislative leaders, members of the present Cabinet and elder statemen, could prove the most destructive of all plans to "help the President." In the legislators, the public would see a body of men who had actually been elected to posts of authority. And because they are so closely identified with the lawmaking process, if they gave the President advice and he ignored it, there would be a great outcry that the President had willfully violated orders. Moreover, many of these men, being ambitious for the presidency in their own right—whether they are of the President's party or of the opposition—would not hesitate to betray private confidences and to make political capital out of any discussion that suited their purposes. [1954, pp. 323–24.]

"In the end," Hyman concludes, "either the President would never solicit the opinions of the council . . . or he would find that his role as an Executive had been usurped by the leaders of the Congress" [cf., Fenno, 1958, p. 405]. The latter result is, of course, precisely what the Anglophiles think would be wise.

The criticisms made by Wilfred E. Binkley are characteristic of those who decry as utopian the rational policy of the Anglophiles. Binkley, an historian of both the presidency and the American political-party system, concludes that the ideal of a parliamentary system with legislative supremacy would be not only unattainable, but also undesirable for the United States:

> There are those who confidently propose resort to the magic formula of a parliamentary system in which the executive can dissolve the legislature and "appeal to the country" in a general election. There was an epidemic of such proposals when Roosevelt and Truman in turn were deadlocked with Congress by the alliance of Southern Democrats with Republican Congressmen which prevented enactment of the presidential program of social legislation.
>
> The theory of the English parliamentary system is fascinating to amateurs who know neither its historical evolution nor its prosaic practical operation. Of course it was by no means a product of planning but is instead a natural outgrowth of the experience of Britain's peculiar society groping through the centuries for adjustments, expedients, and makeshifts that would solve immediate governmental problems. . . . The American constitutional system is just as much the product of our own society and environment as the parliamentary is of another. . . . Such is the complexity of American society, with its conflicts of interests and of sections, that a resort to prompt settlement of its major issues by the simple majorities implicit in a parliamentary system might prove positively explosive. Conflicts inherent in our society are not to be resolved by a simple shift in the mechanics of government. [1947, pp. 295–96.]

By far the most trenchant critique of the Anglophile Rationalists, however, has come from Don K. Price, in an article published in the *Public Administration Review* during the middle of World War II. Price undertakes a detailed analysis of the disparate ways in which the American and British systems have actually functioned during the twentieth century. It is against this frame of reference that he evaluates the proposed reforms of the Anglophiles. Among his findings are [1943, p. 332]: (1) many Britons are (in turn) enamoured of the presumed superiority of many of the distinctive characteristics of the American political system; and (2) "Neither nation can really make [the classic theory of parliamentary government] work under twentieth-century conditions, but both are curiously fascinated by it and judge the systems as they actually exist in terms of patterns that are now dead." American Anglophiles are pursuing, therefore, a will-o'-the-wisp:

. . . in the United States the traditionalists and the innovators, among our academic and journalistic critics, argue for what will amount to the same thing. Our traditionalists want to go back to the American practice of the days of Buchanan and Grant and Harding— a weak executive and government by congressional committees—while our innovators, who always seem to turn to the classic theory of parliamentary government for their arguments, want to go back with Lord Eustace Percy to the House of Commons of the middle of the nineteenth century; but the specific steps that they usually propose could only serve to weaken the executive and lessen the unity of the legislature. . . .

It is odd enough to find Americans who seek to increase legislative control over the executive arguing for the system that in Britain has given the executive control over the legislature, or Americans who seek to remove unpopular department heads arguing for a system that in Britain keeps the administrative heads from being known, much less responsible, to the people. . . . The assumptions that the legislature alone represents the people and that the administrative officials and departments are responsible to the people only through the legislature served the cause of democratic government well when the executive departments were under a hereditary monarch. They are the classical assumptions of the parliamentary system. Under the presidential system they can only set up an impossible relationship as the ideal to be attained. [Price, 1943, pp. 332–33, 334. Cf. Laski, 1944, pp. 347–59, and Price, 1944, pp. 360–63.]

A final variant of the weak-presidency argument is that of persons whom I shall call the "Faithful-Execution" Rationalists. This, too, is an old school of thought, with strands that go back to the colonial period of American history [Thach, 1923]. The essence of the argument is that the intent of the Constitution was to vest in Congress both the power to make laws and the power to supervise the administration of laws by the executive branch. According to this view, the president is supposed to be a kind of chief clerk, in so far as domestic administrative functions are concerned, and his basic responsibility is to see that the other clerks carry out the orders of Congress. He has no policy-making authority or responsibility, *under the Constitution*, except to the extent that Congress has seen fit to delegate such authority to him, or to subordinates whom Congress has *explicitly* subjected to his power of administrative direction. In practice, however, this becomes a doctrine which subjects the presidency to the power of administrative direction of the judiciary: it is the courts who undertake to referee—although to a very limited extent [Schubert, 1957a, chap. xii.]—disputes in which it is claimed that the president has failed to carry out, or to make his subordinates carry out, the will of Congress.

Thus, the Anglophile Rationalists would make the president the captive of Congress; while the Faithful-Execution Rationalists would subordinate the president to the veto power of the Supreme Court, whose job it is "to interpret and to enforce the law"[14]—an assumption that we shall examine presently.

D. Administrators

THE STATUS of the so-called "independent federal regulatory commissions" represents a "problem"[15] in constitutional theory only from the Rationalist point of view. So far as Idealists and Realists are concerned, the decision-making of federal regulatory commissioners is not significantly different from that of federal administrators generally. Idealists place the commissioners on their own individual hillocks. Realists place the commissioners on the same continuum of discretion with departmental administrators and judges, reacting to the same kinds of forces and playing what is essentially the same type of role. Hence, in the two chapters that follow, I shall make no particular attempt to differentiate between regulatory commissioners and other federal administrators.

In Rationalist theory, however, the "anomalous" position of the regulatory commissions is as abhorrent as a vacuum is said to be to Nature. The very idea of agencies entrusted with mixed functions—partly executive, partly legislative, and partly judicial—violates the symmetry of the principle of separation of powers; and the American pragmatic expedient of delegating

---

14. Perhaps the classic statement of the latter position is that of Mr. Justice Black, in the Opinion of the Court in the Steel Seizure Case, 343 U.S. 579, 587–89 [1952].

15. It has been suggested that many "problems" of this type might better be termed "fictions." See Beard [1948, p. 216].

powers which are "only softened by a *quasi*"[16] is not good enough. The commissions cannot be left "independent." They must *belong* somewhere, with clear lines of responsibility and accountability. Obviously, their organizational status could be rationalized by placing them *within* any one of the three major branches of government. *Then* the lark would be back on his wing, and God restored to His heaven.

The original theory was that the regulatory commissions were to be agencies of Congress, not the president; the job of the courts was to ensure that the commissions "faithfully executed" the law. What has been widely interpreted as the demonstrated incompetence of Congress to supervise even its own committees, to say nothing of ancillary agencies, led in time to considerable disenchantment with the theory of congressional supervision of regulatory administration. Therefore, during the modern period, with which we are concerned, Rationalist theory has pointed to two diametrically opposed alternatives, each of which has found proponents urging one or the other nostrum as *the* solution to the supposed dilemma. The historically prior solution is that of executive integration of the regulatory commissions, as proposed by the Brownlow Committee. More recently, there has been somewhat greater vocal support for judicial integration of the regulatory commissions, as advocated by the Second Hoover Commission.

In a passage of purple prose, the Brownlow Committee designated the federal regulatory commissions as "a headless 'fourth branch' of the Government." Naturally, this colorful phrase attracted considerable attention, at least for a time. It may still be relied upon by lawyers and political scientists, whose professional memories are long, to jazz up a lecture or to add a risqué touch to what are usually otherwise dull discourses on administrative law. The dozen independent regulatory commissions constitute, the President's Committee continued,

. . . a haphazard deposit of irresponsible agencies and uncoordinated powers. They do violence to the basic theory of the American Constitution that there should be three major branches of the Government

---

16. Mr. Justice Holmes, dissenting in *Springer* v. *Philippine Islands*, 277 U.S. 189, 210 [1928].

and only three. The Congress has found no effective way of supervising them, they cannot be controlled by the President, and they are answerable to the courts only in respect to the *legality* of their activities. [1937, p. 40.]

The remedy proposed by the Brownlow Committee served as a partial answer[17] by F.D.R. to the Supreme Court's decision announced a year or so earlier, which held that the president could not remove a Federal Trade Commissioner on the basis of partisan politics.[18] Since the president could not control—according to the *Rathbun* decision—the exercise of *judicial* discretion by the commissions, the Brownlow Committee [pp. 40–41] took the tack that half a loaf was better than none: all functions of the regulatory commissions *except judicial functions* should be transferred to the corresponding executive departments, where they would (the committee assumed) become subject to the presidential power of administrative direction:

> Any program to restore our constitutional ideal of a fully coordinated Executive Branch responsible to the President must bring within the reach of that responsible control all work done by these independent commissions which is not judicial in nature. . . . Under this proposed plan the regulatory agency would be set up, not in a governmental vacuum outside the executive departments, but within a department. There it would be divided into an administrative section and a judicial section. The administrative section would be a regular bureau or division in the department, headed by a chief with career tenure and staffed under civil-service regulations. It would be directly responsible to the Secretary and through him to the President. The judicial section, on the other hand, would be "in" the department only for purposes of "administrative housekeeping," such as the budget, general personnel administration, and matériel. It [the judicial section] would be wholly independent of the department and the President with respect to its work and its decisions.

It seems tolerably clear that the half a loaf demanded, in form, would most likely have become the lion's share in practice; but this particular vision of the good life was not destined to become

---

17. The rest of Roosevelt's reply to the Court came in the following month, when the President announced his "Court-packing" proposal for the administrative reorganization of the federal courts.

18. *Rathbun* (Humphrey's Executor) v. *United States*, 295 U.S. 602 [1935].

a reality. Thus far, presidential control over the commissions has been extended primarily in three respects: (1) the original Civil Aeronautics Act of 1938 pretty much followed these recommendations, and the president was granted direct power of approval over decisions of the Civil Aeronautics Board affecting the licensing of *foreign* air commerce; (2) there has been some, but limited, extension of budgetary, personnel, and other "housekeeping" controls over the commissions generally; and (3) a series of presidential reorganization plans has centralized internal administrative authority in the chairmen of most of the commissions, which, combined with presidential power to designate the chairmen, has provided a closer link between the regulatory commissions and the White House. Theory, however, has not yet caught up with even these limited changes in practice, as the Schwartz-S.E.C.-Goldfine-Adams fiasco of the spring of 1958 amply demonstrates. Attempts at executive influence in the decision-making of the commissions are still looked upon as generally pernicious, and the Supreme Court recently has seen fit to reaffirm its holding of the *Rathbun* case,[19] relying upon the same rationale employed by the Nine Old Men twenty-three years ago.

The Brownlow Committee's theory of executive integration appears to have become the dogma of most political scientists. Among those, for instance, who in recent years have written most extensively upon organizational problems in federal regulatory administration are Emmette Redford and Marver Bernstein, both of whom have argued *in extenso* in behalf of presidential domination of the commissions. Redford has urged that

. . . the whole executive branch should be integrated under the President so as to give him the opportunities for influencing the direction of policy. *I mean by this to attack the principle of independence of regulatory agencies as it developed in this country.* Independence, if it was ever justified, is now an anachronism. . . . Independence and plural headship [of commissions] . . . have insulated regulatory agencies against a responsible exercise of democratic control. [1954, p. 112.]

The primary justification for placing the regulatory commissions within the ambit of the president's power of administrative direction, in Redford's view, is not the traditional reformer's gambit

---

19. *Wiener* v. *United States,* 357 U.S. 349 [1958].

of "economy and efficiency." For Redford, integration "has a moral purpose"; or, as he restated his position in a subsequent essay:

The argument for integration assumes that the responsibility of all units points upward to the President. To many this is merely an argument for co-ordination. Or it is an argument for democratic control since the presidency is the only representative organ which can supply continuous and unified direction and control of administration. Here integration is argued as a route to the public interest. The argument is based on recognition that many bureaus, commissions, and even departments are clientele-oriented, and that this clientele orientation is often reinforced by associations with friendly elements in the Congress. It is based on recognition that the perspective of organizations is set, and therefore limited, by the functional allocations to them. It is based on the fact that the President is the only official of the government who is forced by direct responsibility to the one great public constituency to try to keep his mind on the public interest. [1958, pp. 128–29.]

In his book on the federal regulatory commissions, Bernstein arrives at similar conclusions, in a chapter which he entitles "Independence, Responsibility, and the Public Interest":

Under prevailing conditions a regulatory commission's view of the public welfare is inevitably limited to its own sphere of experience. Parceling out regulatory tasks to a number of independent commissions makes administration in the public interest extremely hazardous if not impossible. As long as each agency administers its regulations without regard for programs of other agencies, the welfare of the regulated industry becomes a standard of reference for determining the public interest. . . . One of the significant limitations of the commission in its search for the public interest is inherent in its independent status. . . . The public interest can scarcely be identified and defined short of effective coordination of the various regulatory programs with each other and with national economic policy. As regulatory policies are fitted into a coherent program of national regulation of economic affairs, the nature of the public interest becomes less abstract and less dependent upon the limited experience of the individual commission. [1955, pp. 161–63.]

Bernstein does conclude, somewhat pessimistically, that even executive integration would not solve the basic problem, in view of the lack of effective central planning and supervision of a coherent program of national regulation of even those national economic policies that clearly are, at the present time, under the president's power of administrative direction.

The other solution to the problem of regulatory-commission independence is that of judicial integration, and this has been the recurrent gospel of the organized legal profession. On its face, the plea of the Second Hoover Commission [1955b, p. 84] for the "Transfer of Judicial Functions of Administrative Agencies to the Courts" looks like nothing more than the other half of the loaf demanded by the Brownlow Committee. Closer inspection, however, reveals that the Commission, echoing its Task Force on Legal Services and Procedure, really covets the same prize as the Brownlow Committee: control over regulatory-commission policy, with the significant difference that the Hoover Commission would give such policy control to the courts instead of to the president. Moreover, the Hoover Commission asked for more than the "judicial functions" of the independent regulatory commissions: the Commission proposed to raid several of the major executive departments, with the objective of transferring the enforcement of certain statutes from the executive branch to the judicial branch. The avowed emphasis of the Commission was not upon the more vigorous prosecution of "the public interest," but rather upon the more effective protection of private rights.

"Where functions performed by administrative agencies may not be readily imposed upon the existing courts of general jurisdiction, but should nevertheless be removed from administrative control," said the Commission, "we propose that they be placed in a court of special jurisdiction, to be known as the Administrative Court of the United States" [1955b, pp. 85–86]. The major functional areas which, in the judgment of the Commission, presently are ripe for such judicialization are those of taxation, trade regulation, and labor-management relations [pp. 87–88]. The agencies whose functions might, in part, be subjected to judicial integration include the following:

Federal Trade Commission
Interstate Commerce Commission
Federal Communications Commission

    Civil Aeronautics Board
    Federal Reserve Board
    United States Tariff Commission
    Federal Power Commission
    Department of the Interior
    Department of Agriculture
    National Labor Relations Board
    Tax Court of the United States.

It should be noted that the former Board of Tax Appeals of the Treasury Department already had gone through this metamorphosis, having become the Tax Court of the United States in 1943; all that was recommended in this regard was that the Tax Court be reorganized as the Tax Section of the proposed new Administrative Court.

As noted by the Task Force in its own report to the Commission:

> One of the difficulties in proposing judicialization of the administrative process is that it is bound to affect primarily those agencies which have been the longest established and have developed the soundest methods of administration. It is only after a period of experience that separation can readily be accomplished. The divestment of judicial functions is thus not a criticism of the agency, but an acknowledgment of its ability to handle the problems of adjudication within its jurisdiction. It is a recognition that the governmental function has attained sufficient maturity and stability to warrant its future treatment in accordance with the more traditional concept of the separation of powers.[20] [1955a, p. 242.]

From this point of view, judicial integration of administrative functions is a form of accolade, a reward bestowed for distinguished service, like the traditional gold watch conferred by the general manager upon the retiring employee in recognition of his many years of faithful service.

The Hoover Commission itself, like its Task Force, was quite candid in pointing out that the proposed Administrative Court was to be thought of only as the chrysalis stage in the metamorphosis of judicialization:

---

20. Cf. Bernstein [1957] chap. iii: "The Life Cycle of Regulatory Commissions."

... once it is established the Administrative Court will provide an instrumentality to which, from time to time in the future, additional adjudicatory functions in special areas might be transferred. Additional Sections of the Court could readily be established. The Administrative Court thus would serve as an intermediate stage in the evolution of administrative adjudication and the transfer of judicial activities from the agencies to courts of general jurisdiction. [1955b, p. 87.]

Every administrative worm could look forward to the happy day when it would become a judicial butterfly!

Apart from its concern for reorganizing the federal regulatory commissions, Rationalist theory has expressed little concern for the public interest in administrative decision-making. Perhaps this seeming neglect reflects the major influence that the scientific-management movement has exerted upon the development of American public-administration theory [Waldo, 1948, chap. iii]. Although the management scientists developed quite elaborate theories of administrative decision-making, they produced no articulate theory of the public interest. This is hardly surprising, since they assumed that adoption of their proposals necessarily would produce the best possible results; it was not considered necessary to offer scientific proof that it would be in the public interest to have the best results. The management scientists assumed an ethical basis for their value-free propositions about administrative behavior, and they found this moral basis for an amoral society in the Public Will. As Norton Long has commented,

The legitimacy of the will, like the concept of sovereignty, provides the basis for a logical deductive system moving from the first principle—be it the will of the people via Congress, or the will of the people via Congress through President, or the will of the people via President. In any event, *the prime problem of administration is to give effect to this will* [according to the Rationalist theory of management scientism]. [Emphasis added; 1954, pp. 24–25.]

The general position of the scientists is well represented by the work of Luther Gulick, who stated the fundamental credo in his essay, "Science, Values, and Public Administration" [chap. xi in Gulick and Urwick, 1937], although a decade was to pass before Herbert Simon made explicit the implications, for this theory of administrative decision-making, of the dichotomy between "ought" and "is." As Gulick put it, " 'should' is a word political scientists should not use in scientific discussion!" [Gulick and Urwick, 1937, p. 192]. Such dogmatism was certain to provoke rebuttal; and probably the most perceptive of Gulick's critics has been Norton Long. Although he makes no specific reference to Gulick, Long has written that:

> The attempt of some writers, influenced by logical positivism, to construct a value-free science of administration may well have the unintended and logically unwarranted result of reviving the policy-administration dichotomy in new verbiage. Policy would become a matter of determining values, a legislative-political matter; administration would consist in the application of the values set by the political branch to sets of facts ascertained by the administrative. . . . However attractive an administration receiving its values from political policy-makers may be, it has one fatal flaw. It does not accord with the facts of administrative life. Nor is it likely to. In fact, it is highly dubious even as an ideal. Though the quest for science, mathematical precision, and certainty has an undeniable psychological appeal, it runs the risk of becoming a fastidious piece of ivory-tower escapism. It is this psychological thrust of logical positivism as vulgarized in the social sciences that constitutes its greatest danger to responsible inquiry. [1954, p. 22.]

If Luther Gulick was the prophet of the new science of management, Herbert Simon has become its Messiah. According to Simon the application of management science to the behavior of human beings in administrative organizations is essentially a problem in engineering:

> The theory of administration is concerned with how an organization should be constructed and operated in order to accomplish its work efficiently. A fundamental principle of administration, which follows almost immediately from the rational character of "good" administration, is that among several alternatives involving the same expenditure the one should always be selected which leads to the greatest accomplishment of administrative objectives; and among several alternatives that lead to the same accomplishment the one should be selected which involves the least expenditure. Since this "principle of efficiency" is characteristic of any activity that attempts rationally to maximize the attainment of certain ends with the use of scarce means, it is as characteristic of economic theory as it is of administrative theory. The "administrative man" takes his place alongside the

classical [and equally mythical?] "economic man." . . . Perhaps the simplest method of approach is to consider the single member of the administrative organization, and ask what the limits are to the quantity and quality of his output. These limits include (a) limits on his ability to *perform*, and (b) limits on his ability to *make correct decisions*. To the extent that these limits are removed, the administrative organization approaches its goal of high efficiency. Two persons, given the same skills, the same objectives and values, the same knowledge and information, can rationally decide only upon the same course of action. [1947, pp. 38–39.]

Moreover, Simon makes it crystal clear that administrators get their orders from "higher authority," which presumably refers to the representatives of the people at one or the other end of Pennsylvania Avenue. In this regard, Norton Long has remarked that:

The view of administration as sheerly instrumental, or even largely instrumental, must be rejected as empirically untenable and ethically unwarranted. This rejection will entail abandonment, on the one hand, of Herbert Simon's quest for a value-free administration and, on the other, of the over-simplified dogma of an overloaded legislative supremacy of his logical comrade in arms, Charles Hyneman. These two views fit like hand in glove. Legislative supremacy provides Simon with value premises, which can then permit a value-free science of administration the esthetic delight of unique and verifiably determinate problem solutions through the application of the value premises to the fact premises. . . . But, alas, we know this institutional divorce, however requisite for a value-free science of administration, does not exist. [1954, p. 23.]

Whether it exists in the real world or not, Simon has to assume that the institutional divorce has taken place. Furthermore, the organizational progeny who constitute the fruits of this disunion appear to be a society of administrative eunuchs:

. . . The criterion which the administrator applies to factual problems is one of efficiency. The resources, the input, at the disposal of the administrator are strictly limited. It is not his function to establish a utopia. It is his function to maximize the attainment of the governmental objectives (assuming they have been agreed upon), by the efficient employment of the limited resources that are available to him. . . . Once the system of values which is to govern an administrative choice has been specified, there is one and only one "best" decision, and this decision is determined by the organizational values and situation, and not by the personal motives of the member of the organization who makes the decision. Within the area of discretion, once an individual has decided, on the basis of his personal motives, to recognize the organizational objectives, his further behavior is determined not by personal motives, but by the demands of efficiency. . . . The need for an administrative theory resides in the fact that there *are* practical limits to human rationality, and that these limits are not static, but depend upon the organizational environment in which the individual's decision takes place. The task of administration is so to design this environment that the individual will approach as close as practicable to rationality (judged in terms of the organization's goals) in his decisions. [1947, pp. 186–87, 204, 240–41.][21]

It has been said that the working out of Shakespeare's plots required the intervention of fools; it would appear that the administrative ideal postulated by these logical positivists is automation. Simon's "administrative man" turns out to be a robot.[22]

E. The Judiciary

THE EFFECT OF POSITIVISM upon legal theory has been summarized by Wolfgang Friedmann:

21. The text quoted and the page-number citations are identical in the revised edition [1957], both below and for the preceding quotation from Simon.

22. It may be said, indeed, that the robot actually exists! A decade after the original publication of his remarks that are quoted above, Simon wrote that "we are now able to simulate complex human behavior, using [a] decision-making program, with the aid of an ordinary electronic computer. . . . [This is] mentioned here simply to emphasize that I do not regard the description of human rationality . . . as hypothetical, but *as now having been verified in its main features*" [rev. ed.; 1957, pp. xxvi–xxvii; emphasis added]. Cf. Harold Lasswell's recent statement that "the time is approaching when machines will be sufficiently well developed to make it practicable for trial runs to be carried out in which human decision-makers and robots are pitted against one another. When machines are more perfect a bench of judicial robots, for example, can be constructed" [1955, p. 398]. Lasswell does add, however, that "In the meanwhile, before robots have been developed to the necessary pitch of technical perfection, there will be ample room for research on discretion and especially upon relationships pertinent to extending the role of insight and understanding. Even in an automatizing world some top-level choices must be made. In that sense at least discretion is here to stay" [p. 399].

Positivism mistrusts *a priori* assumptions and ideas, it places its faith in observations. The scientific method is extended to "practical reason," including law. Accordingly, the number and variety of positivist legal theories is as great as that of the sciences, each claiming certainty and accuracy in its own field. Therefore, positivism in jurisprudence comprises legal movements, poles apart in every respect, except for their common aversion to metaphysical theories and natural law in particular. As often as not, however, positivist theories substitute for the articulate idealism of the theories which they fight an inarticulate idealism of their own, which is presented as a scientific fact based on observations.

Legal logic dominates analytical jurisprudence . . . [while] psychological and sociological fact-study [dominates] realist jurisprudence. . . . But the antagonism between such movements as analytical positivism and realism . . . is as strong as their common opposition to idealistic theories. [1953, pp. 50–51.]

The Englishman John Austin was, of course, the father of modern analytical jurisprudence. His basic propositions were that (1) positive law is what *is*, not what ought-to-be; (2) positive law is a statement of the will of the sovereign—which, of course, could be a *popular* sovereign, possessed of a "Public Will"; hence (3), positive law is the sovereign's command and is enforced by appropriate authoritative sanctions. Obviously, the public interest is found in inflexible obedience to the public will. Apart from the ruminations of a few judges and law professors, this remains the orthodox theory of law in the United States. Not only does it correspond with the experience, and therefore the beliefs, of the laity; it is also "specifically the faith of the professional lawyer," as Friedmann has pointed out:

The analytical lawyer is a positivist. He is not concerned with ideals; he takes the law as a given matter created by the State, whose authority he does not question. On this material he works, by means of a system of rules of legal logic, apparently complete and self-contained. In order to be able to work on this assumption, he must attempt to prove to his own satisfaction that thinking about the law can be excluded from the lawyer's province. Therefore the legal system is made watertight against all ideological intrusions, and all legal problems are couched in terms of legal logic. . . . The certainty which the analytical positivist pursues as the chief end of law was largely provided by the political and social background against which it could develop. . . . The lawyer, and the private lawyer in particular, could concentrate on legal technique, on craftsmanship rather than design. [pp. 163, 164.]

One conspicuous and well-known manifestation of analytical positivism in the United States has been the official justification by the Supreme Court for its judicial review of acts of Congress, from John Marshall's opinion in *Marbury* v. *Madison* up to the present. However much the Supreme Court has admitted sociology and social psychology into opinions dealing with statutory interpretation and judicial review of state legislation, the "slot-machine theory of jurisprudence" continues to provide the official rationale for judicial veto power over national legislation. Certainly the best-known modern exposition of the theory is that of Mr. Justice Roberts, delivering the opinion of the Court in the decision which invalidated the original A.A.A. program of the New Deal:

> It is sometimes said that the court assumes a power to overrule or control the action of the people's representatives. This is a misconception. The Constitution is the supreme law of the land and ordained and established by the people. All legislation must conform to the principles it lays down. When an act of Congress is appropriately challenged in the courts as not conforming to the constitutional mandate the judicial branch of the Government has only one duty—to lay the article of the Constitution which is invoked beside the statute which is challenged and to decide whether the latter squares with the former. All the court does, or can do, is to announce its considered judgment upon the question. The only power it has, if such it may be called, is the power of judgment. This court neither approves nor condemns any legislative policy. [*United States* v. *Butler*, 297 U.S. 1, 62–63, 1936.]

Twenty-two years later, we find Chief Justice Warren, speaking for the liberal plurality in a more recent Court decision holding an act of Congress unconstitutional,[23] and reciting language that constitutes, at best, a tight paraphrase of words originally uttered by John Marshall over a century and a half earlier:

> . . . we are mindful of the gravity of the issue inevitably raised whenever the constitutionality of an Act of the National Legislature

---

23. *Trop* v. *Dulles*, 356 U.S. 86, 103 [1958]. Cf. *Marbury* v. *Madison*, 1 Cranch 137, 176–78 [1803].

is challenged. No member of the Court believes that in this case the statute before us can be construed to avoid the issue of constitutionality. That issue confronts us, and the task of resolving it is inescapably ours. This task requires the exercise of judgment, not the reliance upon personal preferences. Courts must not consider the wisdom of statutes but neither can they sanction as being merely unwise that which the Constitution forbids.

We are oath-bound to defend the Constitution. This obligation requires that congressional enactments be judged by the standards of the Constitution. The Judiciary has the duty of implementing the constitutional safeguards that protect individual rights.

Then, having stated the argument, Warren proceeded to follow the model (Marshall's opinion) by repeating it:

The provisions of the Constitution . . . are vital, living principles that authorize and limit governmental powers in our nation. They are the rules of government. When the constitutionality of an Act of Congress is challenged in this Court, we must apply those rules. . . . When it appears that an Act of Congress conflicts with one of these provisions, we have no choice but to enforce the paramount commands of the Constitution. We are sworn to do no less. . . . the ordeal of judgment cannot be shirked. [356 U.S. 86, 103–04; and cf. 1 Cranch 137, 180.]

Although there have been a few iconoclasts who have gad-flown about from time to time,[24] the orthodoxy appears to possess great vitality, for one also reads in one of the most recently published text-casebooks in constitutional law to be authored by political scientists that:

Perhaps the most distinctive feature of our Constitution is that it is *law*, paramount, *supreme law*, and hence subject to interpretation by the Supreme Court in cases properly before it. . . . Nor does this power in the Supreme Court give to it any practical or real omnipotence. The Court is simply exercising a power granted by the Constitution—judicial power. The effect, at least in theory, is not to elevate Court over legislature, but rather to make "the power of the people superior to both."[25] [Mason and Beaney, 1959, p. 9.]

---

24. For examples, see Cahill [1952], especially chap. iii and references cited therein.

25. Perhaps it should be pointed out that this statement appears to be in sharp contrast with other views expressed by Professor Mason [e.g., 1953 and 1958].

This is popular sovereignty with a vengeance! Whatever the result of judicial decision-making may be in substantive terms, we can rest assured that it will be in the public interest. It is so by definition.

So the Legal Rationalists tell us that the law (including the decisions of judges) is the vehicle by means of which the will of the people is made manifest. Judges are skilled craftsmen whose expertise lies in their conditioned responses to questions of public policy. Subject to certain corrections emanating from the pinnacle of the judicial hierarchy, these technicians deduce appropriate rules of decision by a logical process, adherence to which assures results—no matter what they may be—that are in the public interest. Rationalist theory postulates a theocracy with a priesthood of the robe; and the only test for the validity of the public interest it defines is the willingness of the investigator to subscribe to the articles of faith.

idealist theory

Who shall speak for the people?
Who knows the works from A to Z
  so he can say, "I know what the
  people want"? Who is this phenom?
  where did he come from?

            Sandburg, *The People, Yes.*

The Idealists are social engineers. They view the public as an inadequate, indeed, as an incompetent source of public policy. The Idealists would substitute hieratics for hierarchy. They are necessarily a heterogenous group, since they reject the single path to salvation of the Rationalists, offering instead a multiplicity of direct channels to Wisdom, Truth, and the Public Good. The positive decisional norms for politicians, legislators, the president, administrators, and judges necessarily are vague and incomplete, since only the natural law (which is anterior to, and higher than, the positive law made by man) is perfect and complete. Implicit in such assumptions is the notion that not only may positive law be an inadequate guide to decision-making because of its vagueness; it may also conflict with the higher law, thus creating additional decisional dilemmas for the public official.

Since each official—whether he be congressman, president, administrator, or judge—inevitably is left with a residue of personal discretion (which we may conceive of as the decisional alternatives regarding which he has received no guidance from higher positive authority), the Idealists suggest that the obviously moral course for the official to follow is to consult the higher law (i.e., his own conscience) in preference to his personal predilections. Idealists castigate the selfish interest groups and the, at best, amoral political parties; they argue that congressmen should let their conscience be their guide rather than constituency pressures. The president should be a man like Washington who belongs to no party but to all of the people.

In direct opposition to the Rationalists, the Idealists would maximize (or, at the very least, expand) the scope of official autonomy and discretion, thus placing all "public servants" in the heart of the policy-making process. This necessitates a highly moral official world, which becomes personified in the image of the Independent Congressman, the Strong President, the Good Administrator, and the Wise Judge. The public interest is created by the imaginative manipulation of not-too-stubborn facts—including other persons, in and out of government—by official Philosopher Kings [cf. Weldon, 1953, pp. 138–43.]

A. Constituency

PERHAPS THE MOST FAMOUS of *The Federalist* papers was No. 10, written by James Madison and published in the *New York Packet*, on Friday, November 23, 1787. I have found no clear-cut statements of the Idealist position regarding constituency political action in the writings of contemporary political scientists, but political scientists do use Madison's essay in their teaching, and under these circumstances, it seems warranted to utilize the classic prototype as an example. Madison argued both against the excesses of political parties and in favor of a system of representation, under which men of good will, rather than the mass of the people, would make political decisions. He deplored the fact that

> . . . the public good is disregarded in the conflicts of rival parties, and that measures are too often decided, not according to the rules of justice and the rights of the minor party, but by the superior force of an interested and overbearing majority. . . . A zeal for different opinions concerning religion, concerning government, and many other points . . . have . . . divided mankind into parties, inflamed them with mutual animosity, and rendered them much more disposed to vex and oppress each other than to co-operate for their common good. . . . But the most common and durable source of factions has been the various and unequal distribution of property. Those who hold and those who are without property have ever formed distinct interests in society. Those who are creditors, and those who are debtors, fall under a like discrimination. A landed interest, a manufacturing interest, a mercantile interest, a moneyed interest, with many lesser interests, grow up of necessity in civilized nations, and divide them into different classes, actuated by different sentiments and views. The regulation of these various and interfering interests forms the principal task of modern legislation, and involves the spirit of party and faction in the necessary and ordinary operations of the government. [Hamilton, Madison, and Jay, 1901 ed., I, 62, 64–65.]

Madison's express opposition to the dangers of *both* political parties and interest groups, which he felt could be equally pernicious and enemies of good government, remains the logical (though often unarticulated) premise underlying the position of contemporary Idealist theorists of the public interest. This is one of the basic distinctions among the three groups of theorists. As we have seen, the Rationalists are pro-political-party and anti-interest-group; as we shall see, the Realists are pro-interest-group (which they define to include political parties); but the Idealists are essentially anti-politics, and as for political parties and interest groups, the characteristic attitude of the modern Idealist is the same as that of Madison: "A plague o' both your houses!" [cf. Berns, 1957, p. 221]. The Idealists also specifically reject the idea of majority rule, which is so central to the thinking of the Rationalists. In the words of Madison, "when a majority is included in a faction, the form of *popular* government . . . enables it to sacrifice to its ruling passion or interest both the public good and the rights of other citizens" [Emphasis added; Hamilton, Madison, and Jay, 1901 ed., Vol I, p. 66]. Madison was contrasting what he called a "pure" or popular democracy with the republican or representative form of government to be established under the proposed Constitution, which offered the great advantage of making majority rule *impossible:*

> The . . . great points of difference between a democracy and a republic are: first, the delegation of the government, in the latter, to a small number of citizens elected by the rest. . . . The effect of the first difference is, on the one hand, to refine and enlarge the public views, by passing them through the medium of a chosen body of citizens, whose wisdom may best discern the true interest of their country, and whose patriotism and love of justice will be least likely to sacrifice it to temporary or partial considerations. Under such a regulation, it may well happen that the public voice, pronounced by the representatives of the people, will be more consonant to the public good than if pronounced by the people themselves. . . . [pp. 67–68.]

The Federalists' expectation regarding the Electoral College provides a good example of the kind of interposition of the judgment of the wise and well-born that Madison undoubtedly had in mind. It is a commonplace, however, that the rise of an opposition party under the leadership of Jefferson brought about an almost immediate extralegal amendment of this aspect of the Constitution; and, for over a century and a half, presidential electors have been political hacks who rubber-stamp the popular vote, rather than wise men of their respective communities who meet together to choose the man best qualified, in their own judgment, to serve as president. Political parties destroyed the Electoral College as a representative institution, in the sense that Madison had in mind. Rationalists applaud the change, and Idealists, to be logical and consistent, must deplore it. The fact of political parties and the theory of independent representation are intertwined, generally as well as in this specific example.

The point has not escaped modern Idealists, one of whom, not too long ago, quoted with approval a dictum of Lord Halifax. The noble Englishman, speaking several hundred years ago, said that "the best kind of party is in some sort of conspiracy against the nation." His follower was Mortimer Adler, lately identified with the teaching of "Great Books" at the University of Chicago, and, more recently, Director of the Institute for Philosophical Research. In Dr. Adler's view, political parties are the enemies of true democracy:

> . . . permanent party organizations, which seek to endure regardless of the solution of specific issues, are contrary to the common good. For what end do they obviously serve by seeking to endure regardless of specific issues? The end of power, not justice; the end of dominating the electorate or legislature. Instead of real issues causing partisanship specifically responsible to them, permanent party organizations cause political issues, which, as a consequence, are often unreal and merely pretexts in the struggle for power. I do not mean to say the permanent parties are totally vicious. They serve the common good in so far as they are instruments of debate and deliberation, and in so far as they are necessary to the machinery of representation. I am saying only that in so far as they are permanent, parties are organized and operate for another end, namely, their exclusive power, power as such divorced from authority, and, therefore, that permanent party organizations are inimical to the common good. . . . I say that there is an essentially vicious element in [the existing party] system. [1939, p. 75.]

Political scientists, however, appear to agree overwhelmingly that political parties are essential for the functioning of political democracy. Only in utopian literature are parties dispensed with. In modern experience, they have been destroyed in fact (excepting the one official party which is infused in the structure of the corporate state) only by the totalitarian regimes of the Communists, Facists, and Nazis. Dr. Adler wrote at a time when Stalin, Mussolini, and Hitler were all at the peak of their power, so it is not unreasonable to suppose that he had some awareness of the practical as well as the theoretical implications of the corporate-will concept, when he wrote that:

> Others [and in context, these obviously include Adler] hold that the essential principles of democracy are not only preserved but better realized in a corporative state . . . [and that] it will be possible for democracy to come to its full fruition in a harmonious union of social and political principles that are essentially democratic. . . . Those who claim that parties are indispensable are merely confessing that they cannot imagine the institutions which will transform representa-

tive government and make it appropriate for the organic democracy of the corporative order.[1] [1939, pp. 80–81.]

It is apparent that one of the things that "the organic democracy of the corporative order" will not tolerate is dissent, because Adler also says that:

> . . . in so far as men are individual members of a community, they *must* be ordered to the common good, which is superior to the private interests of each and every individual. . . . The common good cannot be achieved by a compromise among conflicting private interests, whether of individuals, sects or parties . . . the common good is everywhere the same in essense. . . . The common good by its very nature requires the cooperation of men of good will, as well as *the coercion* or resistance *of their opponents.* [Emphasis added; 1939, pp. 60, 63, 64.]

No amount of casuistry or mouthing of the word "democratic" can disguise the self-evident fact that the systems of government corresponding empirically with what Adler recommends are those of the totalitarian dictatorships, not the United States as it exists at present, and not as it has existed in the past, except, to some extent, in wartime. Adler does not draw the analogy, but Americans who have lived through the past three decades know only too well that the corporate will of an organic democracy of the corporate order must have a human interpreter, who serves as spokesman. As Carl J. Friedrich has asserted:

> Authoritarians have always presumed to answer [the] question [how to create a common public interest] in an authoritative way. From Plato to Marx and Hitler they have been ready to say: I know! Leave it to me and all will be well. [1950, p. 264.]

Pendleton Herring, writing at the same time as Adler, has agreed with Friedrich:

---

1. At least one person, other than Dr. Adler, has possessed the requisite imagination: the late Elijah Jordan, also a philosopher. In his *Theory of Legislation: An Essay on the Dynamics of Public Mind* (1930, and republished in 1952 with a new preface in which the author refutes his critics), Jordan discusses *in extenso* the concept of corporate will and the model of the ideal corporate state. Philosopher friends of mine advise me that they do not consider Jordan to be a totalitarian. I regret to say that I do not understand Jordan, so I cannot very well attempt to explain his theory of the public interest, other than to state that Jordan is an Idealist who identifies the public interest with his notion of Corporate Will.

No ruling group can properly claim the sole right to speak for the people. Hitler apparently has mass support for his regime, but we must deny his right to claim the sanction of public opinion as we understand it under a democracy. Under our political creed power can never be crystallized in a final determinate human will. It rests rather upon an ever fresh interplay of forces. [1940, p. 305.]

Adler's recommendation that force be employed to correct the errors in thought and belief of men who are not "of good will" has been seemingly criticized, at least by indirection: a recent book by McGovern and Collier [1957, p. 138] defends the philosophical position of "conservative liberalism," the label appropriated by the authors to describe their own and related reactionary views. "Practically all conservative liberals," they tell us, "aim not at the greatest happiness of the greatest number but at the greatest possible 'good' or well-being of the community and above this of *all* sections of the community." Turning then to the Adler thesis of enforced enlightenment, although they do not mention Adler by name, McGovern and Collier appear to argue the liberal point of view:

There are some who feel the state can best promote the common good by ignoring the desires and caprices of the individual, and compelling each person to do what he ought to do if both his own and the common good is to be advanced. . . . Such a view is one sided, to say the least. A careful study of history shows that, generally speaking, a community attains a greater knowledge of truth and therefore increases in wisdom when the state steps aside and permits its citizens to form their own opinions after thought, including those which are downright superstitious or silly. . . . The state should indeed seek to promote morality, but it must learn that true morality exists, as Milton pointed out long ago, only when a man is free to choose between good and evil and voluntarily chooses the good. [pp. 138–39.]

However, the argument immediately becomes circular, and we are back in support of Adler; in the very next paragraph [pp. 139–40], McGovern and Collier conclude that "the common good or the public welfare is best promoted neither by extreme collectivism nor by extreme individualism, but by a compromise which might be expressed in the phrase: 'As much individualism as possible, but as much state interference as is necessary to maintain the common good.'" Of course, it would be equally logical to express the compromise between the extremes of individualism and collectivism in the phrase: As much individualism as is necessary to maintain the common good, but as much state interference as possible. Other permutations of the phrases of the sentence would reflect logically possible compromises. The tip-off to the end of the continuum near which these authors' compromise lies is found in their definition of state interference: it is defined as the necessity that supports the common good, while individualism is the enemy of the common good that must be suppressed whenever it tends to get out of hand: "when the [moral] expressions or acts . . . of a person or group of persons threaten the general well-being to the community, it is not only the right but the duty of the state to interfere and put a stop to such expressions or acts." [p. 140.]

Of course, both liberals and conservatives, to say nothing of conservative liberals, can agree to such a proposition as this, in the abstract. Their disagreement comes in applying the rule to concrete cases; those who believe in absolutes find it easier than those who do not to ride roughshod over dissenters expressing evil and dangerous views. In the process of suppressing heresy, are they not really serving the true interests of the suppressed heretics? Do not such Idealists act in the public interest, the interest of all mankind?

Neo-fascist theories of the public interest in regard to constituency political action appear to have disappeared, at least among responsible American spokesmen, with the public discrediting of the Nazi and Fascist regimes at the close of World War II. However, there are still proponents of a polity in which politicians rise above the level of morality possible for their constituents, and define the public interest *for* the people, on the basis of a wisdom revealed only to true leaders. In his recent book, *The Public Philosophy*, Walter Lippmann declares:

Living adults share, we must believe, the same public interest. For them, however, the public interest is mixed with, and is often at odds with, their private and special interests. Put this way, we can say, I suggest, that the public interest may be presumed to be what men would choose if they saw clearly, thought rationally, acted disinterestedly and benevolently. [1955, p. 42.]

Unfortunately, men rarely behave this way, and the American system of government does little to encourage them to do so because

. . . the normal propensity of democratic governments is to please the largest number of voters. The pressure of the electorate is normally for the soft [as distinguished from the hard, painful, unpleasant, tough-minded] side of the equations. That is why governments are unable to cope with reality when elected assemblies and mass opinions become decisive in the state, when there are no *statesmen to resist the inclination of the voters* and there are only politicians to excite and to exploit them. [Emphasis added; p. 46.]

Lippmann continues, at this point citing as an authority none other than Mortimer Adler:

The public philosophy is known as *natural law*. . . . Except on the premises of this philosophy, it is impossible to reach intelligible and workable conceptions of popular election, majority rule, representative assemblies, free speech, loyalty, property, corporations [etc.]. [Emphasis added; p. 101.]

A similar view is entertained by McGovern and Collier, who state that "most students of human relations have concluded that 'the good life' can be effectively promoted only when [the Stoic-Christian] concept [of natural law] is steadily kept in mind" [1957, p. 150]. Precisely which "students of human relations" the authors may have had in mind is a matter of conjecture, but it does not seem likely that they include the behavioral-science prophets of a new "Social Ethic" whose doings are criticized, *in extenso*, in *The Organization Man* [Whyte, 1956].

B. Congress

IF THE LEGISLATOR must choose from among the competing claims and influences of party, constituency, group interests, and his own conscience, Idealists are certain that he can make only one moral choice: to obey the dictates of his own conscience. This is not quite the same as the assertion of Psychological Realists, who argue that he necessarily will interject his own personal value system into his decisions.[2] The Idealists assume that reasonable men consulting the common good enshrined in the higher law necessarily will come up with the *same* answer; and that answer does not represent each individual's own notions of right and wrong, but the absolute truth that has been revealed to him. The Idealists insist, therefore, that congressmen best serve the public interest when each votes his own conscience, rather than following the false gods symbolized by the party whip and by the constituent's or lobbyist's buttonhold.

The classic statement of the Idealist point of view is that of Edmund Burke in his speech to the electors of Bristol, on November 3, 1774, upon being declared by the sheriffs to have been duly elected one of the representatives in Parliament for that city:

Certainly, Gentlemen, it ought to be the happiness and glory of a representative to live in the strictest union, the closest correspondence, and the most reserved communication with his constituents. Their wishes ought to have great weight with him; their opinions high respect; their business unremitted attention. It is his duty to sacrifice his repose, his pleasures, his satisfactions to theirs,—and above all, ever, and in all cases, to prefer their interest to his own.

But his unbiased opinion, his mature judgment, his enlightened conscience, he ought not to sacrifice to you, to any man, or to any set of men living. These he does not derive from your pleasure,—nor from the law and the Constitution. They are a trust from Providence, for the abuse of which he is deeply answerable. Your representative owes you, not his industry only, but his judgment; and he betrays, instead of serving, you if he sacrifices it to your opinion. [1881 ed., p. 95.]

Burke also stated the classic refutation of the Popular Rationalist theory of representation:

My worthy colleague says, his will ought to be subservient to yours. If that be all, the thing is innocent. If government were a matter of will upon any side, yours, without question, ought to be superior. But government and legislation are matters of reason and judgment, and not of inclination; and what sort of reason is that in which the determination precedes the discussion, in which one set of men deliberate and another decide, and where those who form

---

2. For an excellent discussion of the effect on his voting behavior of the "pictures" in the legislator's mind, see Dahl [1950], chap. i, "The Congressman and His Beliefs."

the conclusion are perhaps three hundred miles distant from those who hear the argument?

To deliver an opinion is the right of all men; that of constituents is a weighty and respectable opinion, which a representative ought always to rejoice to hear, and which he ought always most seriously to consider. But *authoritative* instructions, *mandates* issued, which the member is bound blindly and implicitly to obey, to vote, and to argue for, though contrary to the clearest conviction of his judgment and conscience,—these are things utterly unknown to the laws of this land, and which arise from a fundamental mistake of the whole order and tenor of our Constitution. [pp. 95–96.]

It may be worth noting, parenthetically, that the national legislature of the United States *is* called "the Congress." Parliament, Burke continued,

. . . is not a *congress* of ambassadors from different and hostile interests, which interests each must maintain, as an agent and advocate, against other agents and advocates; but Parliament is a *deliberative* assembly of *one* nation, with *one* interest, that of the whole—where not local purposes, not local prejudices, ought to guide, but the general good, resulting from the general reason of the whole. You choose a member, indeed; but when you have chosen him, he is not a member of Bristol, but is a member of *Parliament*. [p. 96.]

"This idealistic conception," Carl J. Friedrich has written [1950, p. 265], "accords neither with the reality of politics, nor yet with the democratic conception of the 'will of the people' " [cf. Eulau *et al.*, 1959]. "Even in Burke's own day," Friedrich continued,

many a listener to his speech must have chuckled inwardly as he reflected upon the complete subservience of most members of Parliament to the great aristocratic landowners, who did not even have to issue instructions, so assiduously did "their" members study their every wish before each vote in Parliament. . . . Burke's doctrine of reason and conscience as applied to representation and electoral responsibility was an untenable idealization even in his own day. [p. 266.]

Obviously, Friedrich is in error when he says that the Burkian doctrine is untenable; it *is* widely reiterated, and generally with approbation, by most of the texts and other books about Congress that have appeared throughout the past generation. Willoughby, for instance, quotes Burke's letter in full, and places the doctrine of "convictions and conscience" first in his analysis of representation theory, saying that,

. . . the member may take the position that, in electing him to office, the electorate has granted to him what, in the legal profession, is known as a full power of attorney to conduct their affairs according to his best judgment. It is the principle of a large body of persons selecting their wise men to act for them. When this principle is followed, the member is a representative in the full sense of the term. He is not a mere delegate or agent in the sense that it is his duty to take orders from or to act in the capacity of a mere agent to execute orders given to him by his principal. This view rests upon the basis that, while the people should have a voice in the conduct of public affairs, their voice can best and most effectively be exercised by a small body of select and highly qualified specialists rather than by the people themselves acting directly in a collective capacity upon specific issues. It is the essence of such a view that the body of wise men shall act upon their own best judgment. While it is their duty to keep steadily in mind the interests of the people and to seek to determine what are their wishes, the responsibility of the final decisions is to be theirs. A body acting in this way is a representative assembly of a pure type. [1934, pp. 38–39.]

Willoughby's theory of representation certainly is "pure," in the sense that no legislative assembly has ever existed, in the western democracies at least, that has behaved according to the theory. Perhaps the closest example that could be found among American political institutions would be the Electoral College, as conceived in the Philadelphia Convention and as described in *The Federalist* [Hamilton, Madison, and Jay, 1901 ed., Vol II, pp. 35–36 (No 68, by Hamilton)]. But as we have already noted, the Electoral College has not functioned according to the intent of the "Founding Fathers" since the administration of George Washington. On the contrary, for a presidential elector to disregard constituency instructions—an event that occurred in 1948 for only the second time since 1824—is now considered to be the height of irresponsibility. Instead of being the wise men in their communities, electors are small-time political flunkies and hangers-on. The rise of the party system had destroyed the Burkian-Federalist concept of the Electoral College before the end of the eighteenth century.

Nevertheless, there is a certain sardonic irony in the fact that the Burkian theory remains today the avowed faith of practicing congressmen [see Dahl, 1950, pp. 13–14, 39–40, 265 n. 5]. Especially when speaking to his constituents, the congressman of today is likely to say that his votes are determined by his personal convictions and best judgment; he is not the sort of man who bows to the whip of party leaders or yields to the selfish demands of lobbyists, even from among his own constituents! The pages of the *Congressional Record* are sprinkled with repeated protestations of this fighting faith. A characteristic example is found in the recent and posthumous collection of the speeches and writings of a well-known, indeed notoriously "independent" congressman, who was originally elected to the House of Representatives as a Republican. In his last term, and shortly before his untimely end, he declared on the floor of the House that: "I have stood by the fundamental principles which I have always advocated. I have not trimmed. I have not retreated. I do not apologize, and I am not compromising." During his first term, when he was still a Republican, he made the speech from which the title of his book (*I Vote My Conscience*) was taken, saying:

> I have followed Mr. Green [President of the AF of L] on matters of labor legislation when I felt that his position was in the best interests of the American workers; but when Mr. Green attempts to throw the weight of the organized workers of America on the side of the Liberty League and the Economy League and other reactionaries who are opposed to this bill, then I refuse to follow Mr. Green's leadership and *shall vote my conscience* on this bill. (Applause.) [Emphasis added.]

The speaker was Vito Marcantonio [1956, pp. 34, 82], former representative of the East Harlem Twentieth New York Congressional District. While Mr. Marcantonio is not presented as a Communist in his posthumous book, he was generally considered to have been one during his period of congressional service, and there can be little doubt that he qualified as a fellow-traveller. Yet, he, even he found it expedient to espouse Edmund Burke's theory of representation. The theory is certainly an important datum of American politics, irrespective of its correspondence to the actual behaviors of congressmen.

Writers of textbooks on the legislative process state, as one might expect, a variety of theories of legislative representation;

but so do other commentators upon the subject. Stephen Bailey, for instance, argues for the Rationalist-majoritarian position throughout the body of his case study to which we have referred; but in his preface, he articulates "certain underlying assumptions" which he holds, and these include espousal of the Idealist cause:

> It is obvious that the public has no right in a democracy to expect unanimity about the "public interest" character of any particular legislative proposal. The disagreement of honest minds about what is best for the country is the priceless condition of democracy. What the public does have a right to expect, however, is that a national legislator will attempt honestly to abide by the campaign promises of his party and, within that general framework, *to analyze a pending national policy in the light of the broadest and highest ethical norms of which he is capable.* [Emphasis added; 1950, pp. ix–x.]

It is possible, of course, to mix Idealism with Popular Rationalism, as well as to mix it with Anglophile (Party) Rationalism (as Professor Bailey does). Harvey Walker, for instance, while in the process of speaking *ex cathreda* in his textbook says that:

> No legislator who expects to seek re-election can ignore the opinions of his constituents. He will assiduously attempt to ascertain what those opinions are, evaluate them in terms of the number of votes and financial support which they represent, and take whatever action seems most likely to promote his career *or the public interest* [sic.] [Emphasis added; 1948, p. 132.]

Obviously, Professor Walker considers the career objectives of legislators to be incompatible with the public interest, a point of view that makes every legislative vote which is in the public interest either a fortunate coincidence or else an abnormality in which the legislator indulges only at personal sacrifice. Nevertheless, Professor Walker thunders, *"When questions involving right and wrong arise, there should be no compromise."* He then goes on to indicate that in his view, fortunately, there are only a few such tough moral issues to be faced, while for the "thousands of questions of expediency which occur in a legislative session," it is all right for the legislator to pursue *both* his self-interest *and* the public interest. This disarming analysis makes it appear that congressmen can have their bread and eat it too, but they must not eat cake. An alternative analogy to the Garden of Eden would appear equally apt.

Other Idealists identify the public interest with the presumed greater inherent responsibility of certain political institutions than of others. There are, for instance, Idealists who are pro-presidency and anti-Congress; we shall consider these at a later point in this chapter. There are also Idealists who are pro-Congress and anti-presidency, such as Ernest S. Griffith, who was Director of the Legislative Reference Service of the Library of Congress at the time that he wrote:

> There are two strands woven into this concept of "public interest," and they lead, I believe, in somewhat different directions. If by "public interest" we imply an over-all vision of a good society, a kingdom of God on earth, we may anticipate political development with more and more leadership centered in the President, and with the chief function of the presidential office coming to be the dramatization of over-all values or objectives and of the means whereby they are to be obtained. . . . This is the New Deal mood . . . [and] fascism . . . and communism . . . have come to be the debased expression of policy-formation of this type.
>
> The second strand in the definition of the public interest . . . would hold the public interest to be the product of the democratic adjustment of group interests by each group participating in decisions significant to it. Down this path lies corporatism, the possibility of a decentralized operation of a pluralistic society. [1944, p. 459.]

This sounds like Realism, and if there were no more, we would so consider it. In his next and final paragraph, however, Dr. Griffith concludes that:

> In both definitions alike, the precise meaning of the "public interest" rests ultimately upon values. . . . [But only] if the values can become community values, perhaps through the reunion of operative political theory with religion and humanism, has the group a chance of becoming functional in its attitude. Then . . . Congress rises to its full stature as the democratic expression of a *consecrated general will.* [Emphasis added.]

In a subsequent book [1951, pp. 113, 115–16, 117], Dr. Griffith has specified, in somewhat greater detail, the process by means of which congressmen rise to their full stature. The process of "public policy formation," as he sees it, is a kind of morality play, with the Public Interest defending the castle against a horde of savage, ruthless, mercenaries of the selfish interests. Congressmen come to Washington as freshmen, as innocent as Rousseau's *sauvages*, and they become humanized and civilized by the institution to recognize, in time, the true nature of the continuing battle in which they participate. Once having experienced the vision, they should, of course, prefer the Good, and Griffith thinks that this is what they tend to do. Implicit in such assumptions is a strong justification for the seniority system in Congress, for it logically follows that the oldest heads, at least in point of service, will be the wisest, too, and the ones most likely to visualize and to prefer the public interest.

How and how far a more general interest can utilize, discipline, or curb these special interests in the governmental process is a supreme test of a people's economic and political genius. . . . The real nub of the matter is this. While for the most part the beliefs of members sincerely reflect the beliefs of the electorate in their district, especially in the battle of economic interests, nevertheless a process of political and economic education inevitably sets in from the first time a member or would-be or future member gives his attention to national issues. He sees that there are two sides to a question, and, as the years pass, he sees also that there is a transcending public interest greater than and perhaps different from either side *or even any compromise* between the two sides. This realization comes to different persons at different times. . . . To some it never comes. . . . But to many members, now on one issue and now on another—and generally to a different set of members on each separate issue—this realization of the contradiction between the special interest and the general interest surely comes. Their horizons are broadening as they witness the conflicts of interests and as they give thought to deeper analyses of problems and the findings of research. . . . Congress is operating with increasing effectiveness and with an awareness of and conformity to the long-range public interest. [Emphasis added.]

It is comforting to receive assurance, from such an authoritative source, that Congress is approaching nearer to perfection as time goes on, especially in view of the fact that congressmen have a responsibility not only to ascertain public opinion but also to serve as moulders of public opinion. A proponent of the bellwether function of congressmen[3] suggests that:

---

3. For a different use of the concept of the "bellwether congressmen," relating it to functional leadership within each house, see Dahl [1950, pp. 60–61].

[A] true representative of the people would follow the people's desires and at the same time lead the people in formulating ways of accomplishing those desires. He would lead the people in the sense of calling to their attention the difficulties of achieving those aims and the ways to overcome the difficulties. This means also that, where necessary, he would show special interest groups *or even majorities* how, according to his own interpretation and his own conscience, their desires need to be tempered in the common interest or for the future good of the nation. . . . It is in the nature of the Congressman's job that he should determine, as far as he can, public opinion in his own constituency and in the whole nation, analyze it, measure it in terms of the practicability of turning it into public policy, and consider it in the light of his own knowledge, conscience, and convictions. Occasionally he may be obliged to go against public opinion, with the consequent task of educating or re-educating the people along lines that seem to him more sound. [Emphasis added; Galloway, 1953, p. 244.]

The conclusion that the "true representative of the people" does not hesitate to disregard both the "will of the majority" and public opinion, when either of these conflicts with the voice of conscience, is perfectly consistent with the premises and general tenor of Idealist thought. After all, the job of the legislator, according to the Idealists, is not to give the people what they want; it is, rather, to let the people have what will be good for them.

C. The Presidency

AS THE PARTY RATIONALISTS point out, the temptations for a president to agree "to rise above his principles" are many and great, since the resistance of temptation implies his acceptance of the more prosaic role of the instrument by means of which the majority party carries out its pledges to the voters. Indeed, as we have seen, they do not believe that it is possible for any president so to behave, particularly in view of the many defects which continue to mar the potential perfection of the American party system. Their model of rational presidential behavior must remain, for the present at least, an ideal rather than a description of reality.

Even more troublesome, however, is the ephemeral image,

portrayed by the Popular Rationalists, of a president who *follows* electoral majorities, implementing directly the public will. In principle, there might seem to be a vast gulf separating the images of the president who *follows*, from the president who undertakes to *lead*, popular majorities. Idealist thought bridges this chasm without difficulty, however, suggesting that the strong president who leads the people *really* is "giving them what they want"; "doing what is best for the people"; "substituting the common good for the demands of special interests"; etc. If one accepts this metaphysical solution to the problem of political responsibility, then it follows that the responsible president, like the responsible congressman, best serves the public interest when he follows the dictates of conscience and holds fast to his personal vision of the Good, the Just, and the True.

A president who is to be *pater patriae* must be of heroic proportions, a figure larger than life-size. American history provides, of course, an authentic prototype for the Idealist president: a man who was Father of His Country; First in Peace, First in War, and First in the Hearts of His Countrymen; a man who, even as a small child, never told a lie. The vision of the true aristocrat who places love of country before personal desire and the interests of private fortune, and offers himself as a sacrifice on the altar of public good is one of the most enduring of American political myths. The president should be a man like Washington, or De Gaulle, or the Eisenhower of 1952, who rises above the tumult and the shouting of party strife to speak for *all* of the people. He is to be the Citizen King, the Elected Monarch, the physical embodiment of the virtues imagined in one of the oldest dreams of Western political philosophy. He is to be the twentieth-century counterpart of Plato's Philosopher King.[4]

Not all Idealists, however, believe that it is possible to enthrone the president by transcending political processes. As an alternative, they would approach the same goal, establishing what Robert A. Dahl has called a "plebiscitary dictatorship" [1950, p. 64 and chap. vii and viii], by giving the president "the tools

---

4. Cf. August Heckscher's characterization [1958, p. 245] of Woodrow Wilson as "the philosopher [who] really [was] made king."

that he needs to do his job."[5] It is but a short step, as I have suggested above, to move from Popular Rationalism to Plebiscitary Idealism, and the process of metamorphosis is well illustrated in an article by Fritz Morstein Marx [1949, p. 1129]. On the one hand, Morstein Marx appears to advocate congressional supremacy over the president, whose role is first denoted in terms of the "Faithful-Execution" rationale. In a context of frequent references to "the general norm,"[6] Morstein Marx states that: "the axiom of 'government of laws' subordinates government by men to the supremacy of the general interest promulgated in the statutory enactments of the representative assembly." The real test of a "government of laws" lies in *enforcement* of the laws, however, and "the identity of the general interest could easily be lost in the multiplicity of government agencies." This leads, as one would expect, to citations of the Brownlow Committee and benedictions upon the virtues of hierarchical organization and executive integration.[7] All of this seems perfectly consistent with Morstein Marx's early background as an administrator under the Weimar Republic and his more recent experience as a high official in the Bureau of the Budget and the Executive Office of the President.

But Morstein Marx does not leave the president as the servant of either congressional or popular majorities or the majority political party. To the contrary, he appears to recommend the very "plebiscitary dictatorship" decried by Dahl. Although others have pointed to the fact of executive growth, said Morstein Marx, and some have viewed such developments with alarm,

---

5. Cf. the discussion in the preceding chapter of the *Report of the President's Committee on Administrative Management* [1937], and, especially, Norton Long's comments about the implications, from the viewpoint of political responsibility, of the new "evangelism" of executive reorganization.

6. Morstein Marx's "general norm" sounds very much like the *grundnorm* of Kelsen's "Pure Theory of Law," with which Morstein Marx undoubtedly was familiar. See the later section on "The Judiciary" in this chapter.

7. "The necessary cohesion and synchronization between the various elements of the administrative system can be insured only by structural unification of the executive branch. For this reason, the office of the chief executive is an institution of great practical significance for the success of 'government of laws'" [p. 1129].

What has not been adequately stressed is the beneficial effect of a strengthened executive branch upon the coherence of public policies designed to foster the general interest. The matter would be different if our major parties had grown into effective national bodies; but they have not, or not yet. In the national government, the presidency [not "the President"]—*above and beyond* the executive responsibilities vested in it—is today the foremost constitutional device by which the common welfare can be projected into the life of the nation. In contrast with the legislative branch, the President, elected by one single national constituency, can speak with one voice for his entire constituency. The President is therefore better placed than any other spokesman of the people to set forth a reasonably consistent program framed in comprehensive terms. [Emphasis added.]

But whose program? the people's? the president's? or the presidency's? As Bonaparte is reputed to have said, "The tools belong to the man who can use them";[8] and the post-World War II American presidency has the tools[9] [Morstein Marx, 1949, pp. 1130–31]:

Aided by the staff organs at his immediate disposal, the President is equipped to make his influence felt in the continuing contest between the special interests and the general interest. He can play a decisive role in overcoming the obstacles to coherent public policy that arise from "the size of the country and the great variety of interests represented in the Congress. The natural incoherence of national parties is one of the justifications for an independent executive."

In looking at the political balance sheet of executive growth, one must therefore bear in mind the connection between executive unity and the needed articulation of the common welfare. The primacy of the general norm is bolstered substantially by the opportunities for an integrating type of leadership provided in the constitutional status of the President. In large measure, the extent to which such leadership makes itself the arm of the general interest marks our success as a nation in achieving unified political action. . . . The place occupied by the President in the constitutional system renders him particularly qualified to take the initiative in program formulation. His proposals have the greatest chance of sparking widespread public debate. His delineation of basic issues is likeliest to penetrate through the confusion of special pleadings and to rouse the electorate from indecision or lethargy.

---

8. Mr. Justice Jackson, concurring in *Youngstown Sheet & Tube Co. v. Sawyer,* 343 U.S. 579, 654 (1952).

9. Cf. Professor Marian D. Irish's theory of "The Organization Man in the Presidency," which will be discussed in the next chapter.

Many Plebiscitary Idealists would have the president play to the hilt the roles forecast for him (in their view) by the Constitution and by the precedents established by the "great" presidents. He should be not only the leader of the people, but also the leader of his political party; the leader of Congress; the General Manager of the Executive Department; the Chief of State in time of peace and the Commander-in-Chief in time of war; and the "Supreme Organ of the Nation" in the conduct of foreign affairs. He should even be "Defender of the Faith" and "Emperor of the Dominions beyond the Seas," if we take into consideration the widespread views of those internationalists who look upon democracy as a "faith," and the president as the leader of the free peoples (or nations) of the world. This general notion of the president as the Supreme Leader of, at least, the American people has become, without any doubt, the orthodox conception of the American presidency, as an examination of American government textbooks in contemporary usage bears abundant witness.

George Graham expresses, in typical fashion, the views of those Idealists who emphasize the "moral" obligations of the president. Under the heading "Obligations of the Chief Executive: The Public Interest," Graham writes that

The first and primary obligation of the President is to be faithful to the public interest, as distinguished from all of the personal interests, group interests, and special interests that play upon him. A second obligation is to keep his personal integrity above suspicion, even in small matters, as an earnest of his moral discrimination in great issues of policy. A third obligation is to set the moral tone as chief executive for the entire administration. . . . The President's obligation to stand by the interest of the whole public is his paramount obligation. [1952, pp. 157–58.]

As examples of presidential defections in morality, Graham alludes to the "deep freezers" and "mink coats" of the latter days of the Truman administration. If he were writing today, no doubt he would use such examples as "hotel bills" and "oriental rugs." As Graham points out, public discovery of petty chicanery in members of the presidential entourage undoubtedly impairs the effectiveness of presidential leadership. While Realists may discount, or even embrace, the defections of a presidential military advisor or even of an "Assistant President" as a picayune price to pay for the "grease" that helps make the machinery of government work, Idealists cannot countenance them. If the president is to remain a hero, each member of his official family must not only be, but must be thought to be, as pure as Caesar's wife.

It happens that the classic formulation of the Idealist concept of the presidency, as well as its refutation, has come from the writings of three presidents, all of whom had a flair for the literary. These three men followed each other in office after the turn of the present century, and two of them are the great heroes of the Progressive Era. I speak, of course, of "Teddy" Roosevelt, William Howard Taft, and Thomas Woodrow Wilson. Although Wilson was the last to become president, he was the first of the three to articulate his theory of presidential leadership, in a book published five years before he entered the White House. Both Roosevelt and Taft stated their views with the experience of having been president behind them, and at a time when Wilson was serving his first term. I shall turn first to Wilson, whose definition of the role he subsequently attempted to play is as accurate as the blueprint for the Fuehrer detailed by Hitler in *Mein Kampf*. Like Hitler, Wilson took pains also to spell out the steps by which the available man should reach office. The nominating convention, said Wilson, would look for "a man who understands his own day and the needs of the country, and who has the personality and the initiative *to enforce his views both upon the people and upon Congress*."[10] As for the people, continued Wilson, "What the country will demand of the candidate will be, not that he be an astute politician . . . but that he be a man such as it can *trust*." Once the people have placed their trust in such a man, and elected him president,

He cannot escape being the leader of his party except by incapacity and lack of personal force, because he is at once the choice of the party and of the nation. He is the party nominee, and the only party nominee for whom the whole nation votes. Members of the House and Senate are representatives of localities, are voted for only

---

10. This and the next four quotations are taken from Wilson [1908, pp. 65–70]; the emphasis in each instance is mine.

by sections of voters, or by local bodies of electors like the members of the state legislatures. There is no national party choice except that of President. No one else represents the people as a whole, exercising a national choice; and inasmuch as his strictly executive duties are in fact subordinated, so far at any rate as all detail is concerned, the President represents not so much the party's governing efficiency as its controlling ideals and principles. He is not so much part of its organization as its vital link of connection with the thinking nation. *He can dominate his party by being spokesman for the real sentiment and purpose of the country,* by giving direction to opinion, by giving the country at once the information and the statements of policy which will enable it to form its judgments alike of parties and of men.

Not only is the president the leader of his party, he ought also, said Wilson, be a popular leader who serves as spokesman for all of the people:

> For he is also the political leader of the nation, or has it in his choice to be. The nation as a whole has chosen him, and is conscious that it has no other political spokesman. *His is the only national voice in affairs.* Let him once win the admiration and confidence of the country, and no other single force can withstand him, no combination of forces will easily overpower him. His position takes the imagination of the country. He is the representative of no constituency, but of the whole people. When he speaks in his true character, he speaks for no special interest. If he rightly interpret the national thought and boldly insist upon it, he is irresistible; and the country never feels the zest of action so much as when its President is of such insight and calibre. Its instinct is for unified action, and it craves a single leader. It is for this reason that it will often prefer to choose a man rather than a party. *A President whom it trusts can not only lead it, but form it to his own views.*

It is clear, I believe, that Wilson was describing here something quite different from the British system of parliamentary government, responsible political parties, or a prime minister who is *primus inter pares.* Wilson's first hero was Edmund Burke, not Robert Walpole [Heckscher, 1958, pp. 246, 255]. What he recommends is not a collegial executive, but a highly personalized system of executive leadership, in which the president, by the strength of his "moral force," stands astride the political parties [cf. Young, 1958, p. 207], towering over them as he seeks his direct communion with *all* of the people. What Wilson advocates is not a system of political responsibility, with the majority political party as the umbilical cord which binds leaders to followers. Wilson recommends instead that the bond between the shepherd and his flock be one of trust, faith, and love:[11]

> He may stand, if he will, a little outside party and insist as if it were upon the general opinion. It is with the instinctive feeling that it is upon occasion such a man that the country wants that nominating conventions will often nominate men who are not their acknowledged leaders, but only such men as the country would like to see lead both its parties. [Washington? Grant? Eisenhower?] The President may also, if he will, stand within the party counsels and use the advantage of his power and personal force to control its actual programs. He may be *both* the leader of his party and the leader of the nation, or he may be one or the other. If he lead the nation, his party can hardly resist him. His office is anything he has the sagacity and force to make it. . . . The President is at liberty, both in law and conscience, to be as big a man as he can. His capacity will set the limit; and if Congress be overborne by him, it will be no fault of the makers of the Constitution,—it will be from no lack of constitutional powers on its part, but only because the President has the nation behind him, and Congress has not.

When put to what Wilson himself considered to be the supreme test, however, his theory failed, and abysmally. The circumstances under which the Senate rejected the League of Nations covenant is an oft-told tale. It is generally concluded that if President Wilson had been willing to "temper [his] doctrinaire logic with a little practical wisdom,"[12] modern world history might have been significantly different. But he followed his conscience;[13] "a little band of willful men" had their way; and a rather non-charismatic type, Warren Harding, ushered in a dozen years of surcease from the rigors of national life under an Idealist President.

Woodrow Wilson was essentially a man of thought; the man who was president when Wilson delivered his lectures at Colum-

---

11. Wilson's love for humanity in general but not in particular and his craving for adulation are notorious. See, e.g., Link [1958, pp. 8, 9].

12. Mr. Justice Jackson, dissenting in *Terminiello* v. *Chicago*, 337 U.S. 1, 37 (1949).

13. Wilson's belief in predestination and in his own innate superior wisdom, since he conceived of himself as an instrument for the direct fulfilment of the will of God Almighty, has not escaped attention. See Link [1958, pp. 6, 10].

bia University was the very prototype of the man of action. Cowboy, big game hunter, Colonel of the Rough Riders—Roosevelt was in many respects the antithesis of the austere academician. Yet, their respective theories of presidential leadership are very similar. Shortly after both Roosevelt and Taft had been defeated by Wilson in their bids for re-election, Roosevelt published his autobiography in which he stated what has come to be known as the "Stewardship Theory" of the presidency:

The most important factor in getting the right spirit in my Administration, next to the insistence upon courage, honesty, and a genuine democracy of desire to serve the plain people, was my insistence upon the theory that the executive power was limited only by specific restrictions and prohibitions appearing in the Constitution or imposed by the Congress under its Constitutional powers. *My view was that every executive officer,* and above all every executive officer in high position, *was a steward of the people bound actively and affirmatively to do all he could for the people,* and not to content himself with the negative merit of keeping his talents undamaged in a napkin. I declined to adopt the view that what was imperatively necessary for the Nation could not be done by the President unless he could find some specific authorization to do it. *My belief was that it was not only his right but his duty to do anything that the needs of the Nation demanded* unless such action was forbidden by the Constitution or by the laws. Under this interpretation of executive power I did and caused to be done many things not previously done by the President and the heads of the departments. I did not usurp power, but I did greatly broaden the use of executive power. In other words, I acted for the public welfare, I acted for the common well-being of all our people . . . and I always finally acted as my conscience and common sense bade me act. [Emphasis added; 1913, pp. 357–58.]

Roosevelt's stewardship theory evokes memories of the concept of the royal prerogative in English constitutional law. It is particularly appropriate to quote, in this respect, John Locke, in view of Locke's subsequent influence upon the men who wrote the Constitution of the United States. According to Locke [1690, *Second Treatise of Civil Government,* sec. 160], prerogative was the "power to act according to discretion for the public good, without the prescription of the law and sometimes even against it . . . there is a latitude left to the executive power to do many things of choice which the laws do not prescribe."

It was in terms of such notions of executive power as these advanced by Roosevelt and Locke that the Department of Justice sought to defend President Truman's action, in the "government's" argument before both Judge Pine and the Supreme Court in the Steel Seizure case. A majority of the Court, as I have pointed out elsewhere [1953b, p. 73], accepted the theory but were unwilling to apply it to the circumstances of the steel seizure, as they perceived the facts in the case. As we noted in the preceding chapter, the Supreme Court relied upon a Rationalist argument to support its disposition of the case. Locke's position had been upheld by the Supreme Court in 1915, when *Wilson's* Solicitor General used *Roosevelt's* Stewardship Theory as a justification for an action of President William Howard *Taft*, in his argument in *United States* v. *Midwest Oil Co.*, 236 U.S. 459 (1915). As a final irony, we might note that Wilson's Solicitor General, John W. Davis, who persuaded the Supreme Court to accept Roosevelt's views in the Midwest Oil case, was also the chief of counsel for the steel companies who argued, again successfully, but this time against the Stewardship Theory, in the Steel Seizure case.

Professor Taft—he was teaching at Yale Law School at the time Midwest Oil was decided—had no sympathy for the Wilson-Roosevelt position. In a book published the year following the Midwest Oil decision, Taft quotes the same passage from the Roosevelt autobiography that I have used above. After some jovial comments [1916, p. 144] upon Roosevelt's having classified himself among the "Lincoln Presidents," and Taft among the "Buchanan Presidents," Taft goes on to point out that Roosevelt had indicated, elsewhere in his autobiography, that he (Roosevelt) had been prepared to use the United States Army, if necessary, to seize coal mines in Pennsylvania in order to stop a serious strike. Taft looked upon this proposal as "an advocacy of the higher law and his obligation to execute it which is a little startling in a constitutional republic" [p. 146]. Moreover, said Taft,

My judgment is that the view of . . . Mr. Roosevelt, ascribing an undefined residuum of power to the President is an unsafe doctrine and that it might lead under emergencies to results of an arbitrary character, doing irremediable injustice to private right. The main-spring of such a view is that the Executive is charged with responsi-bility for the welfare of all the people in a general way, that he is to play the part of a Universal Providence and set all things right, and that anything that in his judgment will help the people he ought to do, unless he is expressly forbidden not to do it. The wide field of action that this would give to the Executive one can hardly limit. . . .

The true view of the Executive functions is, as I conceive it, that the President can exercise no power which can not be fairly and reasonably traced to some specific grant of power or justly implied and included within such express grant as proper and necessary to its exercise. Such specific grant must be either in the Federal constitu-tion or in an act of Congress passed in pursuance thereof. There is no undefined residuum of power which he can exercise because it seems to him to be in the public interest. [pp. 144–45, 139–40.]

The Taft view has been predominant in recent years, but it is the Idealist concept of the presidency that has defined the role of those presidents whom historians consider to have been "strong," and therefore "great." Clinton Rossiter, for instance, lists seven great presidents: Washington, Jefferson, Jackson, Lin-coln, Theodore Roosevelt, Woodrow Wilson, and Franklin D. Roosevelt [1956, pp. 77–78]. Every one of these presidents acted, and acted conspicuously, in accordance with the dictates of Ideal-ist theory. Rossiter himself, in what is probably the most widely read book on the presidency in recent years, espouses the Idealist theory. After quoting from Wilson's Columbia University lec-tures, Rossiter comments:

Through our history there have been moments of triumph or dedication or frustration or even shame when the will of the people—the General Will, I suppose we could call it—demanded to be heard clearly and unmistakably. . . . no effective President has doubted his prerogative to speak the people's mind on the great issues of his time, to act, again in Wilson's words, as "the spokesman for the real senti-ment and purpose of the country." . . . Sometimes, of course, it is no easy thing, even for the most sensitive and large-minded of Presi-dents, to know the real sentiment of the people or to be bold enough to state it in defiance of loudly voiced contrary opinion. Yet the President who senses the popular mood and spots new tides even be-fore they start to run, who practices shrewd economy in his appear-ances as spokesman for the nation, who is conscious of his unique power to compel discussion on his own terms, and who talks the language of Christian morality and the American tradition, can shout down any other voice or chorus of voices in the land. . . . The President is the American people's one authentic trumpet, and he has no higher duty than to give a clear and certain sound. [pp. 22–23.]

The Presidential Idealists have provided us with both the precept and the practice which characterize the twentieth-century American presidency most of the time, and particularly in time of crisis. Their idea of the public interest is as old as the Platonic quest for justice; and it was Alexander Hamilton who wrote, over a hundred and seventy years ago that

> Energy in the Executive is a leading character in the definition of good government. . . . When occasions present themselves, in which the interests of the people are at variance with their inclinations, it is the duty of the persons whom they have appointed to be the guardians of those interests, to withstand the temporary delusion, in order to give them time and opportunity for more cool and sedate reflection. . . . But however inclined we might be to insist upon an unbounded complaisance in the Executive to the inclinations of the people, we can with no propriety contend for a like complaisance to the humors of the legislature. The latter may sometimes stand in opposition to the former, and at other times the people may be entirely neutral. In either supposition, it is certainly desirable that the Executive should be in a situation to dare to act his own opinion with vigor and decision. [Hamilton, Madison, and Jay, 1901 ed., II, 49 (No. 70), and 60–61 (No. 71).]

To whatever extent the "intent of the Founding Fathers" may be considered to be relevant today, the prescriptions of the Presidential Idealists are in strict accord with the public-interest theory of the leading spokesmen for the "Party of the Constitution."

D. Administrators

THIS IS THE REALM of benevolent bureaucrats, the Guardians of the democratic state [Waldo, 1948, chap. vi]. It is also the area of administrative discretion regarding a vague criterion, where Ernst Freund (as the spokesman for what has become traditional delegation-of-legislative-power thinking) coincides with Dean Leys.[14] In the words of the latter:

> Legislative power is delegated in a few fields where the legislature and the public find themselves unable to define either the rule or the criterion of action. These are the subjects on which most of those in the community do not know even the results which they desire. For a time, at least, the administrator may be free not only to choose the means but also the end of action. [1943, p. 19.]

Since somebody obviously must define the locus of the public interest within the context of particular administrative decisions, and since the "political branches of the government," that is, the presidency and the Congress, have done so in an incomplete and unsatisfactory way, the problem becomes one of divining the public will.

Marver Bernstein, speaking with particular reference to federal regulatory legislation, has emphasized the problem facing commissioners who are required to act on the basis of such vague statutory phrases as "public interest, convenience, or necessity" or "the interest of the public." How are such statutes to be interpreted?

> Discussions of the "public interest" that commissions are supposed to seek frequently seem unreal. . . . Unreality begins to creep in . . . as soon as it appears that the commission's enabling statute may in fact provide only the most general guide to the goals of regulatory policy. . . . At best, it is difficult for a commission to maintain the integrity of the regulatory process even when it is guided firmly by clear Congressional objectives. Difficulties are magnified enormously when the legislative formulation of the public interest is vague or is lacking altogether. [1955, p. 154.]

Such difficulties are minimized, however, by a former Chairman of the Securities Exchange Commission and Dean of the Harvard Law School. In a slim but widely read little volume of lectures, James Landis has advanced what might be termed the Extrasensory-Perception theory of statutory interpretation:

> Phrases such as "public interest," . . . abound in the law. . . . For the administrative [Dean Landis consistently uses this adjective as a

---

14. Dean Leys has insisted that any coincidence between his concept of discretion and Freund's must be entirely coincidental. (Letter to the author, February 27, 1956).

noun] the task of grasping the legislative thought should not be difficult. The meaning of such expressions is, of course, derivable from
the general tenor of the statute of which they are a part. To read them
properly one must catch and feel the pace of the galvanic current
that sweeps through the statute as a whole. [1938, pp. 66–67.]

Landis would solve the problem by sublimating it; most Idealists
prefer a frank recognition of what they perceive to be their obligation to rush into the gap left by the legislature and to forth-
rightly proclaim the public good as it is revealed unto them. For
many Idealists, however, the process of revelation is a function of
the relationship between the administrative and the political processes. Idealists are divided into two camps on this issue. One group,
the Administrative Engineers, finds a solution in the integration of
politics and administration, while the other faction, the Guild
Idealists, urges the opposite course of a politically autonomous and
neutral civil service, somewhat after the presumed fashion of the
British Administrative Class. We shall look first at the Administrative Engineers.

Several political scientists have criticized the widespread tendency of regulatory commissions to become the captives of their
respective clienteles, and the failure of the commissions to vigor-
ously advance the public-policy goals for which the commissions
are responsible. Bernstein has attributed this unfortunate result to
two underlying factors. In the first place, he criticizes the naive
theoretical assumptions upon which American regulatory legislation rests:

> Post-Civil War political thought was heavily biased toward the
> *laissez-faire* approach in economics and politics. In economic enter-
> prise the general welfare was held to be the sum of the efforts of in-
> dividual entrepreneurs in pursuit of their own private interests. Simi-
> larly, the public interest in regulation was usually conceived as the
> aggregate or balance of contending private interests. It was held that
> the public interest in regulation represented an equilibrium of "pri-
> vate" forces; therefore, it had no independent existence of its own
> and could not be discovered by an independent analysis of economic
> situations. The bias of political *laissez faire* led to the expectation that
> the public interest in regulation would be identified automatically as
> the residue of the struggle among the conflicting demands of rival
> private parties. Under this conception the creative search for the
> public interest by government officials became gratuitous. The public

interest, or the proper balance among the private parties, would be produced automatically, provided the struggle was permitted to work itself out without governmental interference. [1955, pp. 126-27.]

In the second place, the commissions suffer from the malaise of the judicial approach, with the result that the typical commission

. . . tends to sit back passively to await the development of the issues and the presentation of the relevant data by the parties. . . . The judicial approach is fully consistent with the view that a commission need not search for the public interest since the public interest will automatically emerge from the conflict of private interests in regulation. [p. 179; and cf. p. 157.]

Bernstein admonishes the commissions to arise from their lethargy and to become "aggressive agent[s] of the public welfare" [p. 266], in an overriding quest for the public interest:

Whatever objectives and policies are set forth by Congress, the overriding task of policy formation in the independent commission is the search for the public interest, that is, *the determination of the goal of public policy* and *the way in which the goal can be achieved.* [Note that this statement corresponds precisely to Dean Leys' second category of discretion.] The agency's attitude toward the discovery of the public interest in regulatory policy is largely determined by its sense of mission. If it has a strong drive to serve the public, if it consciously embraces the task of determining the best way in which it can contribute to the welfare of the public interpreted in the light of democratic political values, it goes far toward meeting the responsibility laid upon it by its enabling statute. [Emphasis added; pp. 154-55.]

I have cited Bernstein first among the Administrative Engineers, not because of the novelty of his views, but, to the contrary, because of their orthodoxy. His recent book reviews the literature in this field, and Bernstein mirrors perfectly the consensus of most political scientists on the theory of the public interest in regulatory administration. More seminal, from the point of view of *formulating* the Administrative-Engineering concept of the public interest, have been the writings of Merle Fainsod and Emmette Redford.

In a well-known and frequently cited essay, Fainsod has stated the case for creative administrative manipulation:

The growth of administrative discretion has emphasized the creative role which regulatory agencies can play in defining the scope and direction of public policy. In theory at least, and frequently in practice, they are capable of recognizing some interests as more "public" or more "general" than other interests and of adapting, fusing, and directing group pressures toward such a recognition. In the process of exercising their discretionary power, regulatory agencies are often in a position to create some pressures and to extinguish others, to stir dormant parties in interest into activity and to anesthetize others, to mobilize groups to come to their support and to penalize opposition. Investigation may deflate pretensions and reveal divisions and minorities within groups which are spoken for as units. The impact of the articulate may be softened by the gentle ministrations of discreet inquiry. The manipulative power of regulatory agencies may be utilized to maintain an existing equilibrium of interests; it can be used to tilt the scale and create a new equilibrium. Within limits, the strategic discretion vested in regulatory agencies can become a real creative force in determining the substance of public policy. . . . The conclusion which suggests itself is that the degree of manipulative power which commissions can achieve in defining public policy is in large part dependent upon the strength and clarity of the communal purpose which initiates and sustains them. [1940, pp. 320–21; cf. Bernstein, 1955, pp. 265–66.]

Although Bernstein criticized laissez-faire theories as "naive" as applied to regulatory administration, Fainsod, in effect, defines the role of the commissioners to be that of political entrepreneurs:

When the purposes which various interest groups proclaim are in partial conflict, there may still be sufficient common ground to permit regulatory authorities to perform their task of adjustment. The skill with which they build on shared purpose will determine the degree of manipulative power which they can acquire. Where common purpose is in process of emerging and consensus begins to be widely shared, the manipulative power of regulatory authorities can be exercised with growing confidence. In emergent areas of community they may count on a swelling reservoir of public support. There are other areas where "the notion destined to prevail" is still far from clear. Crystallization of common purpose has not yet taken place. Regulators are still groping in the dark—confined by circumstance to tentative and hesitant efforts to gauge pressures and movements, risking action if they are bold, standing pat if they are timid. Here are the frontiers of control where an articulate common impulse has not yet emerged from the subsoil of human aspirations, where a new law is an adventure, and administrative agencies experiment at their peril. Daring leadership may arouse hitherto inarticulate desires and carve out a new pattern of public interest. But it may also meet the inertia and hostility which invite repudiation. [p. 322.]

Fainsod took pains to distinguish his position from that of Arthur F. Bentley, whom I shall discuss in the next chapter. Fainsod criticized Bentley's theory on the grounds that it was too mechanistic and that it postulated too negative and passive a role for the administrative bureaucracy:

> In so far as institutional arrangements exist which allow free play for shifts in the balance of forces, the pattern which emerges is essentially a dynamic or moving equilibrium. At any given moment, public policy is the resultant of a parallelogram of operative forces; the substance of public policy is the resultant of the balance of power shifts. Government institutions thus tend to be transformed into mere pawns in a struggle for supremacy. Deprived of independent creative force, the purposes which they serve simply mirror the changing fortunes of battle. The energizing pressures of particularistic interests claim the center of the stage. The idea of public interest becomes a fiction used to describe an amalgam which is shaped and reshaped in the furnace of their conflicts. [p. 298.]

Dwight Waldo has suggested that this is a distinction without a difference, remarking somewhat acidulously that: "The fact that regulatory bodies may have more prime force in making policy decisions than some have supposed (which [Fainsod] concludes) is significant from an ethical viewpoint only if their force is different in quality from other forces; otherwise, public policy will still be only 'the resultant of a parallelogram of operative forces.'" [1948, p. 82.]

Although Fainsod appeared to recognize that his administrative manipulators would need to relate their creative insights to some source or sources of power that would be willing to foster their creations,[15] he failed to explain how the administrator would commune with his sources. Another decade was to pass before Emmette Redford was to take up the cudgels ("Fainsod's conclusions carry conviction" [1952, p. 229]) and attempt to provide a

---

15. See Long [1949, pp. 257–64]; cf. Redford's statement. "An administrator who operates without political support from above will find that his manipulative powers are weakened and that capitulation to group demand is unavoidable" [1954, p. 1113].

natural-law[16] justification and source of inspiration for creative administrators. According to Redford,

> . . . the central need is a publicly-oriented or publicly-conditioned expertness. The words require explanation and the concept of public purpose is admittedly vague; nevertheless, the idea here presented has a sufficient core of clarity and captures the heart of administrative purpose in policy development.
>
> By publicly-conditioned expertness we mean a capacity for finding solutions in government action which accord with the thread of unity in the community ideal and the possibilities for effect on the economic organism. There are at a given period certain unities in community purpose. . . . For the administrator these purposes may be expressed in preambles of statutes, in statutory standards like the "public interest" and "public convenience and necessity," or may be derived by implication from statutes as a whole and the legislative and historical background of these. All the administrator's efforts should be oriented toward such public purposes. Their translation from vague expression into substantive action is the motive which conditions his search for solutions. [pp. 229–30.]

Redford uses a biological analogy to define the function of expert manipulation:

> This translation requires expert consideration of the possibilities for change in the operation of the economic organism. This organism is a complex of technologies, institutional framework, and behavior patterns. Within this complex the administrator finds points of resistance and of pliability. *Expert analysis consists in the discovery of the areas of pliability and the means of manipulating these. The maximization of this ability and its conscious utilization for the community ideal provide the best attainable measure of the public interest.*
>
> On a narrow plane, publicly-conditioned expertness is the ability to resist the pressure for a decision in favor of a particular party or interest which is contrary to the statement of the public interest which delimits and prescribes the area of expert decision. But the concept we are urging has a broader significance. In the broad sense in which we have described it above, *publicly-conditioned expertness consists in finding ways to make the economic organism yield to community purpose.* [pp. 230–31.]

16. Friedmann: "Natural law terminology . . . may disguise the fundamental affinity between all those modern legal theories which, in opposition to positivism, stress the need of legal ideals. . . . Pound's 'social engineering' . . . and a host of others are natural law ideals in the modern relativist and evolutionary sense, whether they choose to adopt the term or not" [1953, p. 71].

Redford recoils from the full implications of his thesis, however, for he hastens to add the qualification that:

... the ideals of democratic government also demand that the administrator shall not try to take the full responsibility for the manipulation of interests. His directives set the vague line of division between his responsibilities and that of his political superiors. If he has integrity and is loyal to the ideal of democratic government, he will recognize that, beyond a certain point of reasonable adjustment to practicalities, the responsibility for restricting a public program through concession to the interests should rest with the top political, not subordinate administrative, organs. Anything more than this is "administrative absolutism" in a negative form and destroys the integrity of administration by asking too much of it. Also, if the administrator understands the meaning of democratic government he will reach to the political superstructure for a guide on community purpose. [p. 233.]

But what of the administrator who does not become "publicly-conditioned," who lacks integrity and loyalty to democratic ideals, the dedicated zealot, or the upward mobile whose primary concern is personal power and pelf? Redford's answer seems to be that such a person does not qualify as a creative, intelligent administrator, and he has no business to be in the federal civil service.

In a paper delivered subsequently at a panel session of a convention of the American Political Science Association, Redford restated the argument of his book. This time, however, he paid considerably more attention to Realist (group) theory, which he accepted as valid up to a point, but incomplete. "Realism and idealism both have a place in the study of political science," he said [1954, p. 1103], but "analysis of the upward impact of interest pressures and their accommodation through government policies should be supplemented by a search for the best means of strengthening the impact of the concept of the common weal in the decision-making process." Redford's Realism seems half-hearted, however, a kind of genuflection to ideas that are current and influential in the profession but that are not, to him, a satisfactory explanation of how officials *ought* to behave. Thus, he posits [p. 1104] a kind of "Sociological Adminis-prudence" (after the fashion of Roscoe Pound, *infra*), suggesting that "one element in the idea of public interest is that of broad, inclusive, or widely-shared interests, called variously general, common, or public interests. Another is the idea of enduring interests." In the next breath, he speculates that "the best attainable in the pursuit of the public interest may be a compromise among varied and perhaps conflicting interests, *subsumed possibly under some standard of community purpose*" (emphasis added). The italicized words constitute, of course, an Idealist qualification of what started out as a Realist assertion; his ensuing discussion makes it clear that the exception swallows up the rule.

"There is danger," says Redford [p. 1106], "that the emphasis on interest groups will lead us to overlook other factors which are important in policy making." On the other hand,

> There is little chance that the immediate interests of organized groups will not receive adequate attention. The real danger is that the interests of the unorganized and weak, the shared interests of men generally, and the interests of men for tomorrow will not have proper weight in government councils. [p. 1109.]

The appropriate response to these dangers is "social engineering," since "the process of government itself would be threatened with stalemate if based at every turn on the adjustment of the separate interests rather than on the discovery of the common interests and ideals, and the necessities arising from the circumstances" [pp. 1106–7].

Redford's obeisance to natural-law ideals is made perfectly clear in his complimentary reference to Roscoe Pound. Since the law will inevitably leave the administrator with "a wide area of free discretion," it becomes important for the administrator to become "oriented to think in terms of the broader identities of social interest and purpose." These identities, Redford insists, "do exist." He then notes that:

> Pound spent many years developing a list of the social interests embodied in the law, and his list reveals the existence of many social interests. No one has made such a search in our legislation, but if made it might uncover more identities of interest and purpose than we are immediately conscious of. It would help reveal, in Pound's phrase, the "received ideals" of the nation, which political scientists have sought too exclusively in judicial decisions. But though our tools of instruction are inadequate, it can be stated that the conditioning of the administrator to look for common and enduring interests is an essential safeguard for the public interest. [p. 1108.]

Redford does not say where or how the administrator is to discover the "received ideals of the nation." One supposes that he must look in his own conscience. And it is against this backdrop that Redford ventures another attempt at defining the public interest: "[The public interest] *may be defined as the best response to a situation in terms of all the interests and of the concepts of value which are generally accepted in our society*" [p. 1108].

Redford does not explain, in operational terms, how administrators may discover the ideals that they are supposed to subserve, but he does suggest a verbal formula to bridge the gap: "creative intelligence." Creative intelligence is apparently akin to a first cause, and it is too subtle a notion to be confined by definition. In any event, Redford does not attempt to define it, but it obviously has something to do with functional expertise, because Redford does say that: "the *primary* needs, in my judgment, are to recognize the complexity of problems which must be faced and to emphasize the part that creative intelligence can play in the solution of problems" [p. 1107]. And again:

The first need is to adopt *every expedient* which promises to increase the amount and to raise the quality of creative intelligence available to government. . . . It is through *the expert* that we can expect to find ways of preventing the use of government for narrow aims, for only an expert can have the competence to discover workable solutions and thus show the ways to manipulate discordant elements toward public ends. [Emphasis added; p. 1109.]

Give continued emphasis to the task of developing a flexible, transferable group of experts for service at top levels in administration, a group of "experts in social engineering—the men *who are skilled in the process of finding, within the framework of institutional organization and process, solution to public problems.*"[17] [p. 1110.]

Redford's confidence in experts might seem to place him among the Guild Idealists (whom we shall consider presently, *infra*), were it not for the broad definition he has given to his use of the term "expert." He does not refer to administrators alone:

---

17. The internal quotation, to which Redford has given the emphasis, is from his book [1952, p. 369].

I am using the word "expert" comprehensively to include every form of intelligence which can be employed efficiently in the solution of problems. There are experts in technical detail, experts in analysis of facets of problems, experts in synthesis and the choice that forms decision, and experts in human (including group) relations. The highest level of expertness is the point where synthesis is reached as a result of juncture of analysis of the obstinacies and flexibilities of organic factors with analysis of the obstinacies and amenabilities of people. This gets close to or includes the expertness of the statesman, whether administrative or political [or even judicial]. [p. 1109.]

Redford has continued "The Never-Ending Search for the Public Interest," the title of a chapter in a book of his lectures [1958, chap. v], published within a few months of the time of this writing. To a large extent, this essay represents but a third variation on the same theme originally stated in his book six years earlier. Nevertheless, it warrants our consideration; Redford is both the most persistent and the most prolific writer on the subject of public-interest theory among contemporary political scientists, as well as those of the past generation.

As before, Redford feels that the group-theory approach is incomplete. He finds "the reality of the public interest" in the quest for "shared interests which arise directly out of organic developments and shared purposes." Redford feels that his approach, which represents his quest for "the essence of rationality," will often reveal that the public interest involves "more creative imagination and origination than umpiring" [p. 115]; and he devotes another half dozen pages [pp. 130–35] to a discourse on creative intelligence, public "braineries," etc. "The emphasis on the function of creative intelligence at the administrative and political levels is not," he adds, "anti-democratic." To the contrary, "the juncture of creative intelligence and the various forms of political responsibility which exist is essential for joint satisfaction of society's yearning for responsible government and for that rationality and fraternity which underlie the public interest."

The only conspicuously new emphasis appearing in this essay is Redford's articulation of ideas very close to those of Administrative-Due Process theory, which, as we shall see in the next chapter, lies at the heart of the Realist concept of the public interest. As Redford puts it,

[Another] approach is to look at the need for machinery for representation of interests and for weighing and deciding issues. There is a public interest in the availability of adequate organization and process, *measured by the needs and ideals of society*, for representing claims and resolving issues. . . . This need for public mechanism (organization and process) is the highest level of the public interest and justifies our continued concern with political "science." . . . for every type of problem there should be a jurisdiction which is inclusive enough to insure that all the interests involved will have a chance to be fairly considered. [Emphasis added; pp. 113, 126.]

He is speaking here, however, of governmental decision-making in all branches and at all levels, rather than with particular reference to public administration. Note, particularly, the italicized clause—as in his article, an Idealist exception to a Realist rule, which results in the tail wagging the dog. Moreover, these remarks are interspersed [pp. 113, 114, 115] with various (and, in Realist theory, incompatible) defenses of the public interest as a higher ethic:

"There is nothing mystical about the concept of shared interests within the political society."
"The public interest . . . is no myth."
"There are deep moral connotations in the concept of the 'public interest.'"

Nor does Redford's conclusion [p. 137] suggest his conversion to the Realist point of view, which he has come increasingly to recognize but which he still considers to be unsatisfactory: "man . . . may hope . . . that much rationality and fraternity are embodied in the order and regularity already achieved, and that creative intelligence and broad sympathies working through institutional organization and process will yield a satisfactory measure of public good tomorrow." This concluding sentence to his essay is a mixture of Rationalist, Idealist, and Realist word images, which seem to leave him eclectically poised astraddle all Gaul but with his eyes fixed on the vision of the Good Life that may yet come to pass by grace of the efforts of Administrative Engineers.

Dean Paul Appleby infuses even more moral fervor into his discussion of this question than does Redford. In Appleby's hands, the concepts of public will and public interest take on an unmistakably metaphysical glow:

The public will is flexible and ever subject to change, learning by its own action and by its own experience, so shot through with discretion that it cannot be predicted as though automatic. It is subject to influence by leaders but is capable of discarding leaders. It is energized just as everyman is, by trial and error that is its own, capable of highly enlightened self-interest, capable of devoted altruism, prone to error and given to profiting from and correcting its own mistakes. It is not inherently and invariably right; perhaps it is never right except in its own time and terms. It is not the sum total of all private wills. It is not even the total of all the private wills after canceling out the pluses and minuses of those wills. It is not distilled in a simple, definite, mechanical way, easy to see and easy to weigh in some merely mechanical weighing machine. It is not to be expressed in terms of some near absolute that leaves no questions to be answered; rather, it is eternally inquisitive. It becomes definite only as a majority will, and since there are many possible majorities, it does not uniformly derive from a particular majority and is not something fixed. It is often expressed only as consent and at times only as a veto. In many instances it is a thing not developed at all, withheld, even nonexistent. . . . The public will, then, is a force, largely potential, definite only as majorities form, but always subject to influence of members and leaders. Its capacity to be, more than its being, is the crux of democratic reality. This capacity penetrates the reality of American government. [1952, pp. 34–35.]

"The public interest," adds Appleby, "is a related phrase of a similar character."

. . . the public interest is never merely the sum of all private interests nor the sum remaining after canceling out their various pluses and minuses. It is not wholly separate from private interests, and it derives from citizens with many private interests; but it is something distinctive that arises within, among, apart from, and above private interests, focusing in government some of the most elevated aspiration and deepest devotion of which human beings are capable.

Unlike the conditioned expertise of Redford's manipulators, however, for Appleby, the administrator's role is an intensely political one:

. . . generally there are very real public interests not readily brought into contrast with acute and strong private interests, and almost throughout the area of public administration officials must struggle with the problem of how much, how far, and in what way to insist upon these public interests. The inner moral satisfaction of responsible administrators turns on the degree to which they have been able to inject consideration of the public interest in the face of a natural inclination of spokesmen for private interests to see those interests as the undiluted public interest.

Neither the simple reconciliation of private interests nor their reconciliation modified by considerations of public interest is in the end a technical performance, no matter how many technical factors may figure in it. It is a political function, involving essentially the weighing of forces and the subjective identification of the narrow area within which these forces may be balanced and the exercising of discretion concerning the point within that area at which acceptability and public interest may be effectively and properly maximized. [pp. 163–64; cf. p. 175.]

This emphasis upon the political function of bureaucracy is a major theme in all of Appleby's writing, and would place him among the equilibrium theorists (to be discussed below) were it not for Appleby's invocation of what Bentley would call "spooks" and "ghosts" in order to give content to the "plus factors" of the public interest.

Like Fainsod and Redford and several of the Administrative Realists, Appleby suggests a principle of the bureaucracy as countervailing force, with the administrator in the role of champion of the unorganized, the underprivileged, "consumers," and other underdogs. This is a strange identification for one whose orientation is so enthusiastically political, in the absence of a better theory of relationship between the administrator and his wards than the notion that the bureaucracy will tend to reflect the representative character of the presidency. Unless one has a theory that can explain, in operational terms, how and why bureaucracy *must* (not "should") represent the inarticulate interests of inchoate masses, reliance must be—as it so largely is—upon teleology.

Dean Appleby also takes issue with the Psychological Realists, who argue that an administrator necessarily projects as his concept of the public interest the image of his own individual attitude structure and value system. The Dean warns specifically against this sort of behavior, when he urges that "there must be care not to confuse one's professional viewpoint, functional preoccupation, or personal prejudices with the public interest" [p. 176].

In effect, Fainsod, Redford, and Appleby tell us that the public interest would be realized if bureaucrats would abjure administrative delinquency and obey the exhortations of these moralists, which may be paraphrased as: "Be clever! Be wise! Be good!"

Above and beyond the Administrative Engineers are the exponents of Guild Idealism, of whom I shall discuss two leading spokesmen: Carl Friedrich and Nathan Grundstein. Although Friedrich [1940] recognizes "that administrative officials participate continuously and significantly in [the] process of evolving policy," which is defined as the close linking of politics and administration, his basic argument is that political direction and control of administration is necessarily incomplete and inadequate, and that it must be supplemented by the "new imperative" of "functional responsibility." By the latter, Professor Friedrich means professionalism. "The will of the people" is a myth, and

> A modern administrator is in many cases dealing with problems so novel and complex that they call for the highest creative ability. This need for creative solutions effectively focuses attention upon the need for action. The pious formulas about the will of the people are all very well, but when it comes to these issues of social maladjustment the popular will has little content, except the desire to see such maladjustments removed. [p. 12.]

Consequently, although the responsible administrator is one who shows a "proper regard for existing preferences in the community, and more particularly its prevailing majority," he must also be "responsive to these two dominant factors: technical knowledge and popular sentiment." "Whether we call it 'objective' or 'functional' or 'technical,' " Friedrich writes,

> the fact remains that throughout the length and breadth of our technical civilization there is arising a type of responsibility on the part of the permanent administrator, the man who is called upon to seek and find the creative solutions for our crying technical needs, which cannot be effectively enforced except by fellow-technicians who are capable of judging his policy in terms of the scientific knowledge bearing upon it. [p. 14.]

As for "popular sentiment," Friedrich seems to have had in mind such devices as the U.S.D.A.'s straw votes in conjunction with marketing controls, and apparently he would not shrink from the official electioneering which has played such a conspicuous role in the marketing referenda:

> . . . administrative officials have begun to tap independent sources of insight into the views and reactions of the general public which are increasingly important in guiding them towards the making of public policy in a responsible fashion. . . . it is the function of the administrator to make *every conceivable effort* toward the enforcement of the law which he is called upon to administer. . . . Instead of administering according to precedent, the responsible administrator today works according to anticipation. [Emphasis added; pp. 16–17.]

It would appear that we have here another bit of advice for administrators who would advance the public interest: "Be zealous!"

From his premises of professional and direct popular responsibility, Friedrich arrives at the conclusion that "instead of subserviency to *arbitrary will* we require responsiveness to commonly felt needs and wants" [emphasis added; p. 20]. For this sacrilege to the official theory of Parliamentary government, Friedrich has been taken to task severely by Herman Finer. This (at least, then) English majoritarian insisted upon official subservience to the public will, as expressed by the legislature and political parties:

> Who would define the public interest—who could define it? Only the public, I believe, or its deputies. . . . I shall again insist upon the subservience [of the permanent civil service] for I still am of the belief with Rousseau that the people can be unwise but cannot be wrong. [1941, pp. 347, 339; cf. 1936, p. 569.]

Finer's rigid monotheistic conception of the public will and public interest places him, at least for purposes of our present frame of reference, among the Administrative Rationalists—where, indeed, all absolute majoritarians repose.

The natural-law foundation of the Administrative Idealists' position is most clearly evident in a paper by Nathan Grundstein, which he presented originally at a panel meeting of the American Political Science Association, in August, 1952, and presented a second time (after the paper had, in the meantime, been published in a law journal) at a panel meeting of the Midwest Conference of Political Scientists, in May, 1956. Under these circumstances, it seems fair to consider that this paper represents

Grundstein's considered views. Grundstein's *bête noire* is Appleby (to whom he consistently refers as "contemporary administrative theory"), whose book had just been published at the time Grundstein wrote. For Appleby's thesis that "the path to the fullest realization of the public interest is in a union of politics and administration," Grundstein would substitute their divorce:

> Administration has the problem of protecting its craft, which centers on the creation and operation of an effective hierarchy and the enlightened application of science to social problems, from the perversions of politics (both the politics of party and the politics of group interests). . . .
> In the quest of administrative theory for an alliance with a disciplined, hierarchically organized, centrally controlled political power—in short, for a political organization with which an administrative organization can do business on terms that will stick—theory jeopardizes the craft of administration by exposing it to an irresistible pressure from without. Its asserted ideals will become meaningless in the face of the unchallengeable authority of the leaders of the disciplined majority party in power, whose handmaid administration must become. The fact is that professional administration needs and wants room for the exercise of its craft, and this requires a core of independence from politics. Essentially, this is the meaningful nub of Goodnow's separation of politics and administration, and modern administration theory cannot get away from it lest the craft of administration be imperiled. [1953a, pp. 282, 286.]

Grundstein leaves the administrator to find his criteria for decision in "civilization ideals" and to rely upon the still, small voice of conscience for his accountability to society:

> In craft there is a foundation for conscience, and a conscience, as a self-limitation on the exercise of power, is the first step towards a morality for administration. . . . Contemporary administrative theory places administration squarely in the middle of the intense conflicts of material interests in society. It talks of morality, but in reality it sees only conflicting group interests, and the search is for some advantage for administration in this situation. . . .
> To the extent that administration becomes a craft, it will have to have ideals. To protect its ideals and to further its craft, it must have an area of autonomy from law and from politics. Administration will best serve society when it sticks firmly by its craft and its ideals and by so doing supplies a yardstick by which to measure how far law and politics fall short of civilized social ideals. [pp. 293, 303, 310.]

For Appleby's "Be good!" Grundstein would substitute: "Be God!"

E. The Judiciary

GRUNDSTEIN APPARENTLY THOUGHT he was recasting administrative theory on the model of the contemporary theory of the public interest in judicial decision-making.

. . . while administrative theory points administration toward a union with the locus of power in politically organized society, contemporary juristic theory points law toward civilization ideals. . . . to the extent that administrative theory attempts to define the content of the "public interest" of administration, it does no more than redraw an image already existent in contemporary juristic thought. . . . insofar as an effort is made to concretize the content of "public interest," the drift, on the one hand, is toward packing it with the social interests recognized by sociological jurisprudence as the concern of law in society and, on the other hand, toward identifying it with the values of contemporary legal idealism. Either way it goes, morality in administration will find its image in juristic theory. [1953a, pp. 268, 273.]

Just as Grundstein necessarily erred in tending to identify "contemporary administrative theory" with one of Paul Appleby's books, he appears here to identify "contemporary juristic theory" largely with those two aspects of it that coincide with his own value preferences: sociological jurisprudence and legal idealism.

Sociological jurisprudence is a development of the twentieth century in the United States. From the early writings of Dean Emeritus Roscoe Pound, of the Harvard Law School, up to the Research Training Institutes in Law and Social Relations, sponsored by the Social Science Research Council beginning in the summer of 1956, an interest in the human-relations aspects of the work of courts and judges (as distinguished from historical and logical studies) has characterized the research and writing of many leading American law professors and judges. For our present purposes, the principal differences between the sociological jurists and the legal realists are essentially two-fold: (1) the sociological jurists invoke natural-law ideals as the ultimate touch-stone of judicial decision, while the realists exclude such ghosts from their theories; and (2) the first group defines the task of judicial discretion as one of the concretizing vague generalizations, while the realists define the problem as one of choice among definite but conflicting alternatives.

Pound developed an elaborate calculus of interests—somewhat reminiscent of the "metaphysical individualism" of Jeremy Bentham's "hedonistic calculus" [see Grundstein, 1953b, pp. 350–51, 355]. This was intended to assist the judge in his task of "social engineering," by which Pound meant the creation and maintenance of the proper balance among the public, social, and private interests:

> If we look at the actual working out, development, and application of legal precepts rather than at juristic theory, we may say that three methods have obtained. One is a finding out by experience of what will achieve an adjustment of conflicting and overlapping interests with the least impairment of the scheme of interests as a whole and giving that experience a reasoned development. Thus the measure becomes a practical one of what will adjust relations and order conduct with the least friction and waste. . . . It is in this way that the legal order actually functions. This is what courts do and judges and jurists have been doing at least since the Roman jurisconsults of the first century. . . . There is at any rate an engineering value in what serves to eliminate or to minimize friction and waste.[18] [1942, pp. 109–12.]

This concept of the judicial function as interest-balancing bears an obvious affinity to the equilibrium theory of certain of the Administrative Realists to be considered in the next chapter.[19]

---

18. The other two methods to which Pound referred were "reason" and "a received, traditionally authoritative idea of the social order and hence of the legal order, and of what legal institutions and doctrines should be and what the results of applying them to controversies should be" [pp. 112, 118]. Cf. Cahill [1952, p. 77].

19. Cf. Berns: "The only 'value' in the Poundian scheme is the assumption that the scheme of interests as a whole should not be disturbed. But Pound does not solve this 'value'; he *assumes* it" [1957, p. 143]. This is, of course, a criticism of Pound by a Straussian Idealist, who complains that Pound is not idealistic enough. If Berns were correct—and he is not—Pound would have to be considered a legal realist. See also ftn. 24, *infra*.

Pound's notion of "public interests," however, was limited to the legal personality of the state—which Pound identified [1942, p. 75] with such technical juristic doctrines as sovereign immunity from suit, the preferential status accorded the claims of the state as a creditor against private property, etc. Professor Julius Stone has suggested that the explanation for Pound's peculiar notion of the public interest lies in "his admiration for the ancient maxim that the king is *parens patriae,* and for the fruitful applications of this maxim at his own hands" [1950, p. 492 n. 24]. Be that as it may, Pound's definition of "public interests" is much less relevant to our concern in this book than is his theory of the basis for "*de facto* interests," which has had much greater influence. He has made quite clear his position on this point:

> There is so much truth in the old idea of a state of nature and theory of natural rights. . . . We must begin, then, with the proposition that the law does not create these interests. . . . It works out the means by which the interests may be secured when recognized and delimited. [1940, pp. 60, 68.]

Pound spoke as an academic. The other leading spokesman for American sociological jurisprudence was a practitioner, Benjamin N. Cardozo, Associate Justice of the United States Supreme Court during the dynamic years of the middle thirties. It may be worth noting, however, that his major writings on the judicial process all appeared during the twenties, and they reflect his experiences on the somewhat more serene bench of the New York Court of Appeals. Cardozo wrote that the judge was a lawmaker;[20] and that the public interest was in part defined by the judge's creative acts in crystallizing what he perceived to be the public will:

> The final cause of law is the welfare of society. The rule that misses its aim cannot permanently justify its existence. . . . Logic and history and custom have their place. We will shape the law to conform to them when we may; but only within bounds. . . . I do not mean, of course, that judges are commissioned to set aside existing

---

20. Cf. Dewey: "Judges make rules of law. On the 'will' theory this is an encroachment on the legislative function. Not so, if the judges further define conditions of action" [1927, p. 55 n. 2].

rules at pleasure in favor of any other set of rules which they may hold to be expedient or wise. I mean that when they are called upon to say how far existing rules are to be extended or restricted, they must let the welfare of society fix the path, its direction, and its distance. . . .

We must keep within those interstitial limits which precedent and custom and the long and silent and almost indefinable practice of other judges through the centuries of the common law have set to judge-made innovations. But within the limits thus set, within the range over which choice moves, the final principle of selection for judges, as for legislators, is one of fitness to an end. [1921, pp. 66–67, 103.]

To paraphrase Clausewitz, we might say that Cardozo believed that "judicial decision-making is the continuation of legislative policy-making by other means":

We do not pick our rules of law full-blossomed from the trees. *Every judge consulting his own experience must be conscious of times when a free exercise of will, directed of set purpose to the furtherance of the common good, determined the form and tendency of a rule which at that moment took its origin in one creative act.* . . . The standards or patterns of utility and morals will be found by the judge in the life of the community. They will be found in the same way by the legislator. . . . *If you ask how he is to know when one interest outweighs another, I can only answer that he must get his knowledge just as the legislator gets it, from experience and study and reflection; in brief, from life itself.* . . . I will not hesitate in the silence or inadequacy of formal sources, to indicate as the general line of direction for the judge the following: that he ought to shape his judgment of the law in obedience to the same aims which would be those of a legislator who was proposing to himself to regulate the question. [Emphasis added; pp. 103–4, 105, 113, 120.]

It is apparent that Cardozo's idealized conception of the role of the legislator is in perfect accord with the postulates of Edmund Burke and an age which knew neither political parties (in the modern sense) nor suffrage of the masses. Putting this aside, Cardozo's non-operational notion of "community ideals" as a criterion of judgment seems to be at one with Redford's and Grundstein's exhortations to administrators. It would not be fair to Cardozo, however, to fail to point out that intermixed with his social idealism there was a strong thread of psychological realism[21]—which in more skeptical hands was to produce the so-called "bellyache" theory of adjudication.

The Supreme Court of the United States provided Cardozo with an ideal forum for translating his theories into practice. As Friedmann has pointed out, "natural law thinking in the U.S. undoubtedly inspired the fathers of the Constitution, and it has dominated the Supreme Court more than any other law court in the world" [1953, p. 67]. Although adjudication in conjunction with the contract clause, freedom of property under the due-process clause of the Fourteenth Amendment, and many other examples might be used, I should like to suggest, as a case in point, the incorporation issue as this relates to personal liberty under the due-process clause of the Fourteenth Amendment. Cardozo's view was that the due-process clause subsumed those rights (or, in Pound's phrase, those *de facto* interests) which are "of the very essence of a scheme of ordered liberty" [*Palko* v. *Connecticut*, 302 U.S. 319, 325 (1937)]. The First Amendment was in—or, at least, largely in—by 1937; the Bill of Rights as a whole—Amendments I to VIII—was out. The job of the Supreme Court was to give effect to a "rationalizing principle" that would give "to discrete instances a proper order and coherence." This would be done by deciding on a case-to-case basis which, if any, of the rights specified in the Bill of Rights, in addition to those preferred by the First Amendment, should be read into the requirements of a system of ordered liberty, as implicit in the "fundamental principles of liberty and justice which lie at the base of all our civil and political institutions." The alternative doctrine of full incorporation had been argued fruitlessly for years by the first John Marshall Harlan, who had joined the Supreme Court less than a decade after the Fourteenth Amendment was adopted. Then too, there was the celebrated Delphic dictum of Justice Stone, coming on the heels of Cardozo's formulations in the Palko case. Stone said:

---

21. "The spirit of the age, as it is revealed to each of us, is too often only the spirit of the group in which the accidents of birth or education or occupation or fellowship have given us a place. No effort or revolution of the mind will overthrow utterly and at all times the empire of these subconscious loyalties" [pp. 174–75].

There may be narrower scope for operation of the presumption of constitutionality when legislation appears on its face to be within a specific prohibition of the Constitution, such as the first ten amendments, which are deemed equally specific *when* held to be embraced within the Fourteenth [Emphasis added; *United States* v. *Carolene Products Co.,* 304 U.S. 144, 152n (1938).]

This eventuated, during the middle forties, in the Court being divided into three factions: (1) the majority bloc, which refused to extend "substantive due process" beyond the First Amendment; this group included Professor Frankfurter, who frequently found it necessary to make available an independent expression of his own views, as the self-appointed legitimate expositor of what Cardozo really meant; (2) Black and Douglas, who argued for full incorporation; and (3) Murphy and Rutledge, who wanted the Bill of Rights (as the legacy of eighteenth-century libertarian ideals) PLUS some unspecified but potentially significant twentieth-century natural rights. The deaths of Murphy and Rutledge left the Court with only the two factions, and, with the minority so small, full-fledged attack seemed hopeless during the early years of the decade following the disposition of *Adamson* v. *California,* 332 U.S. 46 (1947). The more recent appointments of Warren and Brennan, however, have restored the libertarian bloc to a position of real importance; and full incorporation is a goal that might be attained at any time the Court is confronted with a really persuasive case and the libertarians succeed in co-opting a fifth vote.

In the process of rationalizing, in the Adamson case, the counting-out of the self-incrimination clause of the Fifth Amendment, Justice Reed, speaking for the majority, remarked that it was obvious (as well as settled law) that the privilege against testimonial compulsion was not "*one of the rights of man* that are listed in the Bill of Rights" [emphasis added; p. 51]. Justice Black seized upon the phrase, rejecting the theory that:

This Court is endowed by the Constitution with boundless power under "natural law" periodically to expand and contract constitutional standards to conform to the Court's conception of what at a particular time constitutes "civilized decency" and "fundamental liberty and justice." . . . the Court concludes that although comment upon testimony in a federal court would violate the Fifth Amendment, identical comment in a state court does not violate today's fashion in civilized decency and fundamentals. . . . I think [this] decision and the "natural law" theory of the Constitution upon which it relies degrade the constitutional safeguards of the Bill of Rights and simultaneously appropriate for this Court a broad power which we are not authorized by the Constitution to exercise. . . . And I further contend that the "natural law" formula which the Court uses to reach its conclusion in this case should be abandoned as an incongruous excrescence on our Constitution. . . .

I fear to see the consequences of the Court's practice of substituting its own concepts of decency and fundamental justice for the language of the Bill of Rights as its point of departure in interpreting and enforcing that Bill of Rights. . . . To hold that this Court can determine what, if any, provisions of the Bill of Rights will be enforced, and if so to what degree, is to frustrate the great design of a written Constitution. [pp. 69, 70, 75, 89.]

The issue is thus clear. Cardozo's theory of the judicial process has become the official dogma of the Supreme Court for adjudication in this area; the judge is a legislator who reads the contemporary norms of civilized society into the Fourteenth Amendment as benchmarks of the scope of personal liberty under due process of law.[22] As a libertarian living in a civilized society which obviously places a much higher value on "order" and a much lower value on "liberty" than did the forebears of a revolution—unless we assume that the Supreme Court has done a very bad job of tuning in on the conscience of contemporary American society—Black has argued that judicial discretion should be canalized within banks that would keep it from overflowing and not be left unconfined and vagrant, to borrow Cardozo's own phrases anent the quite

---

22. In this regard, Ernst Freund has argued that "to oppose legislative discretion by undefined judicial standards of reasonableness is to oppose legislative by judicial discretion, and constitutional doctrines so vaguely formulated cannot be expected to command confidence" [1917, p. 5]. A recent example of an attempt to foment such distrust is found in Governor Faubus' argument that the Supreme Court's decision in the School Segregation cases is not "the supreme Law of the land," but that an act of Congress decreeing public school integration would be entitled to respect under Article VI of the Constitution. Putting Faubus' motives to one side, and granting his unspoken assumption that it would be politically impossible to enact such legislation, is this not the point? Freund was thinking primarily of judicial review of legislation; but much of the current criticism of the Court is directed against Supreme Court law-making *in lieu of* statutory legislation.

different matter of executive discretion.[23] Black would do this by substituting the specific language of the Bill of Rights—together, of course, with the barnacles constituting its impedimenta of case law—for the narrower ideals of human liberty which, demonstrably, lie within the wave lengths to which a majority of the Supreme Court is attuned.

In view of the clear-cut dominance of sociological jurisprudence in this area of constitutional politics, it is surprising to find Walter Berns venturing the strange criticism that the Court has no ideals of its own; that it is subservient to the whims and caprices of popular majorities; and that it is not sufficiently tough-minded in rejecting libertarian claims.[24] Much more to the point, in my opinion, is Cahill's summation of the contribution of Pound and Cardozo:

> Their basic interest in the interrelationships between law and society ought to have led the sociological jurists into an intensive search for some method of demonstrating those relationships. If the judiciary are to keep law in touch with life, we might hope for a clearer indication of how the judges themselves are to be kept in touch with life. [1952, pp. 95–96.]

In a broad sense, American sociological jurisprudence and realism have dominated the intellectual legal horizons in the United States during the twentieth century. A philosophy of legal

---

23. *Panama Refining Co.* v. *Ryan*, 293 U.S. 388, 440 (1935); *Schechter Poultry Co.* v. *United States*, 295 U.S. 495, 551 (1935). Cardozo, in turn, appears to have borrowed these riparian phrases from John Dewey, who had written that "rules of law . . . are structures which canalize action; they are active forces only as are banks which confine the flow of a stream, and are commands only in the sense in which the banks command the current" [1927, p. 54].

24. "With no clear idea of the good, beyond democracy as freedom and equality, and adamantly denying that any agency of government may interest itself in the determination of what is right, [the liberal justices] must perforce allow this to be determined by the people as a whole, by public opinion. And the process by which this opinion is formed is, to repeat, no concern of the law, just as the opinion itself may not be tested by moral principle. Democracy is government by public opinion, which can be anything so long as it is freely formed. This is the ideal. The end of government for these liberals is a certain process. The end is government *by* the people—not necessarily of and for the people." Berns [1957, pp. 170–71; cf. p. 172].

idealism was being developed at about the same time by European theorists. As Friedmann has written of these "free law" theories:

> In its scepticism against the analytical explanation of law and the legal process this Continental movement is the counterpart of the American realist movement in jurisprudence; but where American realists concentrate on the analysis of the law as it works in fact, leaving aside what it ought to be, the *Freirechtslehre* has a definite idealistic bend. It discards legal logic as a fiction and an illusion, but it is not content to analyze the legal process as a matter of social reality. It has a philosophy and ideology of its own, that of the creative lawyer who, free and untrammelled by *Paragraphenrecht*, finds the law in accordance with justice and equity. [1953, pp. 244–45.]

Such theorists appear to have no counterparts among American writers [Cahill, 1952, pp. 134–36], with the possible exception of Fred Rodell, who, having exorcised legal rules as a guide to decision, has advocated:

> Wherever written laws cannot or do not contain the answer, *somebody* has to make a decision. And that decision might better be made on grounds of plain, unvarnished justice, fairness, humanitarianism—amorphous though it be—than on any other. [Emphasis in the original; 1939, p. 252.]

Another form of European legal idealism, Scientific Idealism, has had somewhat more of an impact upon American thinking, perhaps because its principal spokesman has been a professor at American universities during most of the past two decades. Although Hans Kelsen, a devout positivist, would doubtless be shocked to find himself classified in such close association with natural-law advocates, he belongs here for our purposes since he views the function of judicial and administrative decision-making as being that of filling in a vague criterion. His conception of administrative and judicial decision-making as constituting variations on the same basic theme is very close to the assumption on which this book is based. But he makes no attempt to correlate his theory of judicial/administrative discretion with his theory of the interest-group–conflict basis of politics. This leaves the judge a free agent in exercising the discretion allotted to him. In sharp contrast to Pound, who is concerned with elaborate specification of the substantive content of legal norms, Kelsen leaves the norms indeterminate. He has summarized his theory of judicial discretion as follows:

> The individualization of a general norm by a judicial decision is always a determination of elements which are not yet determined by the general norm and which cannot be completely determined by it. The judge is, therefore, always a legislator also in the sense that the contents of his decision never can be completely determined by the pre-existing norm of substantive law. [1946, p. 146.]

It is humorous to note that, while the logical positivists and in particular the neo-Bentlians have employed the dichotomy of "is" and "ought," while focusing upon the data of politics, to discount and debunk legal rules as "spirits," "ghosts," "spooks," etc., Kelsen applies the same technique to the data of law with the result that he has to exclude political behavior to keep his theory pure. For Kelsen, it is the interest group which is the "spirit," "ghost," and "spook"!

Kelsen has explained why he has to keep interest groups out of his system in these terms:

> . . . it is the ideal of juridical positivism to preserve the theory of positive law from the influence of any political tendency or, which amounts to the same, from any subjective judgment of value. The purity of its knowledge in the sense of political indifference is its characteristic aim. This merely means that it accepts the given legal order without evaluating it as such, and endeavors to be most unbiased in the presentation and interpretation of the legal material. In particular, it refuses to stand for any political interests under the pretext of interpreting the positive law, while in reality it conflicts with it. Just the same, the critical positivist remains entirely conscious of how much the content of the legal order with which he is concerned is itself the result of political efforts. The question as to where the content of the positive legal order has originated, as to what factors have caused this content, is beyond this cognition which is limited to the given system of positive legal norms in its "ought" quality. [p. 438.]

This does not mean, however, that Kelsen has no notions about the behavior of interest groups and other political spooks. The pure theorist, it appears, can entertain very orthodox—that is, orthodox Bentlian—ideas which may float around, however unscientifically, in his own mental stratosphere:

If the question is raised, the answer lies in this *none too fruitful* insight: every legal order which has the degree of effectiveness necessary to make it positive is more or less of a compromise between conflicting interest-groups in their struggle for power, in their antagonistic tendencies to determine the content of the social order. This struggle for power invariably presents itself as a struggle for "justice"; all the fighting groups use the ideology of "natural law." They never represent the interests which they seek to realize as mere group-interests, but as the "true," the "common," the "general" interest. The result of this struggle determines the temporary content of the legal order. It is, just as little as its component parts, the expression of the general interest, of a higher "interest of the State," "above" interest groups and beyond political parties. Furthermore, this concept of the "interest of the State" conceals the idea of the absolute value of justice, the idea of a natural law as the absolute justification of the positive legal order personified as the State. The conception of an order which realizes the "common" or "general" interest and constitutes a perfectly solidary society is identical with the utopia of pure natural law. The content of the positive legal order is no more than the compromise of conflicting interests, which leaves none of them wholly satisfied or dissatisfied. It is the expression of a social equilibrium manifested in the very effectiveness of the legal order, in that it is obeyed in general and encounters no serious resistance. [Emphasis added; pp. 438–39.]

Although one man's insight is another man's science, Bentley and Kelsen have at least one spook in common: for both of them, the concept of "the public interest" is a haunting apparition, playing a role that is more than casually reminiscent of Hamlet's murdered father.

If an outsider were to superimpose an operational concept of public interest on Kelsen's pure theory (which knows it not), one might find it in the maintenance of whatever legal order may have been established under the basic norm of any particular State. But Kelsen cannot admit to his system the public interest as an ethical norm, for he has substituted in its place the key concepts of *power* and *obligation*. As Ebenstein has pointed out [1945, p. 114], these "ought" elements get into the system via the basic norm, which Kelsen must *assume* to be valid.[25] In Kelsen's own words:

---

25. It has been argued that, although Kelsen is a "positivist" in the *jurisprudential* sense, he is not a "philosophical positivist" but rather is an "ethical relativist." See Bergmann and Zerby [1945, pp. 124–26].

It is postulated that one ought to behave as the individual, or the individuals, who laid down the first constitution have ordained. . . . That the first constitution is a binding legal norm is presupposed, and the formulation of the presupposition is the basic norm of this legal order. [1946, p. 115.]

So far as decision-making is concerned, however, the judge is left as a relatively free agent to utilize myths, such as "the public interest," as rationalizations for the policy preferences that give content to his choices. According to Ebenstein, in Kelsen's system:

The lawmaking activity of the judge is a function of will and not of cognition. . . . It is not *better knowledge* but *more authority* that fits a judge or any other executive agent to say what law is. . . . The law itself can give its agent, whether in his lawmaking or in his executive capacity, no guidance in the use of his discretion, for discretion means absence of determination.

The conclusion emerges, then, that the evaluation of interests is no solution, only a formulation of the problem at issue; the norm itself cannot provide a standard for the conflicting interests. The judge cannot find a standard in the law, which leaves the decision open among the various interests, leaves it to the free discretion of its agent. The agent can evaluate the interests according to ethical and moral values, under such names as public policy, progress, etc., but never according to the law itself. [1945, p. 196.]

Thus, concludes Ebenstein, Kelsen leaves the judge to perform the same role attributed to him by Cardozo. I think it evident that this is the case.

Legal Idealists thus reject the myth that the law is a "seamless web," and they define judicial office as a role which frequently demands that a choice of public policy be made among indeterminate alternatives. The job of courts is not to discover the public will, but to make it. The problem, of course, is how to discriminate between the will of the judge as an individual and the will of society in the abstract. The missing link is found in natural law. The Legal Idealists do not explain how courts attune themselves with the infinite; but they assure us that wise and good judges do this sort of thing all the time. It is especially important that the Wise Judge purify himself from political influences, since man—a political animal, according to the pupil of the progenitor of this school of thought—is peculiarly subject to the corrupting influence of politics. It is not what litigants want that is in the public interest; it is what the judge thinks will be good for them. There is, therefore, a close functional analogy between the creative jurists of Legal Idealism and the creative manipulators of Administrative Engineering.

realist theory

"The people is a myth, an abstraction."
And what myth would you put in place
    of the people?
And what abstraction would you exchange
    for this one?
And when has creative man not toiled
    deep in myth?

Sandburg, *The People, Yes.*

The Realists are skeptics and sophisticates who have put behind them myths which postulate any independent substantive content for such notions as "the public will" and "the public interest." For them, the alternatives for official choice are concrete but ambiguous. The supreme virtue of a democratic system of government is the multiplicity of points of access that it affords for the manifold conflicting interests which necessarily arise in a pluralistic society. The function of government officials is to facilitate the continuous readjustment of conflicting interests, with a minimum of disturbance of existing equilibria.

Congressmen are themselves spokesmen for dominant constituency and pressure-group interests; congressional committees—like political parties, administrative agencies, and courts—are conceived of as being, at one and the same time, groups of government decision-makers with mediatory functions to perform *and also* as a kind of interest group themselves. The Realists draw attention to the institutionalization of the presidential office, and to the substitution of administrative decision-making processes for the personal judgment of the man who is president. The mechanist faction of this school assumes the irrelevancy of the official's individuality as well, at least in a statistical sense and in the long run. The public official is thus a catalyst by means of which conflict among special interests is transformed into the public interest.

There is a psychological deviation that sublimates aggregates of individuals in favor of emphasizing the conflict among the multitude of stimuli perceived within the mind of the official. For the Psychological Realists, the public interest is served by the self-awareness of the official, who plays his role self-consciously and recognizes the full implications of his choices. Finally, there are Due-Process Realists, who find the public interest in the structuring of decisional processes to insure full consideration of the facts, hypotheses, and values relevant to the particular decisions involved.

A. Constituency

FOR ARTHUR FISHER BENTLEY, the public interest and the general welfare were "mind-stuff," appropriately discussed by writers of fiction who spun phantasies of a nether world, but with no place in the reality which it is the social scientist's business to explore. As Richard W. Taylor puts it [1952, p. 215], "the ghosts of 'national interest' and 'general welfare' are unfrocked; these phrases come to have no more authority over inquiry than a divested priest has over the faithful." The essence of Bentley's theory is distilled, in his own words, in the statement that:

As for political questions under any society in which we are called upon to study them, we shall never find a group interest of the society as a whole. We shall always find that the political interests and activities of any given group—and there are no political phenomena except group phenomena—are directed against other activities of men, who appear in other groups, political or other. The phenomena of political life which we study will always divide the society in which they occur, along lines that are very real, though of varying degrees of definiteness. The society itself is nothing other than the complex of the groups that compose it. [1949 ed., p. 222.]

As applied to official decision-making, this meant for Bentley that discretion (in the subjective sense of being an attribute of the official) is an illusion. What *really* happens is that the field within which interest groups might maneuver, in their attempts to maximize their influence over the official, contracts or expands; the official's decision, in actuality, is an expression of the action necessary to bring about a new equilibrium among the groups whose interests are in conflict:

> It is so with every public official in every function. Perhaps he has little discretion and we can easily watch the pressures operating through him. Perhaps he has great discretion, and we have difficulty to keep ourselves from being led astray by his prominence as a technical process. But in either case we must push the analysis down to the groups represented, and in either case we shall on the test find that our fullest and richest statement of the law is in terms of the group activity tending to spread itself, with allowance for the differences of technique in the governing organ through which it functions. [p. 292.]

The implications of Bentley's views on the public interest were spelled out, somewhat more clearly than Bentley himself had done, by David B. Truman, whose restatement of the Bentlian view of the public interest is that:

> Many . . . assume explicitly or implicitly that there is an interest of the nation as a whole, universally and invariably held and standing apart from and superior to those of the various groups included within it. . . . such an assertion flies in the face of all that we know of the behavior of men in a complex society. Were it in fact true, not only the interest group but even the political party should properly be viewed as an abnormality. . . . Assertion of an inclusive "national" or "public interest" is an effective device in many . . . situations. . . . In themselves, these claims are part of the data of politics. However, they do not describe any actual or possible political situation within

a complex modern nation. In developing a group interpretation of politics, therefore, we do not need to account for a totally inclusive interest, because one does not exist. [1951, pp. 50–51.]

Stigmatizing "public will" and "public interest" as political myths is characteristic of Bentley and his disciples. But the alternative concept of the public interest that is entertained, however implicitly, by the Bentlians, is a purely mechanical one, reflecting the *Weltanschauung* of Newtonian physics rather than that of the age of nuclear fission. The mechanism of Bentlian theory has frequently been criticized, particularly by Idealists, as we have already seen. There are, of course, Realists who are group theorists but not followers of Bentley; Bentley's influence upon the profession of political science is largely limited to the past decade. These non-Bentlian Realists agree, in many respects, with the ramifications of Bentlian public-interest theory, but their analysis is somewhat more sophisticated and they would qualify, in some respects, the Bentlian dogma.

Pendleton Herring, for instance, agrees that the idea of "public interest" is a myth, but, in his view, the political myth of the public interest has significance other than that of merely being "part of the data of politics" and reflecting only logomachy as a tactic of competing groups:

Under democracy rule by public opinion provides those conditions whereby special interests are free to seek a working compromise harmonious with the values prevailing in the community. . . . [But how] can we get democracy to work in terms of a balance of interests and still evolve public policy? Government, whether by party, president, or bureaucracy, must have a basis in some combination of group interests. These interests can be rationalized in various ideologies. I would defend the myth of the public interest because by its very vagueness it permits the freest interplay of group interests. The dominant combination at any one time can claim that its program expresses the public interest. Yet such a power combination is always contingent. Our loose party system offers an institutional framework suitable to this interplay of forces. [1940a, pp. 313, 424–25.]

Herring cited and appeared to follow John Dickinson, who had written somewhat earlier that "the task of government, and hence of democracy as a form of government, is not to express an imaginary popular will, but to effect adjustments among the various special wills and purposes which at any given time are pressing for realization" [1930, p. 291]. In particular, it should be noted that Dickinson said "to *effect* adjustments," which implies a positive role for government officials rather than the essentially negative, passive function attributed to officials—other than when they themselves act as representatives of "special interest groups"—by Bentlian theory. In the same paragraph in which he described the popular will as "imaginary," Dickinson emphasized the importance of the concept as a popular myth: "if the time should come when this illusion was dispelled, the result might well be a general breakdown of faith in the whole idea of democratic government."

The above comments came at the end of an extended discussion, in which Dickinson refuted the Rationalist concept of popular sovereignty:

A system of democratic theology has grown up; and the temptation to take it seriously and apply it literally can be held responsible for many, if not most, of the things which bring democracy into disrepute.

The first and broadest tenet of this theology is that in a democracy "the people rule." This is explained by saying that while in many matters of government it is obvious that the "people" cannot act directly, they choose by election the officials who are to act in their place and name, and by this process preserve such direct and immediate control over government that its actions are guided by the popular will, or as it is now more fashionable to say, by "public opinion." The keystone of this doctrine is the assumption that there exists in every political society a "will of the people" which declares itself at elections and operates through the instrumentality of elected officials; and it is thought to be the object of democracy to see that this "popular will" gets itself translated into governmental action, and that governmental action is determined by nothing else. The whole theory and strategy of the democratic movement is generally directed toward this single objective; by it is tested the worth of governmental mechanisms, to the almost complete exclusion of other standards of good government. One of the principal grounds of attack on democratic institutions is that they do not achieve this aim—that instead of ensuring that governmental action shall be guided solely by the popular will, they permit it to take its direction from the will of small groups or special interests. . . . The cure for the ills of democracy is thought to be more democracy, in the sense of increasing the number of points at which the electorate can bring its "will" to bear on the organs of government. . . . [But] it seems paradoxically true that the more efforts are made to elicit and give effect to the will of the people, the more power is placed in the hands of special groups and interests. . . . The central insight which emerges . . . is . . . that, after all, the larger number of members of any political society have no opinion, and hence no will, on nearly all the matters on which government acts. The only opinion, the only will, which exists is the opinion, the will, of special groups. [pp. 288, 289, 290, 291.]

Dickinson was equally critical, however, of the Idealist concept of a public interest which is declared "for the people" by wise statesmen. In effect, he rejects the proposition that democracy can pull itself up by its own bootstraps:

It would seem clear that in the long run, no matter how absolute is the power of a government, it cannot make a community develop in directions in which there is no will in the community to develop; sooner or later government sinks to the level of those whom it governs. The picture of a community of unruly children being permanently guided by the disinterested wisdom of its best intellects is an idle dream. Government, whatever its form, is bound to be in the long run far more a reflection of the balance of interests in the community than an agency capable of making the community reflect the independent will and purposes of the governors. This being so, it would seem better in the ordinary case that the influence which the various interests and purposes in the community exert on government should be organized into the orderly processes of democracy than allowed to assert themselves irregularly and sporadically through the methods of absolutism. As an argument against democracy in advanced communities, the need for intelligence in government fails to make out its case.
But this is not, as votaries of democratic dogma are too prone to suppose, the end of the story. If it is desirable that government be democratic, it is equally desirable that it be intelligent; and every democratic government faces the challenge so to organize itself as to introduce into its processes the largest amount of intelligence which the effective wills at work in the community are willing to tolerate. [pp. 304–5.]

Implicit in Dickinson's remarks is the germ of what I shall call "Due-Process theory," to be considered later in this chapter. Another respect in which Dickinson differs sharply with the Bentlians is in his concern for the political ecology of governmental decision-making. The Bentlians describe the group struggle as though it takes place in a political vacuum, into which groups pour, eager for the fray, contracting and expanding more or less in correspondence with Boyle's Law. Political scientists generally, however, appear to agree with those Realists who insist that there must be a general political consensus to accept the decisions of public officials, if a democratic polity is to exist. The alternatives to such a general consensus are anarchy or the despotism of a police state. Dickinson identifies the public interest with such a consensus, saying that there must be a

. . . general will, in the sense of common willingness on the part of all groups and individuals who can make their will effective, to acquiesce in the decisions of the community organ of decision. Political authority can function only in an atmosphere where such a general will prevails. In this sense it is not inaccurate to describe political society as resting ultimately upon agreement—upon a common pact, voluntarily recognized and observed, to abide by the conditions essential to the existence of political order. [1929, p. 632.]

Although Arthur Holcombe indulges in such un-Realistic phrases as "the common good of the whole body of the people," he appears to accept the consensus concept of public interest when he writes that:

Action in the public interest means an adjustment of the conflicts between special interests in such a way as best to serve the common good of the whole body of the people. The public interest is more than a particular special interest which is able to prevail in the adjustment of a conflict with other special interests. It is more than the sum of the special interests which gain recognition in a particular process of adjustment. It is more than the bare fact of a temporary equilibrium among a group of special interests. *It is nothing less than such an adjustment of conflicting special interests as can give the people durable confidence in the stability of the state itself.* [Emphasis added; 1950, p. 426.]

Defined thus broadly, the only test of the public interest is pragmatic. Only decisions so extreme, in terms of the prevailing system of shared values in the community, that they are likely to, or do, succeed in provoking a revolution are contrary to the public interest. It is difficult to point to examples of such decisions emanating from the so-called political branches of the national government, but the Supreme Court's decision in the

Dred Scott case is doubtless in point. It is possible, of course, to apply this "survival" concept of the public interest to subordinate bureaucratic structures, and we may find that at that level it has greater relevancy to recurrent governmental behaviors.

A corollary of this "survival" concept is that any decisions within the extremes of societal tolerance are "in the public interest." This implies an emphasis upon the amorality of the group struggle that is readily found in Realist literature. Thus, Dickinson himself writes that

Government . . . is primarily an arbitrator, and since practically every arbitration must result in giving to one side more of what it thinks it ought to have than the other side is willing to admit, every governmental act can be viewed as favoring in some degree some particular and partial "will," or special interest. It is therefore meaningless to criticize government, whether democratic or not, merely because it allows the "right" side, the "right" special interest to win; and the "right" special interest means only the one whose will is most compatible with what we, as critics, conceive to be the right direction for the society's development to take. [1930, p. 292.]

Bertram Gross, a Bentlian who writes primarily as a practitioner rather than as an academic, has said the same thing, somewhat more bluntly: "the only final decisions are made on the basis of power in one form or another. Once they are made, it is then the province of historians to carry on endless debates on whether Might made Right"[1] [1953, p. 10].

Another major theme in Realist thought is the idea of *catalysis* in the adjustment of interest conflict. There are two different ways in which this is generally conceptualized as taking place. According to one theory, a given special-interest group may function as a catalytic agent, broadening the area of "public debate" by deliberately arousing the interest (and, preferably, the support) of other special-interest groups, with the objective of building a coalition adequate to provide the necessary "public" support for a favorable decision. The leading proponent of this point of view [but cf. Truman, 1951, pp. 358ff.; and Key, 3d. ed.; 1952, pp. 172–74] is probably Fred W. Riggs, who defines the function of catalysis as follows:

---

1. By permission from Bertram M. Gross, *The Legislative Struggle.* Copyright 1953, by McGraw-Hill Book Company, Inc.

Those who share a common primary interest will not only seek to coordinate their own pressure activities, but also to engage the support of all potentially sympathetic groups. The first function we shall refer to as coordination, and the second as "catalysis." The term "catalytic group" will be used to refer to any instrumentality which carries out these functions. . . .

. . . although *rejection* of a proposal might be widespread, the lack of an *opposition* will enable a small *supporting* group to obtain favorable legislation, and vice versa. At first look such an arrangement seems "anti-democratic" in nature. On second look, however, it is apparent that if some of those who *reject* a given proposal become sufficiently aroused to organize a catalytic group, they may precipitate an active opposition. Pressure politics, then, may encourage legislation for minority interests but, if this view is correct, it does not necessarily permit legislation sharply inconsistent with the general interest. If "democracy" requires government by popular majorities, then the American pressure system is not "democratic." If the term can be more broadly used to include a form of responsible government which permits concessions to, and compromises among, strongly felt interests—in contrast to domination by any one special interest—then pressure politics may be considered an essential part of the American type of "democracy." [1950, pp. 44, 198.]

The second variant of catalysis theory looks to the public official rather than to the interest groups themselves, and attributes to him the role of *mediating* rather than *arbitrating* interest conflict. As a mediator, the official is concerned with the effect of his decision upon parties who may be affected even though they are not pressing for consideration or, possibly, even aware that a decision is pending. In such a role, the official himself functions as a catalytic agent to arouse the interest of an enlarged but concerned "public." Thus, John Dewey, having defined "the state" as "the organization of the public effected through officials for the protection of the interests shared by its members," suggests "a criterion for determining how good a particular state is," namely, "the degree of organization of the public which is attained, and the degree in which its officers are so constituted as to perform their function of caring for the public interests" [1927, p. 33]. There is, however, not a single public; there are many publics, reflecting the differentially anticipated *and* unanticipated consequences of a host of decisions; furthermore, publics are constituted by recognition of extensive and enduring indirect consequences of acts. . . . The only constant [among states] is the function of caring for and regulating the interests which accrue as the result of the complex indirect expansion and radiation of conjoint behavior. [p. 47.]

In Bentlian theory, official mediation involves the concept of "unorganized" or "potential" groups. As explained by David B. Truman:

> The strength of the broad general interests supporting the "rules of the game" varies, and the claims based upon them change from time to time as do the strength and the claims of other political interest groups. These persistent interests are not invariably dominant, and, although they are widely shared at any given point in time, they are not held universally throughout the society. These notions of fair play are represented largely by unorganized or potential groups; the generality of their acceptance is such that their claims do not require organized expression except when these notions are flagrantly violated or when they are in process of alteration. In a sense one may think of the principal governmental leaders—legislative, executive, and judicial —as the leaders of these unorganized groups. Part of the official's task is the regular representation of these potential groups in the actions of government. If officials fail to do this adequately, alternative leaders in or outside the government may attempt to organize a following and seek adequate expression of the interest either through the established processes or through violence. [Citing Bentley.] [1951, pp. 448-49.]

Realists who are not tied to Bentlian dogma find it possible to express the same idea while thinking of public officials just as public officials, without trotting in the apparatus of leadership of unorganized groups. (The latter circumlocution is necessary for the Bentlians, of course, so that they can remain faithful to the categorical imperative of a *group* interpretation of all aspects of the political process.) John Dewey, for instance, takes pains to differentiate his theory of the public from the pluralistic conception of the state:

> Our doctrine of plural forms is a statement of a fact: that there exists a plurality of social groupings, good, bad, and indifferent. It is not a doctrine which prescribes inherent limits to state action. It does not intimate that *the function of the state is limited to settling conflicts among other groups,* as if each one of them had a fixed scope of action of its own. *Were that true, the state would be only an um-*

pire to avert and remedy trespasses of one group upon another. Our hypothesis is neutral as to any general, sweeping implications as to how far state activity may extend. It does not indicate any particular polity of public action. At times, the consequences of the conjoint behavior of some persons may be such that a large public interest is generated which can be fulfilled only by laying down conditions which involve a large measure of reconstruction within that group. [Emphasis added; 1927, p. 73.]

"The essential need," concludes Dewey, "is the improvement of the methods and conditions of debate, discussion, and persuasion. That is *the* problem of the public" [p. 208]. Dewey's conclusion is a good summary of the Realist concept of the public interest in constituency political action.

B. Congress

THE FIRST MAJOR STUDY of the relationship between special-interest groups and legislative decision-making was Pendleton Herring's doctoral dissertation [1929]. As his concluding chapter bears evidence, Herring had already developed the pluralistic and Realist frame of reference that was to characterize his subsequent writings on the relationship between interest groups and the administrative process [1936] and between interest groups and the political parties [1940a]. In his introductory chapter, however, Herring called attention to the seeming anomaly, in terms of orthodox representation theory, of the *direct* representation of interest groups in the Congress:

Under the theory of representative government the legislators are presumed to hold to a broad national point of view and think in terms of the public good. These organized groups oftentimes succeed in affecting this detached point of view by skillful pleading; sometimes they succeed in sending their representatives to the legislative bodies. . . . When such delegates do succeed in obtaining seats in a legislative assembly they appear to contravene the theory of representative government when they act as spokesmen for their group. Legislators theoretically are spokesmen for the people as a whole. [1929, p. 11.]

To the extent that special interests succeed in gaining direct representation by having their representatives nominated and elected as congressmen or, what is probably much more common, to the extent that special interests are successful in persuading or conditioning congressmen to function as their spokesmen, the public interest will suffer accordingly—according to Rationalist or Idealist theory. Not so, according to the Realists, since direct group representation merely brings into the open the struggle among group interests that is taking place in any event. Indeed, it is considered conducive to responsibility that legislative adjustment of competing, including built-in, interests should take place subject to public, i.e., multigroup, scrutiny.

There is also an empirical dispute regarding the way in which congressmen actually do behave. Let us examine the larger issue in the more specific context of the activities of members of congressional investigating committees, an aspect of legislative behavior not without interest to the public in recent years. As Dr. Griffith sees it, the congressional committee hearing places the congressman in the role of a defender of the truth in the face of the calumnies of "the pressure boys." On the one hand, says Dr. Griffith, the hearing gives the witness an opportunity to present his case; and "on the other hand, under questioning by a skilled exponent of the public interest, such sophistries and rationalizations as may underlie even the most plausible presentation may be exposed" [1951, p. 113]. Similar views have been expressed by Professor Joseph P. Chamberlain, who has compared committee members to the judges of a plural court who listen to the evidence and legal arguments presented by the parties to a case and then announce their dispassionate judgment as to what the law—that is, the public interest—requires.

The committee itself must be the guardian of the general public interest, too large and too vague to be organized. What is in the general interest is for the committee to determine, after hearing advocates of the special interests who appear before it" [1936, p. 79, and cf. pp. 72–73; quoted in Huitt, 1954, pp. 341–42.]

These Idealist notions have been treated as an hypothesis for investigation by Ralph K. Huitt, who undertook a detailed analysis of hearings conducted in 1946 by the Senate Committee on

Banking and Currency, on the question of the extension of price controls. Huitt's findings and conclusions fail to support the Idealist theory, but they do support the Bentlian thesis which portrays congressmen as actors in the group struggle:

> The committee members are not judges, discovering the general interest; they are themselves participants in the political struggle. . . . The Committee members seemed most impressive when they were acting as representatives of specific constituency interests in their states. Here they seemed to speak as experts in their own right. The cliches fell away, the fuzziness and amateurishness disappeared; there the facts were clear and the grasp was sure. . . . In the price control controversy (and surely in others like it) the senators were not sitting as arbiters of the group struggle, but as participants; it flowed through them. . . . It is generally accepted that there are many opinions, but not that there are many versions of the facts—or at least, not that there is no single *true* one. This is the crucial problem of communication between social groups, as it is, to a greater degree, of intercultural communication. Given its own version of the facts, and believing it to be the only true one, each side could fight for the general interest and impute bad motives to its opponents in all sincerity. In this sense the Committee *was* concerned with promoting the general interest, but so were most of the spokesmen of special interests who appeared before it. [1954, pp. 342, 347, 364.]

Huitt's fact skepticism provides an emphasis that is lacking in most of the writings about investigating committees. We shall find that this same point of view constitutes an important strand of legal realism, most conspicuously, perhaps, in the prolific writings of the late Judge Jerome Frank.

A second thread of Legislative Realism emphasizes the effect of each chamber, as a group, in conditioning the behavior of the individual members. In an epigrammatic phrase attributed to Speaker Sam Rayburn, "To get along, go along" [Robinson, 1958, p. 84]. Each group has its own informal norms as well as formal rules, to which a member must conform in order to obtain enough power and influence to accomplish much of anything. William S. White [1956, chap. vii and pp. 110–16] has dwelt at length on the "Inner Club" of the Senate, and he has used Hubert Humphrey as an example of the process of personal accommodation which can convert a freshman outcast into a "good senator." Essentially, in Humphrey's case, this involved personally cultivating the Southern conservative leaders of the Senate, willingness to compromise, proper respect for the sacred cows of the leaders, and technical skill in the tactics of legislative procedure. All of this may be a somewhat elaborate way of repeating the old adage, "If you can't beat 'em, join 'em."

White's rambling book is folksy in tone and journalistic in treatment, but a recent behaviorial study of decision-making in the House Rules Committee arrives at similar conclusions on this question of the significance of group norms. The latter study concludes that the primary influences upon the decision-making of the Rules Committee's members are the wishes of the members' constituencies and of the House leaders, but these factors are discussed as findings which summarize the way the members behave in fact, rather than as statements about the way they ought to behave:

> When a member's constituency clearly has an interest at stake, no competing claim is likely to receive priority. Survival is valued more, even by the leadership, than any single vote. The philosophy is that a member who ignores the obvious needs of his district will not return another term to cooperate with the leadership on other issues. Where the district's interests are not so clearly involved, the leadership's views are likely to prevail, providing they are firmly expressed. [Robinson, 1958, p. 86.]

Neither the pressures of constituency nor of organizational leaders are linked by James Robinson to Rationalist theories of majoritarian control or public will. Instead, he states a number of propositions which purport to summarize the most important variables in the committee's decision-making. Most relevant to the question of legislative responsibility are the following:

> When spheres of competence of a decisional unit are not explicitly or completely prescribed, individual members of the unit are required to interpret their competences for themselves. [p. 78.]
> When spheres of competence are not clearly defined, diverse loyalties compete for an individual's allegiance. [p. 80.]
> The values and objectives that guide individual decisions in organizations include organizational values and objectives. [p. 84.]

It is the last proposition that supports White's discussion, and Robinson adds, by way of explanation, that

Apparently the predominant organizational value within Congress is cooperation with the majority. . . . Among the membership of the Rules Committee there is a strong inclination to cooperate with the leadership in reporting rules favored by the Speaker and the majority leader. During interviews, ten of the twelve members of the committee offered cooperation with the leadership as one of the expectations of their role, and they are quite predisposed to act in accordance with this expectation. [p. 84.]

The three remaining propositions are:

The values and objectives that guide an individual's decisions in organizations include his previous life experience or social background. [p. 84.]
Organizational values and objectives may conflict with nonorganizational values and objectives. [p. 85.]
Resolution of conflict between organizational and nonorganizational values depends on one's estimate of the strength of the competing demands. [p. 86.]

The latter propositions place the same kind of emphasis upon psychological conflict within the individual decision-maker that we shall find among some of the Administrative Realists and Judicial Realists. This point of view, like Realism generally, points to conflict among competing interests that must be compromised, preferably with a minimum of stress and disaffection among those affected by the decision. The conflict is perceived, however, as an internal problem within the mind of the official; while the Sociological (i.e., group) Realists describe a conflict external to the official, in which he interacts with other persons. Indeed, for the Bentlians, it is the interaction *between* groups of persons, not *among* persons within a single group, that is of primary political significance.

Emmette Redford has defended the single-member district system and geographical representation on the grounds that the existing American system provides more flexibility for expressing the diverse interests of a pluralistic society than would a system of functional representation:

Sectional or geographical representation may . . . approach comprehensive representation through the single-member constituency. The Congressman representing such a constituency may find that there are many diverse interests within his district, that no one of these has a majority, that there is much overlapping of memberships and many unorganized voters. As a result he becomes a moderator among group demands and searches for answers for public problems which have a broad appeal. True, the Congressman is sometimes a virtual captive of a particular functional interest, or sometimes strongly affected by class demands, and ofttimes is representative of a sectional viewpoint. But it remains true, nevertheless, that there are many districts which are almost as pluralistic as the nation and that the single-member constituency is more favorable to search by the individual representative for the public interest than any other form of representation could be. [1958, p. 129.]

Other pluralists, such as John Dickinson, focus upon the mediatory role of each legislator, as well as that of the legislature as a group. In rather sharp conflict with the Rationalists, who conceive of a conflict between political parties which is definitively resolved at the polls (at least until the next election), Dickinson's legislative model suggests the dynamic and continuous resolution of a vast number of group conflicts which can be compromised, but only by processes of interaction more intimate and sophisticated than the dichotomization of issues that makes possible choice by the voters:

Government by elected representatives ordinarily affords opportunity for practically every interest of importance in the community to find somewhere in the representative assembly a spokesman to voice its claims. It is possible for these representatives to meet and work under circumstances making for the mutual understanding of different points of view and for the attainment of compromises designed to provide for the future of all interests in the community important enough to take account of. Conflicting interests, instead of standing apart and testing their numerical strength at the polls, are supplied with means for coming into contact, consultation, and adjustment in a way that can conceivably allow something to each. Each may have some share in moulding the adjustment and consequently be supplied with a motive for abiding by it. Every representative is a potential mediator for the interest which has the strongest control over him in the face of other interests; and in this way opportunity is given for bringing interests into touch and convincing each of the advantage of accommodating itself to the others with which it has to live. These are the substantial merits of representative democracy—these, and not the realization of a supposed "popular" will. [1930, pp. 295–96.]

Dickinson's theory is given substantial support by a more recent case study, by Earl Latham, of congressional action on proposed basing-point legislation during the 1948–50 sessions. The purpose of the bills was to reverse a recent decision of the Supreme Court; in the end, the compromise measure that eventually cleared both houses of Congress was nullified by a presidential veto.

Latham's concept of "official groups" appears to coincide with the distinction that I have made between the Constituency component and the remaining factors of our decision-making schema, which deal with governmental or official behaviors. Latham says that

> The designation "official" is the sign which manifests that the bearer is authorized by the social understanding to exercise against all groups and individuals certain powers which they may not exercise against him. The concept of officiality, then, is the sum of the technical differences which are rooted in the social understanding as to who does what to whom; and the difference between the public and private groups is the "officiality" of the former. . . . the principal function of official groups is to provide various levels of compromise in the writing of the rules, all within the body of agreed prinicples [*sic*] that forms the consensus upon which the political community rests, and . . . each of the three principal branches of government has a special role in performing this function. [1952b, pp. 389–90.]

As an "official group," the legislature is both a participant group in the struggle with other groups and, at the same time, a mediatory or "catalytic group" (although Latham does not use this term) in accommodating conflicting interests of *other* groups within the framework of the legislature's own special competence, in terms of both authority and expertise.

Although Latham identifies [1952a, pp. 3–4, 13–16] with John Dewey and other non-Bentlian pluralists, he comes up with a mechanistic concept of the process of legislative policy-making replete with a Newtonian equilibrium [see also Wilson, 1908, pp. 54–56; Waldo, 1948, p. 106; and cf. Robinson, pp. 252–66], characteristic of the Bentlian model:

> The legislature referees the group struggle, ratifies the victories of the successful coalitions, and records the terms of the surrenders, compromises, and conquests in the form of statutes. Every statute tends to represent compromise because the process of accommodating conflicts of group interest is one of deliberation and consent. The legislative vote on any issue tends to represent the composition of

strength, i.e., the balance of power, among the contending groups at the moment of voting. What may be called public policy is the equilibrium reached in this struggle at any given moment, and it represents a balance which the contending factions of groups constantly strive to weight in their favor. [1952a, pp. 35–36.]

A consistent Bentlian would be content to let the matter rest here, with an analysis of basing-point legislation in terms of group interaction. But like so many political scientists, Latham is not content to close his book on such an amoral note. He yields, in the end, to the compulsion to pledge allegiance to our free democratic institutions, which somehow have produced an over-all harmony in the form of rationalized issues making possible the dichotomous choice of the final roll call. Thus, he concludes, a rational decision was possible, not for the voters, it is true, but for their duly elected representatives in Congress assembled. The appendage of a Rationalist conclusion in the final paragraph of a book whose preceding 225 pages is filled with Realist theory and analysis is more than a *non sequitur;* it tends to make this case study something of a shaggy-dog story:

. . . it is impossible to witness the process in Congress without admiration for the strength of this vital institution of a free people in a democracy. Congressmen looked and sounded inept, and even silly and confused, in various stages of the passage of S. 1008 from committee consideration to final enactment. And many would have disagreed with the way in which Congress finally acted on this particular issue. But when so much is said, the fact remains that a fantastically complicated question of public policy was refined and sifted as it went through the mechanism of legislative procedure, at each stage reducing the number of alternatives to be decided, until the final stage was reached, and it was then possible for Congressmen to say "aye" or "nay" to a specific and simplified, even oversimplified, choice about which they could make up their minds. [1952a, pp. 226–27.]

For a consistent Realist, the final and formal roll-call vote on a bill is not the culmination of an *essentially* rational process that results in a clear-cut choice between two alternative policy goals. For a consistent Realist, the final roll call, more often than not *pro forma* in any event, is merely one of a host of accommodations and compromises that have occurred during the legislative consideration of the policy issues; it is by no means necessarily the most important decision. Nor are the issues necessarily "simpler" to comprehend at the end of the group interaction—in the legislature—than they were at the beginning of the legislative struggle. To the contrary, the effect of more and more groups entering the debate, with further recognition of diversity in the consequences of decision, is usually one of immensely complicating rather than simplifying "choice" in an ultimate sense. Of course, the Realist solution to this problem lies in the argument that choice is never made in an ultimate sense. Accommodation is the product of a sequence of interrelated decisions, and the chronologically "final" decision merely ratifies, as Latham himself has said, "the victories of the successful coalitions" and "the terms of the surrenders, compromises, and conquests."

Moreover, the adoption of any particular statute, or the defeat of any particular bill, marks no more than a particular stage in the on-going process of group interaction. Both Bentlian and non-Bentlian Realists agree that statutes result in the delegation, to other governmental officials, of the ambiguous discretion postulated in Dean Leys's third category. Latham's study, concerned with proposed amendments to a statute for which the primary administrative agency was the Federal Trade Commission, led him to remark that "administrative agencies of the regulatory kind are established to carry out the terms of the treaties that the legislators have negotiated and ratified" [1952a, p. 38]. Bertram Gross, with an eye on judicial enforcement of legislation, suggests that judges—like regulatory commissioners and other administrators—are frequently faced with the same unresolved issues that Congress had considered but evaded by using ambiguity in the statutory language; in addition, of course, there are new "issues," i.e., conflicts between groups, that have arisen since the enactment of the statute:

> . . . "the intent of Congress" is little more than a method of rationalizing the views of the judges themselves. Every statute leaves broad room for interpretation. The issues litigated before the courts are usually ones which never arose during the course of the legislative process, were scarcely considered by the legislators, or upon which the Congress as a whole would certainly never have had an

"intent." In fact, many issues which are determined "in accordance with the intent of Congress" were in the first instance deliberately left unsolved because any effort to resolve them in Congress would have made too many people unhappy.[2] [1953, p. 106.]

The most general and yet succinct statement of this point is that of David B. Truman, who writes that

The imperative of compromise among groups, between group demands and the "rules of the game," explains various aspects of the legislative process. . . . One of these is the ambiguity of many legislative formulas. The variety of meanings that can be read into the verbal formulations and other behavior of governmental officials is often derided by those who project their own interest affiliations upon the whole polity. But ambiguity and verbal compromise may be the very heart of a successful political formula, especially where the necessity for compromise is recognized but is difficult to achieve in explicit terms. Ambiguity may postpone or obviate the necessity for a showdown and as such has an important political function. [1951, p. 393.]

From this point of view, congressional decision-making constitutes one stage of the policy-making process, and it frequently results in temporary or inadequate accommodations of the contending group interests concerned with any particular issue. Even if the legislative compromise re-establishes an acceptable equilibrium for a given issue, the passing of time and the dynamics of group interaction on *other* issues, to mention only two possibilities, may lead, just as much as preferred ambiguity in statutory language, to a re-opening of the group struggle before other official decision-makers, such as administrators, judges, and the president.

C. The Presidency

BOTH RATIONALISTS AND IDEALISTS, we have found, divide into one or the other of two opposing camps: they are either for presidential supremacy, which they define as a system in which the president dominates his party and Congress; or they are for

---

2. By permission from Bertram M. Gross, *The Legislative Struggle.* Copyright 1953, by McGraw-Hill Book Company, Inc.

congressional supremacy, wherein party leadership is put in collegium in Congress, and Congress dominates the president. Rationalists and Idealists differ on the question whether the president (or Congress) should be dominated by the people, or whether the people should be dominated by the president (or Congress). However, they both want to have *somebody* in ultimate as well as proximate charge, to serve as the fountainhead of authority and legitimacy. They cannot accept or be at ease in a world or polity in which

The actual art of governing under our Constitution does not and cannot conform to judicial definitions of the power of any of its branches based on isolated clauses or even single Articles torn from context. While the Constitution diffuses power the better to secure liberty, it also contemplates that practice will integrate the dispersed powers into a workable government. It enjoins upon its branches separateness but interdependence, autonomy but reciprocity. Presidential powers are not fixed but fluctuate, depending upon their disjunction or conjunction with those of Congress.[3]

After having examined the relationship between special-interest groups and the Congress [1929], the regulatory commissions [1936], and the political parties [1940a], Pendleton Herring brought forth a small volume on the political relations of Congress and the president [1940b]. He found that the same kinds of group pressures that focus upon Congress and administrative agencies converge upon the presidency as well. As for presidential-congressional relationships, Herring's proposal was characteristic of the Realist orientation of his thought and work. He proposed that, given the American party system as it then was and the institutional practices of the presidency and Congress as they then existed, a large measure of presidential leadership was required, but that it must be based on a high degree of interaction with Congress (to speak only of executive-legislative relationships for the moment). "Our presidential system cannot function," Herring wrote, "unless based on common underlying loyalties that induce unity up to the top." On the other hand, "it cannot be left to one man—the symbol—in the White House to

3. Mr. Justice Jackson, concurring in *Youngstown Sheet & Tube* v. *Sawyer*, 343 U.S. 579, 635 (1952).

'save the nation' or to 'make democracy work.' " Assuming (as, at least, the non-Bentlian Realists generally do) that agreement on fundamental values exists, then

> To reconcile our differences we support political institutions which prescribe a procedure for peaceful adjustment. The presidential office is one such institution. The man in the White House is to guide the nation towards its common purpose. To the framers of the Constitution the chief magistrate was to be a moderator, not a crusader. Time and events have built the presidential office into a foremost position for national leadership. Yet the leader, to be effective, in a democratic society must remain a moderator at least in part. [p. 144.]

There are clearly Idealist elements mixed in Herring's statement, but his emphasis is upon compromise, moderation, and co-operation, rather than upon presidential evangelism. Robert A. Dahl [1950], writing a decade later, and with particular concern for presidential-congressional relationships in regard to foreign policy, came to conclusions very similar to those of Herring.

Although Louis Brownlow is a strong exponent of the Constituency-Rationalist concept of the presidency, he does not limit to the electoral process his analysis of the ways in which the people express their will. In describing the other ways in which the public gives its orders to the Chief Magistrate, he states what is clearly Realist doctrine:

> . . . the machinery with which we control the President is by no means confined to [the] formalized system of checks and balances. We undertake to control him by custom and tradition and by subjecting him in many ways to the direct impact of the voice of the people as interpreted by this, that, or the other special interest. . . . we expect of the President . . . that he be a faithful representative of the opinion of the people. [But the] people are neither so naive nor so doctrinaire that they imagine the existence of one general opinion that reflects the views of the whole country. Rather they are insistent in their diverse groups that each group has the right opinion; that contrary opinions held by other groups are wrong; that the opinion of their group is right and should prevail as the national opinion; and that the way to bring about that desirable end is to persuade the President to go along with them. . . . It is a centripetal . . . force. Whether they meet as three people in a room or as 3,000 in a convention, the groups pass resolutions telling the President what to do; if they publish a journal, they publicly advise the President how to

conduct himself; if they fear a rival group in a particular field, they
hasten to claim from the President sole recognition as the representatives of their bailiwick. [1949, pp. 78, 69.]

Charles A. Beard has written that, notwithstanding the pressures for what we would call today a "bipartisan foreign policy,"
the interplay of group pressures upon the president's decisions
affecting foreign affairs is no less than in regard to domestic
affairs. What is different, as Dahl has emphasized, is that the
pressures of both party and constituency may be much less
sharply defined and persistent regarding questions of foreign
policy, thus making the personal attitudes of presidential [Payne,
1949, p. 91] and congressional [Dahl, 1950, pp. 13, 44, 200–4]
decision-makers *and* interest-group pressures [Dahl, 1950, pp.
52–57] all the more important in defining the public interest in
foreign affairs. As I pointed out in the introductory chapter,
when we speak of the public interest in foreign affairs, it is
customary to use the term "national interest," as Beard does:

> What any particular President may do in fact depends upon his
> training, personality, and sympathies, upon the pressure brought to
> bear upon him by private interests, economic and moral, organized
> and unorganized. His interpretation of national interest in particular
> cases will not be derived from abstractions alone; it will be the result
> of complex forces, among which corporate and individual private
> interests must always be reckoned. He is as much subject to the
> pressures of lobbies in his sphere as Congress is within its domain—
> through the leaders of his party and through personal connections.
> He brings a heritage of theories, sentiments, ideas, and attachments
> with him into his office. Though a single person, he often finds him-
> self, as Emerson said of every man, at war with himself in his own
> bosom, balancing conceptions, pressures and appeals over against one
> another. Seldom can his decisions be determined by statistical demon-
> strations or the clear weight of facts duly found by experts. Not
> always can he tell in advance whether any single action will be sup-
> ported by Congress, his party, or the majority of the voters. Yet,
> under the assumption that "politics stops at the water's edge," it is
> widely supposed that the President's determination of national in-
> terest in foreign affairs must receive unconditional support on
> grounds of loyalty. More than one President has taken this position.
> . . . But efforts to throw the protection of lese majesty around
> executive pronouncements on national interest have only a shadowy
> claim to validity in law and none whatever in practice. The President

is merely one of the interpreting agencies in the Federal Government and his efficiency in realizing his decisions depends upon shrewd calculations respecting particular situations and the possibility of winning popular support for his resolutions. [1934a, pp. 418–20.]

Only two years later, however, the United States Supreme Court was interpreting the Constitution, in *United States* v. *Curtiss-Wright Export Corp.*, 299 U.S. 304, 319 (1936), to mean that "the President is *the sole organ of the nation* in its external relations, and its sole representative with foreign nations." This Rationalist dogma was a patently inaccurate and misleading statement when first uttered by Congressman John Marshall in the twilight of John Adams' administration [Annals, 6th Cong., col. 613 (March 7, 1800)]; and it is a fantastically gross oversimplification of the American constitutional system, as it functioned in 1936, or as it operates today. Even in the context in which Mr. Justice Sutherland spoke for the Court, this rationale was inept, for President Roosevelt had acted in co-operation with Congress and under the express authority of a joint resolution. The perspective of the Realists seems much more useful than that of the Rationalists or Idealists, as a basis for better understanding presidential decision-making.

Earl Latham's more recent case study of a problem of domestic policy leads him to conclusions consistent with those of Beard. Latham does, however, suggest an important qualification: that it is much more difficult for any single interest group, or combination of groups, to control the president than to dominate a single congressman, or even a substantial group of congressmen:

Democratic politicians must reflect the consensus, and most of the time of legislators and chief executives is spent in determining what the consensus is. There are no infallible signs, and the White House guess on the balance of power could have been wrong. Congressmen are vulnerable to particular pressures brought by powerful groups who hope to identify their particular group interest with the national interest, and the pressures of these groups are acutely felt in the small constituencies at home. Besides this, Congressmen continually seek to forecast the reactions of incipient and unorganized groups which, although not immediately organized and aroused, might conceivably become so. The President is generally less vulnerable to the direct pressures of organized groups because his constituency is national and not local; and for pressure groups to defeat him

requires an expenditure of effort and money sometimes out of keeping with the value of the prize which this effort wins. But he is not
less responsive than the Congressman in his anticipation of the reactions of incipient and unorganized groups. [1952a, p. 225.]

Latham emphasizes primarily the size of the presidential constituency and the related expense of presidential campaigns as
factors likely to insure that presidential decisions will be based
upon a synthesis of many conflicting group interests. One could
logically argue—and since most writings on this subject seem
to be based upon speculation rather than systematic empirical
knowledge, one man's logical argument is as good as another's
—that the effect of freeing the president from the *control* of interest groups (assuming that this is the case) must widen the
field of discretion for the interplay of other influences. These
influences would be, in terms of our previous analysis, primarily
(1) the presidency's guesses—note that I do not say "the president's"—about the probable attitudes at some future time of
some ten million marginal voters; tempered by (2) the majority-
party bureaucracy's estimate of the same factor plus their estimate
of the atomized reactions of congressional constituencies, both in
relationship to financial and other kinds of group support for the
party; plus (3) the president's personal values and attitudes
toward the commonweal, and this too as a function of the advice he receives from those closest to him in regard to any particular decision. I do not mean to suggest that other factors than
these may not be of great importance to presidential decision-
making. I say only that *at least* these will ordinarily be present.
Assuming that these three factors, plus the interplay of group
pressures by processes that we shall leave unspecified for the
moment, define some of the major components entering into
presidential determination of the public interest, then we can
infer that *all* of these factors will logically tend to condition the
president to seek constantly to forecast the *probable consequences*
of his decisions.

As we noted earlier in this chapter, a concern for the consequences of decision-making is perhaps the primary emphasis in
John Dewey's philosophy of the public interest. It is this aspect

of presidential decision-making that Dean Harlan Cleveland has affirmed:

> Where . . . does the "public interest" appear? Not, certainly, through the organized political parties, which inflate like balloons at election time and are of small consequence in governmental decision making the rest of the time. No, the defense of the public interest rests in the hands of the people as a whole, who cannot do anything much about it, and of the President they elect, who can. . . . Though we sometimes make gods or supermen of our Presidents, they have not generally been more moral than most of us. The difference is that in the White House they are compelled to stand a little higher on the mountain than anybody else, and they consequently see farther at the horizon. It is this unique and lonely vantage point that lends grandeur to the American Presidency. [1956, p. 42.]

Certainly, it seems to be true that the institution did much to shape the man in the case of Harry Truman. The consensus of contemporary observers appears to be that Truman performed very well in making the *big* decisions required by his office; it was his petty decisions that evoked the greatest criticism. Of course, the decisions to drop the first atomic bomb in World War II, or to send troops to Korea, or to veto the Taft-Hartley Act, or to re-call General Douglas MacArthur were the products of a complex institutional decision-making process, in which the President's ultimate choice was made only after he had been exposed to a thorough indoctrination in the relevant alternatives to and the probable consequences of his decision. It was the "snap judgments," the highly personal decisions—e.g., to write critical letters to music critics—that brought the most grief to Truman. This is not to say that decisions arrived at as the result of complex institutional processes, tending to insure a conscious weighing of alternatives and a consideration of consequences, will always prove to be the "right" presidential decisions that are accepted as being "in the public interest." But if Dewey and Cleveland are correct, such presidential decisions are more likely to prove to be in the public interest, than are presidential decisions arrived at according to the prescriptions of the Rationalists or the Idealists.

Let us consider, for example, one of President Truman's big decisions that has been subjected to much criticism by the present generation: his seizure of the major steel mills in the spring of

1952. It seems correct to conclude that the predominant popular reaction at the time was unsympathetic to Truman and adulatory of the Supreme Court. If one is to infer anything about the verdict of the electorate from the Eisenhower triumph at the polls less than six months later, the inference must be that the public upheld the Court and repudiated Truman. The professional opinion of political scientists and lawyers was almost universal in the heaping of laurel wreaths upon the collective heads of the justices, and coals upon the head of President Truman. In other words, the judgment of our times has been that Truman made a bad decision, a decision contrary to the public interest, in ordering the seizure of the steel mills.

In previous chapters, we have noted that the judgment of judicial and other critics of the President was that: (1) Truman *should* have followed Rationalist theory, and obeyed the law as enacted by Congress, thus invoking the Taft-Hartley act; but (2) Truman, it is assumed, had actually followed Idealist theory, substituting his own personal judgment of public good for the substantive policies ordained by Congress and for the procedural policies ordained by the Constitution. In regard to the second point, it should be remembered that we use "Idealist theory" in a special sense that I have attempted to define carefully; what is meant, in this context, is essentially that Truman thought that a strike in steel would be bad for the country, irrespective of the suspicions entertained by some critics that another influence was labor politics in the forthcoming presidential election. The issue was generally described as being one of The Law versus Prerogative Power; thus, Justice Jackson saw the Court in the historic role of Chief Justice Coke defying James I [*Youngstown Sheet and Tube Co.* v. *Sawyer*, 343 U.S. 579, 655n. (1952)]; and Justice Douglas, speaking for the liberals, thought that "today a *kindly* President uses the seizure power to effect a wage increase and to keep the steel furnaces in production. Yet tomorrow. . . " [emphasis added; p. 633].

But there is a third perspective, in terms of which it is instructive to consider the Steel Seizure case. This is provided by a public-administration case study [McConnell, 1960], written by a former member of the White House staff, from the point of view of the presidential staff towards the decision. As a description of the events, the story related by this case study is very different from the "facts" recognized by the Supreme Court, or reported in the press at the time. The case study is written from a Realist point of view, and it describes in considerable detail the interplay of group pressures upon the presidency that culminated, after months of struggle, in the seizure order. According to Grant McConnell, the author of the case study, there was no seizure "policy"—the decision to seize came literally at the last hour before a strike deadline called by the union, and only after other alternatives had become, for one reason or another, no longer available. The seizure order was issued upon the advice of the Attorney General, who informed the President that the proposed action was consistent with both previous presidential practice and with the decisions of the Supreme Court—as, indeed, it was; so the President and his staff assumed that the seizure order would be legal, not *illegal,* and their concern was not with that problem but rather with the question of which alternative, or combination of alternatives, would constitute the best adjustment to a rapidly changing and highly unstable situation.

Early in January 1952, for instance, President Truman had written to Philip Murray of the United Steelworkers, saying in part that:

I believe the national interest requires such a decision [to work after expiration of the contract] by your union at the present time. The nation simply cannot afford a stoppage in steel production, even a stoppage of limited duration [McConnell, 1960, p. 18.]

At this time, Murray acceded to the President's demands in the name of the public interest; and at this time, there was no thought of seizure, although it was thought by some White House staff members that if the Wage Stabilization Board failed to settle the conflict, "the Taft-Hartley procedure might be invoked." Five days before the strike deadline on midnight April 8, four major alternatives were under intensive consideration, including: (1) seizure under Section 18 of the Universal Military Training and Service Act of 1948; (2) seizure under the "inherent powers" of the president; (3) sending a bill to Congress requesting additional and specific authority to seize steel mills; and (4) invocation of the Taft-Hartley Act [pp. 31–32].

On April 7, less than forty-eight hours before the strike deadline, negotiations between the unions and the companies appeared to have reached such a stage that "the Taft-Hartley procedure might prove the only possibility other than a strike," and the seizure alternative would be discarded [p. 34]. Then, on the afternoon of the following day, "it seemed that the strategy would include use of the Taft-Hartley board of inquiry [procedure] as well as seizure" [p. 35].

At 7 p. m. an official of the steelworkers was telephoned and asked to get an authoritative estimate of what would happen to production if a Taft-Hartley board of inquiry were appointed at the same time that the mills were seized. He phoned back an hour later to report that this would probably cause such anger among the men that there would be a rank-and-file walkout regardless of what the union ordered or agreed to. The idea was abandoned.... [p. 36.]

Then, and only then, on the evening of the President's speech announcing the seizure order and only hours before the strike deadline, was a decision finally made *not* to invoke Taft-Hartley and to rely exclusively upon the president's direct constitutional powers to support an order of seizure.

Whether the decision was "right" or "wrong," it was made with an attempt to give full consideration to alternative courses of action and to the probable consequences of choice; and it was made in a maelstrom of group and other pressures, rather than in an attempt to follow *either* the imputation of a previously expressed "will of the people" *or* the personal and private ideas of public good which may have been entertained by the President as an individual. The conclusion at which McConnell arrives is quite different from that of the Supreme Court. As he saw the situation from the perspective of the White House, the situation was tragic. The tragedy, however, lay not in an unbridled quest of the President for dictatorial power; the tragedy lay in the frustration of the presidency which, although held publicly responsible for taking action, was relatively impotent in the face of monolithic combinations of big business and big labor, each of which, from the point of view of economic advantage, had more to gain than to lose by having a strike.[4] In McConnell's own words, this was "the irony that while the White House was convicted by public opinion of the crime of grasping for unchecked power, its troubles in the steel crisis had come from its lack of influence—over public opinion, over labor and industry, and, in the critical early stages of the controversy, over some of its own stabilization agencies" [p. 53]. The President stopped the strike by issuing the seizure order; the Supreme Court reversed the President and the strike took place immediately. As the White House had anticipated, the strike lasted throughout the spring and summer, and its effect upon defense production, if the Korean War had erupted again, could have been disastrous. But the war did not erupt again, and President-elect Eisenhower went to Korea that winter to symbolize the return of peace and prosperity.

With benefit of such hindsight, we can, perhaps, say that President Truman made the wrong decision, that his seizure order was not in the public interest. But this attempt to give substantive content to the concept of public interest, whether confirmed or not by the judgment of future generations, contributes little or nothing to our understanding of the *theory* of the public interest, for reasons that I stated in the introductory chapter. The significance of our analysis of the Steel Seizure case lies, I believe, in its demonstration of the different kinds of understanding and insight that come to those who employ differing concepts of the public interest to interpret the same set of events. By Rationalist standards, Truman was wrong; by Idealist standards, he was right if he did what he really believed was best; and by Realist criteria, the President made his decision in the proper manner but he made a poor decision, in no small measure because of inadequacies in the forecasting of his staff.

The President's advisors guessed very badly regarding two critical outcomes: (1) the reaction of the Supreme Court; and (2) the long-range effect of the strike on national security and

4. The whole episode of the steel seizure raises doubts concerning the wisdom of earlier proposals for having the president "appeal to the nation" in the face of congressional recalcitrance; many such proposals were advanced against a backdrop of Roosevelt and the New Deal. See, e.g., Herring [1940b, p. 74].

on the national economy. In Realist terms, the decision was irresponsible, to the extent that it was based upon a less accurate forecasting of consequences than might have been possible. Such irresponsibility, however, is less attributable to the President's lack of personal judgment, than to the bad judgment of his subordinates, upon whose advice in regard to *technical* matters he necessarily relied. Truman was neither a lawyer, a professional soldier, nor an economist; and these were the three areas of expertise upon which accurate forecasting of consequences depended in the Steel Seizure case, or, at least, these were the areas in which forecasting went conspicuously awry.

The clear implication of the preceding discussion is that a realistic analysis of presidential decision-making must undertake to examine the institutional processes of decision-making at the level of the presidency, of which the man, the president, is an important part, but only a part. This is precisely the tack that characterizes the Realist approach to the presidency in the past few years. This approach is so new, indeed, that almost all of the literature that we shall examine has appeared since the time of the Steel Seizure decision; and one of the principal writers, Richard Neustadt, was a member of the "Murphy group" on Truman's staff at the time of the events discussed above.

Neustadt has written two major articles which describe and explain some of the adminstrative processes which are a part of the modern presidency. In the first article, Neustadt [1954] traces the development of the Budget Bureau's role as the co-ordinating agency for the president for clearing proposed Administration bills to be submitted to Congress and enrolled bills awaiting the president's approval. Particularly during the last decade, the Budget Bureau has come to have a predominant influence, as the broker between the White House and the agencies of the executive branch, in the co-ordination of presidential policy regarding legislation. A critical aspect of such a role is the extent to which all parties concerned—the president and his immediate staff, the agencies of the executive branch, and the Congress—are willing to indulge in the assumption that the Budget Bureau *really* speaks for the president, and "knows" the president's position on all the policy questions that arise.

One commentator, who writes from a Rationalist point of view, has been quite critical of the Budget Bureau's capability for telling the agencies whether or not their proposals are "in accord with the program of the President." This critic has argued that what the Bureau actually does is to function in perfect accord with the general principles of Realist theory, serving as a political mediator among departments with conflicting interests, inducing the agencies concerned to compromise their differences, and then reporting to the president that the interested agencies have agreed upon a policy position. Arthur Maass, the Rationalist critic, feels that in many instances, the Bureau does not know the president's position on such matters, because he has no previously formulated position; the Bureau is in the process of helping to define the presidential position when it engages in such mediation. Moreover, because the Bureau sublimates and compromises much conflict of interest among the agencies, the president is kept from knowing the extent to which apparent harmony masks underlying differences on questions of policy [Maass, 1954, pp. 77–93, esp. pp. 80–82]. Assuming that Maass is correct, a Realist would argue that it is *desirable* for the Budget Bureau to function in such a manner. And Neustadt does so argue:

> The President, as he may choose, gains ample opportunities to make known his desires. But Congress and the agencies are not compelled to notice. And he, meanwhile, retains the right to alter course, or change his mind. The voice that speaks is not the President's; it is the Budget Bureau's. And when need be, the Budget serves as whipping-boy. This is a neat arrangement; it helps preserve the enterprise. But it can do that only so long as the distinction remains more fiction than fact. Were there to be a demonstration, generally and over time, that Budget really spoke not for the President but for itself alone, then the whole game would lose its point and the participants soon cease to play. [1954, p. 671.]

In his second article, Neustadt [1955] discusses the development of administrative machinery for planning the president's annual program. He relates this to the requirement that the president present a number of messages to the Congress at the beginning of each session, which, for the past decade, have included the Economic Report and Budget Message in addition to the message on the State of the Union. Neustadt describes in considerable detail the institutionalization of presidential decision-making and the specification of which legislative proposals were to be advocated as "in the public interest" for the first year of the Eisenhower administration, in the fall of 1953. At least at this time, according to Neustadt, the President assumed a highly important role of personal leadership in the numerous and lengthy conferences in which major policy decisions were made. There were seven "full-scale" cabinet sessions in November and December, and "on each occasion Eisenhower was in the chair, not merely presiding, but actively participating; his questions, suggestions, and advice sparked most of the changes made" [p. 989].

The result of the elaborate integration of agency proposals into a program which the President was willing to sponsor was the very sort of accommodation of conflicting interests which is recommended by Realist theory:

> The presidential role anent Congress, cabinet, and party; the party's general posture anent oppositional gambits of other days, these things were by no means become matters of course or common understanding during 1953—not even, perhaps, in the White House at the time those staff reviews began. Yet the regime's first venture into legislative programming, while in no sense determinative on all scores, was bound to come to grips with such unknowns more directly and on a wider scale than any prior undertaking in the Eisenhower term. The form and content of the annual messages for 1954 thus became matters of considerable moment to Republican office-holders —and their clientele—of all shades of opinion at both ends of the Avenue. The very elaborateness of program processing devices suggests the amount of potential party cleavage they were relied on to contain. The very moderateness of the final product disguises a not inconsiderable amount of prior disputation among protagonists variously placed along the regime's right-left spectrum of opinion (a spectrum obviously centered to the right of that in Truman's time, or in F.D.R.'s, but distinctly observable nonetheless). [p. 995.]

The processes by which the President's legislative program became institutionalized was pragmatic, rather than planned, however:

> The custom of compiling formal agency programs as a preliminary stage in presidential program-making owes very little to procedural initiatives from the departments, deriving, rather, from White House requirements imposed upon them in the four years after World War

II. Those requirements, in turn, reflect a step-by-step accumulation of *ad hoc* responses on the part of Truman's aides to various felt needs arising in the course of readying his annual messages. . . . [p. 1001.]

Neustadt's articles demonstrate that, at least in regard to the major policy decisions which involve interaction with the Congress, there has been increasing reliance during the past decade upon procedures which tend to collectivize presidential judgment, and to make it more accurate to speak most of the time of the *presidency* rather than the president.

A recent article by Louis W. Koenig is, indeed, entitled "The Man and the Institution"; it is part of a symposium on "The Office of the American Presidency." "It is generally agreed," says Koenig, "that the President's staff has played a central part in the Truman and Eisenhower administrations. . . . never before [the Truman administration] had a President . . . relied so much upon collective advice in making his decisions" [1956, p. 14]. Koenig was speaking particularly of the White House staff, as distinguished from the heterogeneous collection of agencies that now comprise "The Executive Office of the President."

We certainly have come a long way from the half dozen administrative assistants with "a passion for anonymity"—one almost blushes at the use of the phrase today, in the light of the conspicuous publicity that has shone in recent years upon presidential military advisors and assistant presidents—proposed by the Brownlow Committee [the President's Committee on Administrative Management, 1937, p. 5]. As Brownlow himself has subsequently revealed [1949, pp. 105–6], the original recommendation of the President's Committee on Administrative Management, tendered in person to the President, was "to adjust the model of the British Cabinet secretariat to fit the Presidential rather than the parliamentary system and then to get one man to head it." In the words of Tom Jones, this would require "a man like [Sir Maurice] Hankey, a man of high competence, great physical vigor, and a passion for anonymity." But F.D.R. would have none of this, so the committee settled for "a corps of administrative assistants instead of an administrative secretariat under a single head."

The Committee's recommendation of not more than six additional administrative assistants—Roosevelt had three secretaries at the time—was in perfect correspondence with the requirements of Graicunas' Law (of the span of control), which was announced in a volume for which the co-editor was Gulick, one of the members of the Brownlow Committee, and which was published in the same year as the report of the Brownlow Committee [see Graicunas, 1937]. In view of the developments of the past two decades, however, it would appear that it is not Graicunas' Law, but Parkinson's Law [see Parkinson, 1957, p. 12], which governs the growth of the White House staff. According to Marian Irish "The [*United States Government Organization*] *Manual* for 1951–52 listed 18 positions for Truman's White House Staff" [1958, p. 267]. Grant McConnell indicates that there were actually 26 names on the routing slip in use for the White House staff in March, 1952, but that among these names "were those of the President's personal secretary, his appointment secretary, and several people with quite specialized duties. On the list also were the names of the military aides and of the Director of Mutual Security" [1960, p. 22]. But Irish notes that "the *Manual* for 1957–58 lists 47 positions in Eisenhower's White House Office [and subsequent additional appointments had] brought the total to 49 in the fall of 1957"; moreover,

The 1958 Budget called for some seventeen million dollars just for the Executive Office of the President. This covered salaries and expenses for more than a thousand full time employees and several more thousand part-time employees. The building which not so long ago housed the entire personnel of the State, War, and Navy Departments, is now considered inadequate for the office needs of the President's managerial staff. [1958, p. 267.]

The recommendations of the Brownlow Committee for the staffing of the presidency, made only a generation ago, have borne fruits that must exceed the wildest expectations of the members of the Committee. Such developments are anathema to the Rationalist and to the Idealist concepts of the presidency, because in the one case, institutionalizing the president's decisional processes comes between the president and the legitimate expositors of public will (party or constituency); and, in the other case, the staff inevitably comes to play much of the role that is supposed to be carried out, in Idealist theory, by the president's conscience. But to the Realists, the interposition of presidential staff provides increased opportunities for the access, accommodation, and satisfaction—of the multiple group interests—which constitute the presidential function.

Professor Irish is among those who feel that things have gone too far in the direction of substituting bureaucracy for what used to be a person, the president. She entitled her own presidential speech to the Southern Political Science Association "The Organization Man in the Presidency"; and she deplored the circumstance that "the President has been so featured as the symbol of national unity, so high above partisanship or even politics, that it is now out of character for him to participate personally in the major decisions of his own administration" [p. 260]. She uses the enforcement of integration in Little Rock as an example:

The decision to federalize the Arkansas National Guard and to send Federal troops to Little Rock was a White House decision. The President was on vacation in Newport, Rhode Island.

The "cease and desist" order to the mob in Little Rock was read by James Hagerty, the President's press Secretary, to the reporters in Newport on the evening of September 23rd. It is unlikely that the President had any part in the writing of the order which appeared above his initials. [p. 259.]

Of course, one could readily reply that it made no difference whether the president had helped to draft the order, so long as it *did* appear above his initials and he necessarily assumed the responsibility for its issuance. One of the public-administration case studies describes an instance in which Truman signed an executive order while still clad in his bathing trunks, down at the beach near the "Little White House" at Key West. According to the author of the case study [Andrews, 1954, p. 9], Truman had been thoroughly briefed on the issues involved, and comprehended fully the significance of the policy he was approving by signing the order.

Professor Irish would not indulge in such an assumption. She argues that the White House has been taken over by two kinds of experts—the public relations experts and the management experts—with the result that

The popular hero, created by public relations, may be a symbol of national unity, but he is no longer Chief Executive. Like the British Monarch, he is head of the state, not head of the government. Relying more and more upon the collective judgment of his staff, the President has virtually ceased to make decisions on his own . . . [but] in the American republic, the abdication of the President from the role of political leader, leaves us with no responsive or responsible head of government. [1958, pp. 275–76.]

As for the public relations experts:

Seated at the policy tables, they pressed for the right to participate in discussions—that they might indicate what policies were most feasible to "equate with the public interest." Admitted to policy participation, they were not only seated with top management—they had, in fact, become top management. From the public relations point of view, the basic problems of modern democracy are twofold: (1) ascertaining what policies are necessary or desirable in the public interest (this calls for opinion analysis, forecasting, planning, and "sociometrics"); (2) engineering the public consent for what the government has decided to do (this involves the methods of wholesale merchandising, the special skills of mass communications, and the newest techniques in hidden persuasion). [p. 265.]

And as for the management experts:

Truman, the first President to use the staff system in the White House, was his own Chief. He met with the staff daily, let each and all brief him, listened to their discussion, and then went back to his own office to digest their information, to assort their various opinions and to make his own decisions. Eisenhower, however, rarely meets his staff. Sherman Adams does it for him. The President insists that conflicts be resolved before they reach his desk; he wants only to hear the consensus, not the discussion, of the staff. . . . It's no secret . . . that Eisenhower calls Adams "the boss." [pp. 268–70.]

It seems most likely that Professor Irish has caricaturized, rather than characterized, the role of the president in contemporary presidential decision-making. But even if she is correct in her description and analysis, the situation should occasion no great disquietude for Presidential Realists. As long as the institution of the presidency accomplishes successfully its task of accommodation, it is accomplishing all that the Realists demand of it. The question remains whether the Realists demand enough of the presidency; and whether the American system could continue to function, without fundamental alterations, if we were actually to put the Organization Man in the presidency.

D. Administrators

PROBABLY THE BEST-KNOWN STUDY of the relationship between pressure groups and administrative decision-making is that of Pendleton Herring, whose book [1936] is based upon a series of case studies of so-called regulatory agencies. Writing at least a decade before the "rediscovery" of Bentley by the political science profession, Herring accepted the premises common to Realist thought, and postulated a role for administrators that thrust them into the vortex of the group struggle:

> Under democracy the public interest is based not upon the welfare of one class but upon a compounding of many group interests. We assume the possibility of achieving a balance of forces, social and economic. . . . [But there has been a] transfer from Congress of much of the direct superintendence of reconciling the conflicting groups within the state. The governmental result has been the creation of a great bureaucracy with wide powers to carry on these functions. . . . We conclude . . . that the purpose of the democratic state is the free reconciliation of group interests and that the attainment of this end necessitates the development of a great administrative machine. [pp. vii, 8, 9.]

Herring's work has the virtue, however, of evincing intellectual concern with the problem of the administrator confronted with the turmoil of group pressures and both a legal and ethical obligation to reconcile them in accord with the public interest. This contrasts fairly sharply with the bland optimism with which Bentley and Truman contemplate the impact of the group struggle upon public policy. Until his final chapter is reached, however, Herring reaches conclusions very similar to those of the Bentlians:

> This increase in administrative discretion, while making possible the more understanding application of rules to concrete situations, nevertheless places a heavy duty on the administrator. The words of the statute delimits his scope, but within the margin of his discretion he must write his interpretation of state purpose. . . . What criteria are to guide him? The *public interest* is the standard that

guides the administrator in executing the law. This is the verbal symbol designed to introduce unity, order, and objectivity into administration.

This concept is to the bureaucracy what the "due process" clause is to the judiciary. Its abstract meaning is vague but its application has far-reaching effects. The radio commissioners were to execute the law in the "public interest, convenience or necessity." The trade commissioners are to apply the law when they deem such action "to the interest of the public." Congress has frequently authorized boards and quasi-judicial commissions to determine the public interest.

Although it is clear that the official must balance the interests of the conflicting groups before him, by what standards is he to weigh their demands? To hold out the *public interest* as a criterion is to offer an imponderable. Its value is psychological and does not extend beyond the significance that each responsible civil servant must find in the phrase for himself. Acting in accordance with this subjective conception and bounded by his statutory competence, the bureaucrat selects from the special interests before him a combination to which he gives official sanction. Thus inescapably in practice the concept of public interest is given substance by its identification with the interests of certain groups. . . . the public interest can be realized only through promoting certain special interests. [pp. 8, 23–24, 259.]

In his concluding chapter, however, Herring seems to yield to the temptation, so seductive for political scientists, to rise above his data and end his book on a cheerful note:

The task of government in a democracy, we assume, is the adjustment of warring economic and social forces. The public interest is the standard that supposedly determines the degree to which the government lends its forces to one side or the other. *Without this standard for judgment between contenders,* the scales would simply be weighted in favor of victory for the strongest. [Emphasis added; p. 397.]

What "standard of judgment"? By his own repeated testimony, Herring has assumed the role of an oath-helper for Thrasymachus. Waldo is of the same view, noting that Herring's

. . . evidence strongly supports the "resultant-of-forces" hypothesis. In practice the "public interest" is given meaning only by the pulling and hauling of private interests—mitigated occasionally by the personal views of the Good Society held by some regulatory commissioners. Admirable as these analyses are, Herring advances us little in the search for a substantive content for the "public interest." [1948, p. 13; see also p. 93.]

A more authentic statement of the Bentlian position is found in David B. Truman's description of the administrator's mediatory role, which is in precise accord with Dean Leys's third category of "discretion as ambiguity":

The administrator's position in controlling the access of competing interest groups is made the more difficult if the terms of his mandate from the legislature are highly ambiguous. . . . Where compromise in the legislative stage is the alternative to temporary failure and where the imperative to compromise is accepted by some participants as a means of avoiding the open frustration of expectations widely held in the community, the terms of legislative settlement are almost bound to be ambiguous. Such compromises are in the nature of postponement. The administrator is called upon to resolve the difficulties that were too thorny for the legislature to solve, and he must do so in the face of the very forces that were acting in the legislature, though their relative strength may have changed. Note that it is not the ambiguities in the law that make difficult the question of what groups shall have privileged access to an administrator. Almost all legislative declarative declarations are ambiguous in part. It is rather the causes of the ambiguity that make the difference. If the administrator holds out for an interpretation of these controverted ambiguous provisions that is not in itself a compromise, he invites the affected groups either to denounce his "dictatorial" methods and his "unscrupulous assumption of powers not granted to him" or to expose his "sell-out" of the "public interest." [1951, p. 443.]

But Paul Appleby, in his second book, has suggested what—taken out of the context of his other writings—appears to be a more mechanistic definition of the public interest than that entertained by the Bentlians. The formula is: Special interests $^n =$ Public interest. In Appleby's own words, administration

. . . is the eighth political process. It is a popular process in which vast numbers of citizens participate, in which assemblages of citizens comprise power units contending with each other, in which various governmental organizations are themselves functional representatives of special interests of many citizens, and in which these organizations themselves contend mightily with each other in the course of working out a consensus that translates many special interests into some workable approximation of public interest. This process is an essential to the evolvement of governmental action as public debate, and closely akin to it. [1949, pp. 43–44.]

Among the problems left unresolved by the Bentlians, however, is that of precisely how and why the bureaucracy may be assumed to fulfill the representative function of articulating the inchoate, unexpressed, and unrealized wants and interests of the public-at-large. It is my opinion that this is one of the weakest points in the Bentlian theory, and that both the master and his followers rely upon "a vague but fervent transcendentalism"[5] in their attempts to infuse "unorganized groups" into the administrative decisional process. Here is an example of this "soul-stuff":

> The broad general interests, whether organized or not, must have a measure of access to the determinations of an administrative agency. The survival of an administrative activity is as certainly dependent upon the adjustment of these as of the more narrowly supported interests that confront an agency in organized form. It does not follow that an administrator in making a decision consciously thinks of himself as a guardian of the constitutional understandings of the American people. Depending upon the nature of his position, he may or may not do so. The influence of these largely unorganized interests is normally of a more unconscious character, however. As Paul Appleby has said in describing the preparation of the budget in the closed hearings at the Bureau of the Budget: "It is not made in a public arena, but the public is somehow well represented. This is one of the most mystifying of governmental phenomena." [Truman, 1951, p. 449.]

I submit that these references to "mysticism," "phenomena," and Dean Appleby are neither accidental nor an adequate substitute for a theory of interaction of "unorganized groups" stated in operational terms. The theory in its present form is susceptible of neither verification nor disproof, although it is entirely possible that other observers or participants might experience revelations similar to the budget hearing to which the Dean testified. This may be administrative realism, but it leaves the public interest in the form of a spirit, which students of administration may, of course, worship in spirit and in truth. It offers little to the scientists who are left to grub around down here on earth.

---

5. The phrase is borrowed from the late Mr. Justice Robert Jackson's dissenting opinion in *Douglas* v. *City of Jeannette,* 319 U.S. 157, 179 (1944).

The most concrete role that Truman postulated for "potential groups"—that they might fall into line behind a leader of the loyal opposition, or possibly even support a revolution—this generalized notion has been related more specifically to administrative decision-making by Harold Stein. His point is illustrated by many of the public-administration case studies published by the Committee for Public Administration Cases and by the Inter-University Case Program. In Stein's hands, this "survival theory" conceives of the public interest as a range of values within which administrative choice can roam; the extent to which the administrator exceeds these limits is an index of the probability that (in an unspecified but potentially menacing way) other forces and factors in the environment will liquidate him. This is something akin to taboo-breaking and the automatic punishment that Nature visits upon those who break her laws. Democracy moves in mysterious ways, its wonders to perform:

> The other aspect of survival [i.e., other than tactics]—values— is also basic to the whole concept. For politics involves ethics and benefits and power; it is the resolution of the contending forces in society. In this light we see the administrator as an agent of society making choices that affect the well-being of society. With the increasing scope of government activity, the range of administrative discretion is enormously broadened. Pre-determined answers become increasingly less appropriate, and self-explanatory and self-executing standards more and more elusive. The administrator must rely on his own system of values—his feeling for what is right—his judgment of what to emphasize, or what to play down—his sense of justice and fair play. The fundamental safeguard against an administrator's arbitrary and unethical conduct is the fact that public administration, especially in a democracy, circumscribes the range of values which the administrator can observe. For the making of value judgments by the administrator is part and parcel of the whole system; every act of political response that can be weighed in terms of its significance for survival has value connotations as well. In our society and particularly in our national government, it is doubtful that any administrator can long survive, no matter how adroit a manipulator, if his decisions reflect values that are sharply at variance with the general standards of society or the goals which society seeks. [Stein, 1952, pp. xvi–xvii.]

Stein may well be correct, but survival theory as he has stated it is of doubtful utility to either practitioners or researchers.

His statement is a form of Social Darwinism; it leaves the individual administrator to hope that he is right in his guesses about the permissible range of society's toleration. Those who guess wrongly obviously are not fit administrators, but one discovers his errors only after the fact of his repudiation and dismissal. Such elimination of the culls may tend to give administrators ulcers, but it is not clear how it will tend to make them more responsible, or to insure that each *individual* decision will be in the public interest.

While group theorists focus upon the dynamic environment confronting the administrator, Psychological Realism focuses upon the administrator himself, as a discrete human being rather than as an arithmetic mean. This suggests, as an initial insight, that "legitimacy," from the point of view of the individual, is a subjective rather than an objective phenomenon:

> To the extent that democracy means to an administrator the formal processes of courts, legislatures, and hierarchy, his democratic beliefs make him responsive to these processes *even beyond* their power to hold him formally accountable. To the extent that the administrator has some conception of a popular will, a general interest, or natural rights that goes beyond the formal political processes, his democratic beliefs may actually make him less responsive and more resistive to judicial, legislative, and hierarchical accountability. Each policy that is imposed on the administrator will be interpreted and executed by him in terms of *his* conceptions of legitimacy. [Emphasis added; Simon *et al.*, 1950, pp. 551–52.]

We have noted John Dewey's emphasis upon the desirability for official awareness of the *consequences* implicit in the alternatives of choice, as perhaps the most important ingredient in responsible decision-making. After citing Dewey, Arthur Macmahon appears to apply it specifically to the administrative quest for the public interest, suggesting that the administrator

> . . . must constantly impose the test of impartiality upon any proposed action by asking himself whether it could be applied to everyone else in similar situation. . . . the essence of public interest is awareness of that web and the constant impulse to trace things as far as possible before acting and as a guide to action where choices otherwise unguided must be made. . . . the deep-lying protection needed for the two-way safeguarding of the role of demo-

cratic administration in a democracy is the ultimate self-identification of administrators with the public interest. . . . [1956, pp. 48, 49, 53.]

Similarly, Dean Harlan Cleveland has written that:

[The political executive] must be imbued with the public interest. . . . Whenever a political executive says, does, or decides anything, he also needs to ask himself a question: Where does the public interest lie? The public interest cannot of course be defined in general. But in our society we have a pretty fair index ready to hand, if we approach each action or decision with the following query in mind: Would this decision—*and the procedures by which it was made*—stand the test of detailed public scrutiny? [Emphasis added; 1956, p. 45.]

Let us assume that our administrator is honest, intelligent, and courageous. Does he face the same basic problem, irrespective of whether he conceives his role as being that of Simon's rational flunkey, Fainsod's creative manipulator, or Herring's bureaucratic centerboard?

. . . in a country where democratic values prevail, most persons who are placed in public administrative positions will feel that in their decisions they *ought* to be responsive to democratic values. They may actively seek out such values as bases for their decisions, quite apart from the power of the legislature, the courts, or their hierarchical superiors to enforce particular values upon them. The difficulty is that even if an administrator most sincerely wishes to obey "the people's will," he will have a most troublesome time discovering just what that will is; and where he will find it will depend on his own particular notions of democracy—i.e., his own particular values. . . .

Of course, when one looks in a mirror, one sees one's own image. Responsiveness to public interest, so defined, is responsiveness to one's own values and attitudes toward social problems. Nevertheless, this responsiveness provides a major channel through which values that are commonly or broadly held through our society (or those parts of society from which particular groups of administrators are drawn) enter into administrative decisions. [Simon *et al.* 1950, pp. 548–49, 551.][6]

6. The same view is expressed by Pfiffner and Presthus, who say that "his feeling for the public interest is an emotive force, bound up with the administrator's personal code of values, which will often, in turn, reflect the dominant egalitarian values of our society. The public interest, in this sense, is a democratic ideal which exerts a varying degree of influence on official behavior" [1953, p. 530].

Here, it seems to me, is the first idea that we have examined that points to a means of bridging the gap between the inchoate interest of unorganized people and its administrative articulation. There are three steps to the theory: (1) each individual administrator will define the public interest in his decisions in terms of his own value system; (2) the public interest as so defined will include, in each instance and in variable degrees, "positive" policy norms, other environmental pressures, and "internal" pressures, which are projections of the administrator's beliefs and attitudes; and (3) to the extent that the bureaucracy is itself a cross-section of society, it necessarily will reflect, in the aggregate, values that are deeply felt and widely shared within a given culture. It has been argued by some, in fact, that the federal civil service—even under present personnel–administration policies—when coupled to the political sensitivity of the presidency, constitutes a "representative bureaucracy" that much more adequately and accurately reflects the interests and values of American culture than Congress can or does.[7] It was probably inevitable, however, that even those who would be prepared to accept the notion that the bureaucracy, as a kind of random sample of society, would have to be representative of it, would not be content to rest with this passive state of affairs. Why not try to structure the situation?[8] Wouldn't a "scientific" sample be better than a random one? (The representative character of the federal bureaucracy taken as a whole, for instance, might not be valid for any single agency, or smaller

7. Long has said, "important and vital interests in the United States are unrepresented, underrepresented, or malrepresented in Congress. These interests receive more effective and more responsible representation through administrative channels than through the legislature" [1952, p. 811; cf. pp. 809, 813, 814, 817]. Wiltse has argued, somewhat to the contrary, that "the unorganized 'public' has no special interest, no lobby, and for all practical purposes, no representation" [1941, p. 515; cf. Dahl and Lindblom, 1953, p. 350].

8. Arthur Macmahon has discounted "any notion about administration as all of one piece, geared to the undifferentiated interest of an amorphous general public. Indeed we may say of legislation generally that the pressures in a pragmatic democracy, sanctioned by majorities and guided by an instinct for equilibrium, are constantly writing a kind of balancing bias into one law or another. . . . Some of the chief problems of public interest inhere in this kind of statutory specialization" [1955, p. 47].

administrative unit.) Furthermore, if personal values are so important, why not try to condition them?

It has been to these problems that those whom I shall call "Due Process" theorists have turned their attention. Apart from the activities of a few professional guilds, of which the International City Managers' Association is perhaps the best-known example, the most serious and thoughtful attempt to promote codes of ethics as a generally usable and potentially significant administrative technique has come from Phillip Monypenny [but see also Morstein Marx, 1949, pp. 1121–26]. Monypenny has emphasized [1953b, p. 429] his view that a code of ethics cannot be relied upon as a device for ensuring the preference of one alternative over another in situations where choice must roam among competing criteria: "its value," he says, "is in assuring the faithful execution of settled policy."[9] Nevertheless, an examination of his draft code, in particular that section entitled "The Public Interest," makes it clear that Monypenny's proposals go considerably beyond the induction of rational choice in the Simon sense. On this point, Monypenny [1953b, p. 441] is, in effect, defining the minimum of procedural due process which is postulated as the right of all who have a stake in the administrator's decision:

[A Projected Statement of Administrative Ethics]
D
The Public Interest

1. It would be presumptuous of a public servant to follow his own conception of the public interest in opposition to or in deviance from the policy of the agency and of the administration in which he serves. But lacking any other guide in law, regulation, order, or instruction, and required to act, he should follow the public interest as he understands it rather than his personal convenience or any private aim or goal.

Admittedly, there is nothing novel in this exhortation. This is essentially what Cardozo [1921, pp. 66–67, 174–75] advises judges to do.

---

9. He has also said that a code would be "useful in reducing to systematic statement the highest standards of perception and devotion which are active within an agency and securing their general adoption" [1953a, p. 187].

2. The primary determination of the public interest for public servants is by the action of his political and hierarchic superiors, acting through the conventional channels, by legislation, and court decisions where applicable. However there will be areas of discretion still, and in the use of these the public servant will be exposed to a relatively small group of persons immediately affected by a proposed action. The public servant must accept their right to speak and even to be consulted, must consider the consequences which they present. But he must remember that there are others unorganized and not directly represented, and as far as he can perceive the consequences to them, he must be their representative also in considering this discretionary action. This will not result in uniformity of action since the frame of reference of the actor will determine his view of the consequences, but it may correct a little the selective effect of direct representation before the agency.

Again, on the face of the statement, we might dismiss this as moralism, were it not for the fact that Monypenny has taken pains to point out that "conformance to an ethical code is a matter of social relationships rather than of individual morality. It is not a matter of personal conversion" [1953b, p. 435]. He expects that the code will be enforced directly by group sanctions, such as being cut out of the office grapevine, and indirectly by official sanctions, such as being denied preference for a merit increase in salary. The effect of this would be to enforce conformity with the (characteristically) many group norms of the public interest, within the area of the group's expertise, even though these attitudes were never put into written form, to say nothing of being issued as official regulations. This would happen to some extent anyhow, but a code would help to clarify the fact situations to which the group sanctions should be applied.

3. No problem is ever entrusted completely to a single administrative organ. In acting on any problem the public servant must consider what effect his action will have on the responsibilities of others and if possible consult with them prior to action. His own action must in the end be consonant with his agency's policy, even though it be adverse to policies of other agencies where it is impossible to harmonize them.

4. A public servant should be always open to representations from those interested in a situation which is before him if discussion will not prejudice the position of other parties to the proceeding. As far as possible those affected should be informed of pending

transactions and time set aside to meet with them so that the public servant is not exposed only to the most aggressive members of his clientele to the exclusion of others. Such meetings between a public servant and those interested in the action should as far as possible take place during ordinary working hours, in the ordinary working quarters which are appropriate, and with ordinary publicity and office records of the event.

These final two paragraphs seem to take us much closer to the concept of "administrative due process," which Norton Long has advocated. The difference would seem to be that Monypenny's concern is with the relationship between the individual and the primary group of which he is a part while Norton Long's published remarks on this point are in much more generalized form, and seem to relate to the rational structuring of expertise, power bases and transmission belts, ambassadors of special interests, etc., into a kind of giant administrative brain which, once properly wired up and plugged in, will grind out responsible decisions on questions of public policy which are fed into the machine. Long has written that:

The will of the people is always expressed by some of the people. It is process rather than substance. . . . The structuring of organization must be concerned with the reflection of values and their implementation. . . . Adequate organization would require that every major question have an institutional protagonist, the securing of every important piece of factual information be an assigned responsibility, and every important point of view have a spokesman built into the proposal-formulating process.

The nature of the policy to be formulated implies the theoretical, factual, and value premises necessary for its rational and responsible development. The institutional structure can then be considered in terms of personnel possessed of values, drives, and skills so structured as organizationally to simulate a reasoned inquiry. . . . [The] organization must be structured for a variety of points of view so that significant values in the community are necessarily considered in the formulation of policy proposals. . . . It requires the building into the organization of a system of values and procedures that will enforce the presentation at the highest level of all the relevant facts— and their most significant possible interpretations.

. . . An organization in its routines and its personnel—their training and values, professional and political—can be so structured as to maximize the likelihood that decisions will be made as a result of full consideration of the relevant facts, hypotheses, and values involved. One might well strive for the acceptance of a "minimum administrative due process." [1954, pp. 25, 24, 30, 29, 26.]

Attempts to build in particular points of view to date do not appear to have met with unmitigated success. On the one hand, experiments with devices for articulating the voice of the partially organized or unorganized, such as the office of "consumers' counsel" or "public counsel," demonstrate the dilemma of the administrator who is forced to lead from weakness [see, e.g., Arnow, 1950, pp. 99, 101; and Dahl and Lindblom, 1953, p. 501]. Norton Long himself [1949] has pointed forcefully to the necessity for effective administration to be supported by adequate sources of real power. On the other hand, building in some organized interests tends to give those included a preferential advantage over those organized interests not given organizational representation; rarely is it possible to include all groups with a legitimate interest. This is not to say that it is futile even to attempt to rationalize the administrative decision-making process, in particular instances and specific agencies, toward the goal of greater "administrative due process." But it is necessary to realize that the model administrative machine that Long has suggested is an "ideal," as Long himself has recognized.

Although several of the pressure-group theorists whom we have considered have spoken of "balance" and "equilibrium," the first to attempt a concise statement of an equilibrium theory was Avery Leiserson. Implicit in Leiserson's theory is an operational definition of the public interest: an administrator best serves the public interest when his action creates or restores an equilibrium among all of the affected group interests, or, if this is not possible, when the disequilibrium resulting from his act is minimized.[10]

---

10. The postulated condition of equilibrium is an attribute of Leiserson's theory, a hypothetical limit rather than a description of what we should expect to find in the empirical world. As Easton has insisted: "instead of viewing the state of equilibrium as a theoretical model, helpful in simplifying reality for purposes of analysis, rather than as an exact picture of reality, [political scientists] have committed the natural mistake of considering the equilibrium a possible condition of the empirical system. . . . To employ a model of a political equilibrium for the purposes of helping us to understand the complicated political system, it would be necessary to reduce the important political elements or variables to measurable terms.

Quite to the contrary of the "countervailing-force" role, postulated for bureaucracy by the advocates of administrative engineering, equilibrium theory posits an essentially negative, conservative task:

> Is there any objective test of such a capacity [the facility for judgment in which the administrative expert's policies and decisions are guided by the test of optimum satisfaction on the part of the groups affected by his administrative acts]? Hypothetically, we shall formulate this test as the acceptance of administrative decisions and policies by the group interests affected or concerned by them. . . . In other words, the political formula or agreement, expressed in legislative enactment, is a suspension of overt political conflict between group interests—a period in which administrators are given the opportunity to devise policies, under and within the law, which influential parties to the political conflict for the most part accept as a working *modus operandi*. These policies are exposed to public (multi-group) scrutiny and may be said to have become accepted if the affected groups no longer agitate before the legislature to obtain amendments or repeal of the law.[11] [Leiserson, 1942, p. 14.]

This need for quantifiable magnitudes is a substantial barrier in the way of equilibrium analysis of the political system. It is conceivable that in some distant future quantification may be much more successfully applied to political data than at the present and in that case, the utility of equilibrium analysis will immediately change. For the present and foreseeable future, however, wanting readily measurable data, we must recognize its limits" [1953, p. 279, 284]. Easton's argument is that Leiserson's equilibrium theory of the public interest, as we have restated it in the text, is *not* operational, because the theory cannot be tested by relating it to *quantifiable* empirical data. See also Easton [1956, pp. 397–405].

11. Reprinted from Avery Leiserson, *Administrative Regulation*, by permission of the University of Chicago Press. Copyright, 1942, by the University of Chicago. Cf. Truman: "it is not altogether out of place to think of a legislature like the Congress as a court from which petitioners seek indulgences and redress of grievances. As a seat of power it is one of many points to which appeals can lie from disturbances in the society at large or from acts of judicial courts and administrative agencies. Especially in a loosely integrated system like that in the United States, the legislative process offers an interest group alternative means of effectively asserting its claims. . . . In recent years it has been somewhat restricted through the growth of administrative discretion in the wake of the increased complexity and technicality of group relationships and adjustments. Any administrator knows, however, that the legislature still is an alternative line of approach to a policy decision, *one of many means of appeal from his own determinations for groups with effective access* to the law-making body" [emphasis added; 1951, p. 394].

It should be added that the test of acceptance extends, in addition to appeals to the legislature, to any kind of agitation intended to bring about a change in the administrative decision at issue.

Dean Leys seems to express the same idea when he says that "the problem is to relate an immediate and pressing interest to a mass of other interests in such a way that the immediate interest somehow 'fits into the picture'" [1952, p. 68]. For the administrator who functions as a charismatic leader of the unorganized public, group-equilibrium theory would substitute the democratic administrative politician. The latter image seems to be in closer accord with common experience.

Like other Realists, the Administrative Realists define the public interest not as essence but as the resultant of the interaction of complex forces. The Due-Process theorists differ significantly from the Bentlians and the Psychological Realists, however. For the Bentlians, the critical struggle is taking place among forces outside the agency, and the administrator is the pawn for whom the gods, i.e., groups, contend. For the Psychological Realists, the forces are found in the constellation of values of the administrator, and the critical struggle takes place within his own mind. For the Due-Process Realists, the agency itself is the battleground, the administrator is a soldier of fortune, and the war games should be so planned that all contenders have a fair, but not necessarily equal, chance to enter the lists.

E. The Judiciary

LIKE OTHER FORMS of positivism, legal realism assumes:

> The *temporary* divorce of Is and Ought for purposes of study . . . value judgments must always be appealed to in order to set objectives for inquiry, yet during the inquiry itself into what Is, the observation, the description, and the establishment of relations between the things to be described are to remain *as largely as possible* uncontaminated by the desires of the observer or by what he wishes might be or thinks ought (ethically) to be. More particularly, this involves during the study of what courts are doing the effort to disregard the question what they ought to do. [Llewellyn, 1931, p. 1236; and cf. Friedmann, 1953, p. 201.]

The philosophical premises of such an approach have been articulated by William James, in his well-known definition of the pragmatist as one who

. . . turns towards concreteness and adequacy, towards facts, towards action and towards power. That means the empiricist temper regnant and the rationalist temper sincerely given up. . . . At the same time it does not stand for any special results. It is a method only. [1948 ed., pp. 144–45.]

On the other hand, "a pragmatist turns away from abstraction and insufficiency, from verbal solutions, from bad *a priori* reasons, from fixed principles, closed systems and pretended absolutes and origins" [James, 1948 ed., p. 144]. As applied to the analysis of the law, this means that

How the rules of law work, not what they are on paper, is the core of the pragmatic approach to legal problems. This, of course, is very general. To concretise what they had in mind, realists turned to those sciences which had begun to explore human behavior in society. In particular they turned to economics, criminology, general sociology and, last but not least, to psychology, and sought to utilise them for the science of law. . . . For the realist movement is not a philosophy of law, it is a modern method of approach which wants to find out what the law is, not what it ought to be. In exploring the law it is positivist, and puts its faith in science. In both these respects it agrees with the adherents of analytical jurisprudence. But instead of the single avenue of logic, realists seek to utilise multiple avenues, which modern science has opened or is opening up, for a more exact and detailed knowledge of the many factors that compose modern life.
The law is both a result of social forces and an instrument of social control.[12] [Friedmann, 1953, pp. 199–200.]

Pragmatism was a new version of positivism—"a new name for some old ways of thinking," as William James put it—and it provided the philosophical basis for the new American legal realism, just as, at a somewhat later time, it was to perform the same function for the Administrative Realists. The other American philosopher whose name should be mentioned in this regard

---

12. For a recent example of the advocacy of the borrowing of the methods of the natural sciences in order to create a "science of jurisprudence," see Beutel [1957, *passim*].

was John Dewey.[13] Dewey, who had been Bentley's teacher and who maintained a close association with Bentley for over half a century [Ratner, 1957, pp. 31, 35, 41, 45–47], provided also the personal link between Administrative Realism and Judicial Realism. In Dewey's view,

The public interest is manifested in formalities which are necessary to make a union legal and for its legal termination. Consequences, in a word, affect large numbers beyond those immediately concerned in the transaction. . . . when consequences concern a large number, a number so mediately involved that a person cannot readily prefigure how they are to be affected, that number is constituted a public which intervenes. . . . the public itself, being unable to forecast and estimate all consequences, establishes certain dikes and channels so that actions are confined within prescribed limits, and insofar have moderately predictable consequences. The regulations and laws of the state are therefore misconceived when they are viewed as commands. [1927, pp. 51–52, 53.]

One of the first, certainly the best known, and probably the greatest among American legal realists was Oliver Wendell Holmes, Jr. As Cahill has pointed out: "Holmes was a striking example of the 'rationalist temper sincerely given up' " [1952, p. 33]. "The prophecies of what the courts will do in fact and nothing more pretentious," said Holmes [1897, p. 461], "are what I mean by law." As for the *making* of public policy, how could a candid judge deny that this was part of his job?

The very considerations which the courts most rarely mention, and always with an apology, are the secret root from which the law draws all the juices of life. We mean, of course, considerations of what is expedient for the community concerned. Every important principle which is developed by litigation is in fact and at bottom the result of more or less definitely understood views of public policy; most generally, to be sure, under our practice and traditions, the unconscious result of instinctive preferences and inarticulate convictions, but none the less traceable to public policy in the last analysis. [Holmes, 1879, pp. 630–31; also in Shriver, 1936, p. 10.]

----

13. See particularly his article [1924] on "Logical Method and Law." There are three footnotes in this eleven-page article; all of them cite quotations from the writings of Mr. Justice Holmes; and the first of these quotations is Holmes' statement that "the whole outline of the law is the *resultant* of a *conflict* at every point between logic and good sense" (emphasis added).

Holmes also had a theory as to why judges were not candid:

> Perhaps one of the reasons why judges do not like to discuss questions of policy, or to put a decision in terms upon their views as lawmakers, is that the moment you leave the path of merely logical deduction you lose the illusion of certainty which makes legal reasoning seem like mathematics. But the certainty is only an illusion, nevertheless. Views of public policy are taught by experience of the interests of life. Those interests are fields of battle. Whatever decisions are made must be against the wishes and opinions of one party, and the distinctions on which they go will be distinctions of degree.[14] [1894, p. 7.]

This would seem to put Holmes pretty close to the general position of Bentley, who did not shrink from consistently applying his theory to the judicial process:

> The courts make this theorizing a dignified portion of their work. But they do not decide cases purely in the highly rarified atmosphere of such theorizing. They decide them by letting the clash of the underlying interests work itself out, and then making the theorizing follow suit (not crudely, remember, but as a representative process). Within fairly broad limits theories will be found available for either apparent alternative of activity. [1949 ed., pp. 294–95.]

Bentley did not elucidate what he had in mind by "a representative process." The known facts of life would hardly support a theory of "representative judiciary," as an analogue to the con-

---

14. Also in Holmes [1920, p. 126]; and quoted in Haines [1922, p. 103]. Cf. Holmes [1920, p. 181]; and Learned Hand: "in one way or another, we set up officials who innovate, and when they do, we call it our common will at work. This we have made the cornerstone of our structure. Our common law is the stock instance of a combination of custom and its successive adaptations. The judges receive it and profess to treat it as authoritative, while they gently mould it the better to fit changed ideas. Indeed, the whole of it has been fabricated this way like a coral reef, of the symmetry of whose eventual structure the artificers have no intimation as they labor. Sometimes for this reason we speak of the judges as representing a common-will, and this was more nearly true before the advent of democracy, since they were of the class which alone had political power. It is a fiction to say so now. . . . The truth appears to be that what we mean by a common-will is no more than that there shall be an available peaceful means by which law may be changed when it becomes irksome to enough powerful people who can make their will effective. We may say if we like that meanwhile everybody has consented to what exists, but this is a fiction. They have not; they are merely too inert or too weak to do anything about it" [1929, pp. 49–50].

cept of a "representative bureaucracy" suggested by some of the
Administrative Realists [e.g., Long, 1952]. It may well be true,
as James Willard Hurst has suggested, that "the ideas and feelings
prevailing in any given generation in those levels of the community from which judges came offered far more convincing
explanations of judicial policy [than did particular methods of
judicial selection]" [quoted by Truman, 1951, p. 490]. There
remains substantial doubt whether "those levels of the community" from which judges come afford a good cross-section of the
community. It is for this reason that, in my opinion, David Truman's discussion of the function of judges, as representatives of
unorganized groups, is even more spectral than his treatment of
this point in regard to administrative bureaucracy:

> *To a greater degree* than legislators or executives they [*judges*]
> *are*, in a sense, *leaders of widely shared but unorganized interests*, i.e.,
> potential groups, which must be effectively represented in court de-
> cisions. One function of the respect for precedents and of the
> juristic talk of certainty, stability, and predictability in the law
> is to help maintain the routine in the relationships of which the
> courts have custody. Both the administrator and the judge, therefore,
> tend to identify themselves with the patterns of adjustment that are
> committed to them. In both cases the relative access of interest
> groups is fixed or controlled by such identification. The adjustment
> becomes an object in itself, reinforced by expectations concerning
> the official role, especially that of the judge. The dynamics are of
> the same kind in both cases; the differences are of degree. [1951, pp.
> 486–87.]

The concept of the judge as one whose job is to adjust conflicting interests that compete for preference, however, is at the
core of the Supreme Court's own official theory of the judicial
process, as this relates to many areas of constitutional adjudication.
This is the same, it seems to me, as the equilibrium theory of
Administrative Realism. In the words of the late Chief Justice
Harlan Stone:

> We are coming to realize more completely that law is not an end,
> but a means to an end—the adequate control and protection of those
> interests, social and economic, which are the special concern of gov-
> ernment and hence of law; that that end is to be attained through the
> reasonable accommodation of law to changing economic and social
> needs, weighing them against the need of continuity of our legal

system and the earlier experience out of which its precedents have grown; that within the limits lying between the command of statutes on the one hand and the restraints of precedents and doctrines, by common consent regarded as binding, on the other, the judge has liberty of choice of the rule which he applies, and that his choice will rightly depend upon the relative weights of the social and economic advantages which will finally turn the scales of judgment in favor of one rule rather than another. Within this area he performs essentially the function of the legislator, and in a real sense makes law. [1937, pp. 140–41.]

An example of the theory in action is provided by the formula still followed by the Court in considering the extent to which the commerce clause should be construed to limit state legislation. Stone spoke for the Court, when, referring to the scope of the commerce clause, he said that: "the reconciliation of the power thus granted [to the national government] with that reserved to the state is to be attained by the accommodation of the competing demands of the state and national interests involved."[15]

As Bertram Gross has noted [1950, p. 743], Bentley was "rediscovered" by Karl Llewellyn [1934], a leading spokesman for the academic realists. This occurred shortly after the internecine warfare between the realists and certain proponents of sociological jurisprudence, in particular, Dean Pound, was raging at its height [see Llewellyn, 1930, Pound, 1931, and Llewellyn, 1931]. For present purposes, Jerome Frank's division of the legal realists into "rule skeptics," whom he accuses of "rule fetishism," and "fact skeptics," for whom he speaks, will do. Although Karl Llewellyn is the best known of the "rule skeptics," I have found in David Truman a clearer statement of this position than in Llewellyn's own writing:

Many of the so-called rules of the law and particularly many of the more sweeping provisions of the Constitution have no very precise meaning. Even more than statutory provisions, they permit an

---

15. *Parker* v. *Brown*, 317 U.S. 341, 362 (1943). The same concept has been applied by the Court in its arbitration of civil liberties problems, as in a recent decision relating to the rights of witnesses before congressional committees, in which the majority announced: "we conclude that the balance between the individual and the governmental interests here at stake must be struck in favor of the latter, and that therefore the provisions of the First Amendment have not been offended."

interpreter to exercise discretion. For judges as for other individuals, the frames of reference within which these provisions are understood and in which the facts of a case are "found," are a function of interest affiliations. The myth of depersonalized and machinelike adjudication upon which rests in part the continued popular acceptance of the judicial function assumes that all such attachments are left behind when a man ascends the bench. . . . Judges do not cease to be human when they don their robes. They do not derive all their premises from the court room. [1951, p. 490; cf. Weldon, 1953, pp. 61–69.]

The "rule skeptics" focused upon the behavior of appellate courts, while the "fact skeptics" turned their attention to trial courts. The leading "fact skeptic" was the late Judge Jerome Frank, [Paul, 1957, p. 143; and 1958, p. 753]. A characteristic example of his Psychological Realism is found in the following statement:

Now the trial judge is a man, with a susceptibility to such unconscious prejudiced "identifications" originating in his infant experiences. Sitting at a trial, long before he has come to the point where he must decide what is right or wrong, he has been engaged in making numerous judgments or inferences, as the testimony dribbles in. His impressions, colored by his unconscious biases with respect to the witnesses, as to what they said, and with what truthfulness and accuracy they said it, will determine what he believes to be the "facts of the case." His innumerable hidden traits and predispositions often get in their work in shaping his decision in the very process by which he becomes convinced what those facts are. The judge's belief about the facts results from the impact of numerous stimuli—including the words, gestures, postures and grimaces of the witnesses—on his distinctive "personality"; that personality, in turn, is a product of numerous factors, including his parents, his schooling, his teachers and companions, the persons he has met, the woman he married (or did not marry), his children, the books and articles he has read. [Frank, 1949, p. 152.]

The relationship between Frank's approach, with its borrowed psychoanalytic theories [see particularly, Frank, 1930], and that of the Psychological Realists among the administrative theorists, is apparent. Furthermore, he comes to a similar conception of the public interest: if I may borrow my own description of an earlier occasion, Frank places "reliance upon the super-ego as a curb on the judge who wittingly wields his quantum of political power in handing down each decision" [Schubert, 1952, p. 1181].

Frank's ideal is Oliver Wendell Holmes, whom he describes as "the completely adult jurist" [1930, p. 253]. Professor Friedmann has come up with iconoclastic musings on this point, suggesting that the extremity of Frank's realism may have pushed him unwittingly into surrealism, and hence, into the camp of the enemy:

> Analytical jurisprudence seeks to achieve certainty by relying on an allegedly complete logical system. Realism uses psychology to demolish this myth of certainty, and the psychologists among the realists, like Jerome Frank, have, at times, appeared to build up this lack of certainty into a philosophy very similar to the *Freirechtslehre*. For what else is the "completely adult lawyer" but the wise and creative judge who, unfettered by paragraphs and precedents, finds justice through a clear and cool perception and valuation of the social issues at stake. The philosopher-king of Plato's Republic appears in the cloak of the modern lawyer. [1953, p. 209.]

The moderates among the legal realists, however, seem to have much in common with the Due-Process theorists of Administrative Realism. Julius Stone, for instance, concludes his work on legal theory with the statement that

> . . . the irreducible minimum requirement of legal justice is in a broad sense procedural. It is that society shall be so organized that men's felt wants can be freely expressed; and that the law shall protect that expression, and provide it with the channels through which it can compete effectively for (though not necessarily attain) the support of politically organized society.[16] [1950, p. 785.]

The emphasis upon process has significance in a double sense: the judicial decision is viewed as an event in an institutional pattern, whose significance cannot be understood out of context; and what the judge will decide, including his constructions of the public interest, will depend upon the factors he recognizes and the forces that impinge upon the decisional process. Felix S.

---

16. After quoting the same statement from Stone, Straussian Idealist Walter Berns comments that "this appears nothing but a legalistic restatement of the William James ethical argument. . . , an argument compounded of enthusiasm and a lack of diffidence out of proportion to its value" [1957, p. 146].

Cohen [1935, p. 843] has criticized[17] the crudity of the "belly-ache theory" of jurisprudence:

The "hunch" theory of law, by magnifying the personal accidental factors in judicial behavior, implicitly denies the relevance of significant, predictable, social determinants that govern the course of judicial decision. Those who have advanced this viewpoint have performed a real service in indicating the large realm of uncertainty in the actual law. But actual experience does reveal a significant body of predictable uniformity in the behavior of courts. Law is not a mass of unrelated decisions nor a product of judicial bellyaches. Judges are human, but they are a peculiar breed of humans selected to a type and held to service under a potent system of governmental controls. Their acts are "judicial" only within a system which provides for appeals, re-hearings, impeachments, and legislation. The decision that is "peculiar" suffers erosion—unless it represents the first salient manifestation of a new social force, in which case it soon ceases to be peculiar. It is more useful to analyze a judicial "hunch" in terms of the continued impact of a judge's study of precedents, his conversations with associates, his reading of newspapers, and his recollections of college courses, than in strictly physiological terms.

Judicial decisions, argues Cohen, are better understood when conceived as points in a sequence of complex social behaviors:

A truly realistic theory of judicial decisions must conceive every decision as something more than an expression of individual personality, as concomitantly and even more importantly a function of social forces, that is to say, as a product of social determinants and an index of social consequences. A judicial decision is a social event. Like the enactment of a Federal statute, or the equipping of police cars with radios, a judicial decision is an intersection of social forces: Behind the decision are social forces that play upon it to give it a resultant momentum and direction; beyond the decision are human activities affected by it. The decision is without significant social dimensions when it is viewed simply at the moment in which it is rendered. Only by probing behind the decision to the forces which it reflects, or projecting beyond the decision the lines of its force upon the future, do we come to an understanding of the meaning of the decision itself.

Implicit in this view is the insight that the identifications of the public interest that are made in particular decisions may be re-

---

17. Cohen was speaking with particular reference to the views expressed in Hutcheson [1929].

shaped or recast precisely to the extent that the environment of decision-making is itself subject to control.

The Judicial Realists scoff at the temples of the Rationalists and the clouds of the Idealists. As in the case of the Administrative Realists, there is a mechanist faction, which assumes the statistical irrelevance of the judge's personality, and a psychological wing, which assumes the irrelevancy of almost everything except the judicial psyche. Since the Bentlians propose that judicial decision-making be investigated in a manner similar to that employed in studying other aspects of the political process, one might assume that here is an area in which political scientists might have an important and peculiar contribution to make, if the time ever comes when the compulsion to imitate lawyers, historians, and philosophers wears thin—and this irrespective of the nuances of Bentlian dogma. It is further conceivable that empirical investigations can be made of the effect of personality upon judicial decisions. But the theory of the Judicial Realists tells us very little about how to proceed with such investigations. It is probably the dearth of research in these areas that explains why the public-interest theory of Administrative Realism is more sophisticated and more sharply formulated than that of Judicial Realism.

In particular, Administrative Realism encompasses a theory of "administrative due process" that finds no explicit counterpart in the literature of legal realism. This is passing strange, since, at least on a verbal level, the concept of administrative due process borrows from a judicial model! The administrative theorists suggest that the decisional processes of an administrative agency might be so structured that all relevant sources of data, points of view, and affected interests are consulted. The theory suggests that the public interest is, in effect, a probability statement: decisions made via decisional processes so structured are more likely to achieve maximal accommodation of the affected individual and group interests with a minimum of stress than will be decisions made in some other fashion. It is, of course, assumed that administrative agencies have an obligation to foster the realization of public-policy goals.

But even though courts and administrative agencies share many functions, working at disparate stages of a common regulatory or service process, it is generally assumed that courts are different in kind from administrative agencies. The historic role of the courts has been to protect private interests. As recently as two decades ago, private parties could bring collusive suits for adjudicating constitutional issues to the Supreme Court, without any provision for the Attorney General's appearance to argue "the public interest" in the question. In 1949, the Supreme Court amended its rules to restrict the filing of *amicus curiae* briefs, thus limiting its exposure to the viewpoints of groups who think they have sufficient interest in a case to undertake the time and expense involved in preparing and filing such briefs. The "law of evidence" and other rules of court procedure may have been designed to assure fairness to the adversary parties, but they have the effect of excluding much, if not most, of the relevant data from the scope of legitimate judicial consideration. The practice, if not the theory, of the adversary process casts opposing attorneys in the role of competing gamesmen, not that of social scientists. In fact, the court trial seems to represent the very antithesis of the concept of "administrative due process," however ironic this may be.

The problems arising out of urbanization, industrialization, and scientific advancement, however, have begun to leave their mark upon the administration of justice. Courts rely less and less upon the participation of grand and petit juries, those non-expert expositors of what is presumed to be the expression of local public interests; the gap thus created has been more than filled by many kinds of experts. Administrative experts have supplanted the courts in many functional areas. In others, expert judges sit on "legislative courts" which exercise jurisdiction to the exclusion of the "regular" courts; expert witnesses speak authoritatively on subjects too specialized for judges or juries to comprehend; the judges themselves become specialists in presiding over a relatively narrow class of cases, as in many functionally organized metropolitan courts; administrative assistants are assigned to help shoulder the labor of federal judges and justices of state supreme courts. Sociologists and psychologists have increasingly taken over the responsibility and authority to make decisions that used to be made by judges in such fields as juvenile delinquency and probation [Beutel, 1957, pp. 132–33]. The scientific-management movement came to the federal courts, at least as a beginning, as one of the fruits of the "Court-packing" fight of 1937—appropriately enough, one might add, since the President chose to argue his case on the grounds of the Supreme Court's failures in administrative efficiency. The "laboratories for social and economic experimentation" began to shuffle slowly and hesitantly in line behind the federal government—as so frequently appears to be their custom—about a decade later. The upshot has been that the courts, like Congress, are becoming bureaucratized.[18]

Administrative Realism postulates an open administrative society, as distinguished from the relatively closed society of the courts. The theory of the public interest advocated by proponents of "administrative due process" presumes a complex and flexible model of organization. The adaptability of such a model to judicial decision-making processes is limited, of course, by the seeming strength of constitutional mores which posit for judges a broad scope of personal discretion, subject to the restraints and distraints of guild ideals. But to the extent that the judicial process becomes increasingly bureaucratized, further limited but potentially significant experiments of a parallel nature might be ventured [Beutel, 1957, p. 378]. From this perspective, the key to more responsible decision-making lies not in the judicialization of the administrative process, but rather in the bureaucratization of the judicial process.

18. It is certainly true that administrative agencies, generally speaking, have much larger staffs than courts, and the effect of hierarchical organization is to disperse and sublimate most agency decision-making among subordinate working groups. But it is also a fact that the federal-court structure as an entirety can be viewed as a single agency with problems of organization and methods, headquarters-field relationships, and highly organized clientele groups, and similar questions of administrative management that have become familiar grist for the mills of students of public administration. Consider, in this regard, the creation of the Administrative Office of United States Courts and the court administrators at the state level during the past two decades, and the substantial movement within the legal profession for the reform of judicial organization and management.

is there a public interest?

You may call spirits from the vasty deep,
Aye, you may—but will they come
When you call them?
You may sell an idea to the people
And sit back satisfied you have them your way
But will they stay sold on the idea?

Sandburg, *The People, Yes.*

Our analysis of the theory of the public interest has revealed a contraiety of assumptions, conclusions, and concepts, all of which are current in contemporary American political thought. We have, however, discovered certain continuities that can be traced through all five factors in our decision-making schema when this is related to each of the three types of official discretion that we have postulated. There remain two tasks: to state the major patterns characterizing Rationalist, Idealist, and Realist concepts of the public interest, and to consider the parallel findings of other contemporary critics of public-interest theory.

A Summary of Public-Interest Theories

THE RATIONALISTS ARE PROPUBLIC, proparty, and anti-interest group. They postulate a common good, which reflects the presumed existence of various common—frequently majoritarian—interests. The common good (or commonweal, to use the older term) finds expression in a popular will (public will; will of the people); the common obligation of all public officials is faithfully to execute the popular will. To this extent, there is consensus among Rationalists. Differences of opinion are many, however, as to the appropriate channels for authentic interpretation of the public will. Basically, there are two factions: Party Rationalists and Popular Rationalists. Party Rationalists defend a stronger two-party system as the chosen instrument for expressing the public will; Popular Rationalists would do away with political brokers and consult public opinion directly in order to discover the will of the people. Party Rationalists tend to be Anglophiles with regard to the political-party system, the relationship between legislators and political parties, and the relationship between the executive and the legislative departments. (As we pointed out in Chapter 2, the model of British political processes envisaged by the Anglophiles bears no necessarily close correspondence to contemporary reality.) The Party Rationalists urge, therefore, that congressmen ought to be the disciplined members of a majority or a minority party, with the two parties dividing over issues of public policy. Popular Rationalists think that congressmen ought to carry out the wishes of their constituents.

The Anglophiles believe that the presidency should be weakened and subjected to the control and policy direction of Congress, which they have already defined as the legitimate expositor of the public will. Other Party Rationalists, however, would link presidential leadership to a stronger two-party system, thus strengthening the presidency. Popular Rationalists would accomplish the same result by casting the president in the role of instrumental leader of direct popular majorities. At this point, the distinction between Party and Popular Rationalists disappears, because all Rationalists agree that the proper function of the bureaucracy is to carry out the policy norms supplied by hierarchical superiors

(Congress and the president). Administrative Rationalists would use scientific management to rationalize the behavior of administrators; Legal Rationalists would accomplish the same result among judges according to the prescriptions of Analytical Jurisprudence. In both instances, administrators and judges are supposed to exercise technical discretion to carry out norms which *they* do not make, but which are supplied to them in the form of constitutional provisions, statutes, and executive orders—made, of course, by the representatives of the people, who implement the public will. There is a schism among Rationalists regarding how best to rationalize the independent regulatory commissions: Administrative Rationalists want to place the commissions within the ambit of presidential control, and Legal Rationalists want the commissions to be subject to the administrative direction of the judiciary. Either way, it is variously argued, the commissions would become subservient to the will of the people, and the common good would be assured.

The Idealists are propublic, antiparty, and anti-interest group. By "propublic," I mean, of course, that Idealists support the *true* interests of the public, which do not necessarily coincide with the interests of the public as perceived by the public itself. Idealists believe that the public interest reposes not in the positive law made by men, but in the higher law, in natural law. They describe the public interest as a thing of substance, independent of the decisional process and absolute in its terms. They advise the public official to excogitate the true essence of the public interest by means of a mental act of extrasensory perception. This does not necessarily imply communion with the public will, because no will may yet have been formulated regarding the relevant issues; in any event, there is no assurance that the public will will be right. The public interest becomes whatever the still, small voice of conscience reveals to each official.

Such an approach renders superfluous, if not downright dangerous, such orthodox appurtenances of democratic politics as political parties and interest groups. These latter are perceived as disturbing interferences with official excogitation of Truth, Virtue, and Justice. According to Idealist thought, congressmen are responsible neither to political parties nor to their constituencies;

they have a higher obligation, to God and to their own consciences. Those who advocate converting the presidency into a plebiscitary dictatorship emphasize the evils of party influence; proponents of the Stewardship Theory of the presidency wish to surmount the pernicious demands of selfish special interest groups. In either case, the president is urged to rise above the mundane level of democratic political processes and to become the Father of his Country, the patron of all of the people, a leader of crusades both at home and abroad who should receive love and adulation—not criticism—from his subjects.

The same images recur in Idealist discussion of administrative decision-making. Administrative Engineers advise administrators to be creative manipulators and to resist the seductions of interest groups. Guild Idealists warn—almost in the words of Madison —of the dangers of party politics, and demand that administrators be given elbowroom for the exercise of craft and conscience. Substituting judges for administrators, equivalent prescriptions are offered by the spokesmen for Sociological Jurisprudence and Scientific Idealism, respectively. Thus, the themes which permeate Idealist public-interest theory are the invocation of natural-law ideals; hostility to the instrumentalities of democratic politics, i.e., political parties and interest groups; elitist notions of superior intelligence and wisdom; and the abetment of public officials, from the president on down, to become aggressive evangelists who will strive mightily—and ruthlessly, if necessary—in behalf of the public interest. The public interest, of course, is what the elite thinks is good for the masses. Idealist dogma, as dogma, is basically antithetical to democratic theories of governance.

The Realists are pro-interest group. It is not accurate to say that they are antiparty or antipublic. However, they define "party" and "public" in such a way that these terms lose the identity that we have ascribed to them in discussing Rationalist and Idealist thought, to say nothing of their usual, everyday meaning in American speech. Political parties become merely a special kind of interest group, and "public" becomes segmented as "publics," in which form it, too, merges in the concept of "interest group." The Realists, in other words, do not *oppose* the public and political parties; they devour them.

There are three major strands of Realist theory, and each of these recurs through all five factors of our decision-making schema. As befits a pattern of thought so colored with pluralism, the three major strands are each primarily oriented to one or more of the other social sciences. Bentlian Realism draws predominantly upon the outmoded sociology of the turn of the century; the source of inspiration for Psychological Realism is self-evident; and law and economics are the wellsprings for Due-Process–Equilibrium Realism.

The Bentlians direct attention to the competition among multifarious interest groups and assert that this is the reality of political behavior at all levels of governmental (as well as nongovernmental) decision-making. The official responds to these pressures; his decisions register the thrust of the balance of power for the time being. It makes no difference whether the decision-maker is a congressman, the president, an administrator, or a judge; his role is essentially the same, although the patterns of access and the particular constellations of groups that enter the lists will vary according to the institutional context in which the official decision-maker functions. To the Bentlians, the public interest has significance only as the slogan which symbolizes the compromise resulting from a particular accommodation or adjustment of group interaction.

Psychological Realists go beyond the essentially mechanical formulations of the Bentlians, and focus attention upon the conflict of interests within the mind of the decision-maker.[1] The rather fuzzy Bentlian notion of unorganized groups is redefined by the Psychological Realists in terms of Dewey's concept of a self-conscious search for the consequences of choice. This point has been well put by Sorauf, in his statement that:

> . . . the public interest, myth or not, serves a "hair shirt" function. It has offered many a public servant and citizen an uncomfortable and persistent reminder of the unorganized and unrepresented

---

1. Cf., in this regard, Leo Strauss's description [1953, p. 124] of the Socratic dialectic as a *process* which leads to the ultimate discovery of the truth; this shaking-down of competing and contradictory half-truths and untruths suggests a technique for accommodating and adjusting ideas that resembles, at least vaguely, the resolution of mental conflict described by the Psychological Realists.

(or underrepresented) interests in politics. It directs our attention beyond the more immediate and toward the often-ignored interests. Especially for the courts and administrative agencies, the public interest may represent the interests of freedom, equality, and opportunity—the widely-held and unorganized interests. The public interest becomes then a symbol for the attempt to recognize and consult interests that might be forgotten or overlooked in the pressure of political combat. [1957, p. 639.]

The role of official mediation described by the Psychological Realists adds a significant factor to the formulations of the Bentlians: the personal value system of the decision-maker. He is limited, of course, to the values that he understands and recognizes, but he is not necessarily limited to the values with which he personally agrees. His acceptance of such broad components of the democratic ethic as the concepts of "freedom, equality, and opportunity" may lead him to take into consideration interests other than those actively pressing in behalf of specific alternatives of choice in a particular decision.

At this point, the line between Psychological Realism and Social Engineering may seem to be pretty shadowy, but the distinction is nonetheless viable. The Social Engineers write on a blank slate: creative manipulation leads to the fabrication of any interest-group pattern needed to support the predetermined goals established by the decision-maker. Official mediation looks to the interstices of a framework provided by the interaction of activated groups and asks what the effect would be, upon this pattern, if certain other interests were weighed in the final decision. In this sense, the official mediator functions as a catalyst; but since the critical conflict is internal to the decision-maker rather than in the external environment, Psychological Realism's search for consequences is a more operational concept than Bentley's mystical notion of the leadership of unorganized groups. Nevertheless, both are different ways of thinking about the same processes.

As we have seen, Psychological Realists apply the concept of official mediation to congressmen, the president, administrators, and judges alike. There is a close functional relationship, however, among politicization, constituency size, and the limits of official horizon. In Harlan Cleveland's image, the president stands a little higher on the mountain than anyone else, and consequently can see further; district court justices and subordinate administrators, presumably, have much more limited horizons. But what of the Supreme Court? Are the justices on a separate alp? I do not think a meaningful answer to this question is possible at the present stage of underdevelopment in the measurement of power by the political science profession;[2] the question raises doubts, in any event, about the application of Cleveland's hierarchical image, rather than about Psychological Realism's concept of official mediation.

The next logical step beyond Psychological Realism is to pre-structure the environment of decision-making and to condition the mental processes of the decision-maker. It is to these matters that the Due-Process Realists call attention. Although all Realists premise their theories of the public interest upon a philosophy of ethical relativism, rather than the absolutism characteristic of Rationalists and Idealists, the Due-Process–Equilibrium Realists lean most heavily upon what is, at least crudely, mathematical-probability theory. According to the theory, people accept democratic decision-making processes because these provide the maximum opportunity for diverse interests to seek to influence governmental decisions at all levels. A plurality of decision-making points afford access to a plurality of interests, which can seek to change or to provoke particular decisions. The job of official decision-makers—irrespective of whether we speak of congressmen, the president, administrators, or judges—is to maximize continuity and stability in public policy; or, in other words, to minimize disruption in existing patterns of accommodation among affected interests. The extent to which agitation continues, before the same or other decision-makers, provides a rough measure of the extent to which adjustment has, in terms of the equilibrium standard, been successful or "satisfactory."

Now this kind of thinking, as I have remarked earlier, is quite conservative in its general overtones. It underscores the adjectives in advocating *gradual, peaceful, evolutionary, orderly* change. It

---

2. But see Shapley and Shubik [1954] and Dahl [1957].

does not tilt, it slants the scales of judgment in favor of the status quo. The votaries of liberalism preach a brand of ethics in which most Americans feel they ought to believe; but it is not a way of life, nor is it the basis for our system of government. It is the Constitution, not the Declaration of Independence, that provides the model for the American political system. The general model leaves largely unspecified, however, the structure and functioning of decision-making processes in Congress, the presidency, administrative agencies, and the courts. It is particularly upon administrative decision-making processes that the Due-Process–Equilibrium Realists have focused their attention.

Instead of leaving the "representativeness" of the administrator's personal value system, or the particular configuration of interests in a specific type of decision, up to chance, Due-Process theory would so structure both of these factors in the decision-making process as to maximize the probability that the resulting decision has been made, in fact, after consideration of all relevant interests and perspectives. Due-Process theorists do not claim that any particular substantive result will automatically be the "right" decision; they do not guarantee that every decision arrived at after such full consideration will be "in the public interest." This is the point that seems so difficult for absolutists, who live in a world of dichotomies, to comprehend. What the Due-Process theorists do claim is that decisions reached as the result of such full consideration are *more likely* to meet the test of equilibrium theory, i.e., "satisfaction," acceptance, etc., and to do so *most of the time*, than are decisions arrived at as the necessary consequence, at least in a statistical sense, of processes that assure less than full consideration. *Decisions that are the product of a process of full consideration are most likely to be decisions in the public interest.*

There has been some, but very limited, application of the concept of "administrative due process" to congressional, presidential, and judicial decision-making. Although some critics have decried placing "the organization man in the presidency," the fact remains that the applicability of the model of "administrative due process" to these other decision-makers is a function of bureaucratization of congressional, presidential, and judicial decision-making processes. Certainly, there is considerable evidence to support the proposition that the *trend* in each of these areas is towards greater bureaucratization. To this extent, the potential extension of the public-interest theory of the Due-Process–Equilibrium Realists is correspondingly enhanced.

The Critics of Public-Interest Theory

TWO DECADES ELAPSED after Beard's historical studies [1934a] of the national interest as a concept, before any systematic analyses of the public-interest concept appeared in the literature of political science. Beginning in 1955, however, several political scientists and philosophers have ventured independent (from each other, and from my own work) exploratory critical essays on the subject of public-interest theory. It seems appropriate, before stating my own conclusions, to undertake a brief examination of the findings and conclusions of these other critics.

a. Banfield.—The first of these was a political scientist, Edward Banfield, who appended a "Note on Conceptual Scheme" to the case study of public-housing policy-making in Chicago which he wrote with Meyerson [Meyerson and Banfield, 1955].[3] In the "Note" [p. 303], he explained that the public interest was one of three central concepts (the other two being "politics" and "planning") "in the light of which the case-material was largely selected, organized, and interpreted." "We are trying," he said, "to establish analytically significant formulations of these ideas." The footnote references to the seven-page section of the "Note" which discusses "The Public Interest" are all citations to the theoretical statements of other writers, however, supporting the inference that Banfield's schema is deduced from his sampling of the literature rather than based upon the observations of behavior analyzed in the case study.

Banfield's basic proposition is that:

---

3. A footnote on p. 303 states that "this supplement is the work of Banfield."

A decision is said to serve special interests if it furthers the ends of some part of the public at the expense of the ends of the larger public. It is said to be in the *public interest* if it serves the ends of the whole public rather than those of some sector of the public. [p. 322.]

He then distinguishes two major categories: Unitary and Individualistic. Unitary, in turn, is divisible into "Organismic" and "Communalist" subcategories; and Individualistic, into "Utilitarian," "Quasi-Utilitarian," and "Qualified Individualistic" subcategories.[4] All of these subcategories are defined, more or less, in teleological terms. But more interesting than Banfield's categories are his remarks about the *uses* of varying concepts of the public interest:

It will be seen that since either the same or different decision-makers may employ opposed conceptions of the public interest, the question of which conception is to be regarded as *the* public interest, either in a specific situation or in general, may itself become a matter of controversy. Moreover, given agreement on any one conception of the formal nature of the public interest, there may be controversy as to its concrete content. Indeed, the agreed upon conception may imply equally any one of a wide range of outcomes. [pp. 326–27.]

Banfield suggests, however, that different kinds of decision-making *processes* are appropriate to differing concepts of the public interest:

A somewhat different decision-making mechanism is implied by each of these conceptions of the public interest. A unitary conception implies a cooperative choice process, i.e., one in which the outcome or settlement is derived from a single set of ends [Idealist or Rationalist, in our terms]. Any individualistic conception, on the other hand, implies a mechanism through which competing ends are compromised [Realist].

Thus, a unitary conception implies central decision-makers who are specially well qualified to know the ends of the body politic or the common ends, who can perform the largely technical function of adapting means most efficiently for the attainment of these ends, and who have power to assert the unitary interest of the "whole" over any competing lesser interests [Rationalist]. The decision-maker whose task it is to spell out the implications for action of the body politic or of the *ethos* ought, of course, to be free to take account

---

4. For a critique of what the authors refer to as Banfield's "sophisticated" Utilitarianism, see Leys and Perry [1959, pp. 17–18].

of the "real" rather than the "apparent" interest of the members of the society and to ignore their preferences in the immediate situation if these are inconsistent with the most general and fundamental ends of the society [Idealist]. [p. 327.]

The ensuing discussion, largely in terms of market and non-market—i.e., political and administrative—choice mechanisms, seems to suggest that for each concept (subcategory) there is *a* choice mechanism which is, more or less uniquely, suitable. This turns out to be the case, since Banfield's conclusion is that:

> An institution may function as a mechanism which asserts at the same time different, and perhaps logically opposed, conceptions of the structure of the public interest. . . . the outcome of a process in which various conceptions of the public interest are asserted is likely to be an analgam [*sic*]. Since the nature of the choice mechanism employed determines in part the content of the public interest, the question of which conception of the structure of public interest is appropriate, in particular circumstances or in general, is suitably discussed in terms of which *mechanism* of choice is preferable. [p. 329.]

Banfield's concluding observation—that an expression of preference among concepts of the public interest should be related to, and based upon, a choice among decision-making processes—implies one possible adaptation of the typology of official discretion that I have employed in this book as the basis for defining the central concepts of public-interest theory. Indeed, Leys and Perry have suggested that my "explication would seem to rest upon an identification of the role of the official who is thinking about the public interest, and the role repends [*sic;* depends] upon the political situation. . . . Depending on one's role . . . one is justified in employing one or another of the three conceptions of 'public interest' " [1959, pp. 35–36].

In other words, if there are three types of discretion that *any* official might be called upon to exercise in certain circumstances—assuming that concepts of the public interest can appropriately be defined in terms of the kind of discretion that any given decision-maker is required or expected to exercise—then:[5]

---

5. In Banfield's terminology, we could change this statement to read: "if there are alternative mechanisms of choice available for preference, then. . . ."

1) No particular theory of the public interest (e.g., Unitary or Individualistic, in Banfield's terms; or Rationalist, Idealist, or Realist, in mine) can be "best" or "correct," because no single class of discretion (technical; vague norms; ambiguous norms) is generally dominant in the empirical world.

2) The selection of a theory of the public interest appropriate to guide any decision in particular ought to depend upon the prior determination of the kind of discretion (or "choice mechanism") required by the decision-making situation.

If this argument is valid, then it necessarily follows that anyone who affirms *any* theory of the public interest, without first having defined the decision-making situation, is putting the cart before the horse. Moreover, any claim that a particular concept of public interest—e.g., "Communalist" in Banfield's terminology, or, perhaps, "Due Process–Equilibrium Realism" in mine—is a panacea, would have to be rejected. The responsible decision-maker first must identify the kind of decision-making process he is expected to employ; the concept of public interest appropriate to guide his decision could then, it would seem to follow, readily be determined.

Pursuing this line of argument one step further, it should of course be recognized that the kind of discretion predominantly associated with some offices differs from that of others. The decisions required of budget examiners are different from those required of clerk-typists. We should expect to find more technical discretion in the decisions of federal district courts, and more vague discretion required in the decisions of the Supreme Court. We should expect to find a great deal of ambiguous discretion in decisions of Congress, but not to the exclusion of technical and vague discretion for certain kinds of congressional decision-making. Even this is a vast oversimplification of empirical reality.

The nub of the issue is that frequently all three types of discretion will be involved in the making of a single decision by a single official. What then? Is it possible for the decision-maker to analyze the component factors in the decision-making situation and to identify particular aspects appropriately calling for particular kinds of discretion? If so, then to the extent that norms are in part supplied by "higher authority," he should follow Rationalist theory. To the extent that the norms are specific but ambiguous, he should follow Realist theory. To the extent that, in part, there remain indeterminate elements of policy which he must make, he would have to follow Idealist theory, and—it could be argued—he might as well do so self-consciously.

The "if" that leads to such conclusions is so big that it really begs the question. Leys and Perry have commented that:

> Doubtless, role theory helps the administrator to make sense of contrasting conceptions of public interest. But it does not remove all difficulties:
>
> (i) *How does one know his proper role?* Instructions do not come from the legislature and the community neatly labelled Type 1, Type 2 and Type 3. What is to keep an administrator from rationalizing his own timidity by seeing a political, mediating situation wherever he encounters a little resistance?
>
> (ii) *Role-theory, furthermore, seems to presuppose some more general theory of the public interest.* [Emphasis added; 1959, p. 36.]

The second point is not really as profound as it may seem to be at first glance; what Leys and Perry apparently have in mind [pp. 36–37] are such notions as "a public interest in the sense of a stake in the whole political system." Of course, role theory— if such it be—assumes that the political actors, and the constituencies they represent, generally accept the functional prerequisites of the relevant political system. And the analysis that we have undertaken in this book has been exclusively concerned with evolutionary, not revolutionary, decision-making processes.[6] The Austinian lawyers with their cult of the literal Word of the Constitution; Kelsen and his basic norm; Dickinson and his "common pact, voluntarily recognized and observed, to abide by the conditions essential to the existence of political order"; all affirm this

---

6. I have, for instance, emphasized the extent to which Due Process– Equilibrium Realism has conservative implications and subserves best the interests of those persons who have the largest stake in the status quo.

kind of a "stake" in the existing political system.[7] Such non-revolutionary assumptions are not, therefore, the basis for "some more general theory of the public interest." To the contrary, they are the essential precondition to sensible discussion of public-interest theory, including role theory.

But how, indeed, does one know his proper role? If each official must decide this question for himself, according to his own best lights, then the only key that has been provided by the public-interest concept (thus defined and employed) has been to Pandora's Box. And if the official is not to decide for himself, who will do it for him? Agency lawyers? Personnel-classification experts? Surely, no more examples are necessary to illuminate further our leap from the frying pan into the fire; one can almost hear the shade of Patrick Henry, shouting again and across the "vasty deep" of two centuries: "Forbid it, Almighty God!"

b. Sorauf.—The second contemporary critic of the public-interest concept is Frank Sorauf, also a political scientist, who identifies and discusses [1957] five categories of public-interest theory. These include the public interest as "Commonly-Held Value," as "the Wise or Superior Interest," as "Moral Imperative," as "a Balance of Interests," and the public interest "undefined." Some of these categories appear to correspond closely to the types that I have identified in this study, and others do not so relate. The apparent similarity between Sorauf's "public interest as a balance of interests" and my own Realist type, for instance, turns out to be spurious—at least in his view—for reasons that we shall examine presently. There is no reason why we should expect very close correspondence between the two sets of categories, since Sorauf bases his, presumably, upon the empirical groupings of the public-interest statements that he examined, instead of dividing doctrines on the basis of an explicit and *a priori* principle of classification such as I have tried to use. The important question is: what kind of findings and conclusions does

7. Only some strands of Idealist public-interest theory, which emphasizes a higher law and a commonweal that may surpass ordinary human understanding, appear to lend themselves to the kind of official behavior that might be considered responsible—at least by the plotters—when revolution is afoot.

Sorauf come to, on the basis of his examination of part of the same literature that I have discussed in the preceding chapters?

Sorauf quickly dismisses his fifth category ("the public-interest undefined") as embracing no theory whatsoever; he then proceeds to reject, seriatim, his other four categories, concluding that "one cannot justify the public interest as either commonly-held value, moral imperative, superior wisdom, or compromise and yet maintain its status as a genuine 'interest,' as a political goal of the great 'public' attached to it in the struggle to influence policy" [1957, p. 638]. Following John Dickinson, the Walter Lippmann of an earlier day, and John Dewey, Sorauf concludes that the only defensible and legitimate concept of the public interest is the ace that he left up his sleeve during the first seventeen pages of his article: an additional category which he calls "compromise-as-method":

> Americans . . . are agreed upon a governmental process that reconciles divergent interests according to established rules and processes. . . . We expect only that this political organization will settle in an orderly, equitable way the differences that divide us. . . . We are bound together, therefore, in accepting the process of democracy and the method of compromise, regardless of the policies it may produce. To this extent we may claim a "public interest"—our interest in the democratic method and in its settlement of conflict by orderly rules and procedures. [p. 633.]

This "modest conception of the public interest," to borrow Sorauf's own characterization, is only dubiously a public-interest concept, however. It seems to hang somewhere between (1) the notion of "a public interest in the sense of a stake in the whole political system," which, as I have just argued, is a precondition to, rather than a kind of, public-interest theory; and (2) a somewhat vague and half-hearted statement of Due-Process Realism. The reason for Sorauf's watering-down of Due-Process Realism, to such an extent that it seems almost eligible for admission to his own fifth category of "the public interest undefined," appears to lie in his distinction between "compromise-as-result," which is bad, and "compromise-as-method," which is good.

He argues that compromise-as-result results in a public interest that is neither "public" nor "interest"; and that:

It ceases, furthermore, even to be a prior standard by which we might evaluate the claims of competing interests. The public interest as compromise is no longer an interest that men strive for, no longer a guide to policy-making, but a *post hoc* label for the product of their strivings. Since it does not exist until after the group struggle is lost and won, it can provide no benchmark for policy formation. . . . The result is a surprising, and unbecoming, political Darwinism that naively presumes that the public interest will automatically be served if all men pursue their own interests. . . . At best the public interest as compromise legitimatizes the political solutions of the moment; its purpose is no longer to guide policy-making, but to gain acceptance and approval for current political compromise. [p. 630.]

Compromise-as-method, in Sorauf's view, is quite different:

Instead of being associated with substantive goals or policies, the public interest better survives identification with the process of group accommodation. The public interest rests not in some policy emerging from the settlement of conflict, but with the method of that settlement itself, with compromising in a peaceful, orderly, predictable way the demands put upon policy. [p. 638.]

In other words, it is more important that issues get finally settled, than that they be settled in any particular way. This seems to be quite as conservative a doctrine as that of Due Process–Equilibrium Realism and much more amoral, since Due Process–Equilibrium Realism argues that it is moral as well as wise for decisions to be based upon a full and fair hearing of all affected interests.

In setting up his distinction, Sorauf states that

Some confusion exists . . . as to whether these men [i.e., Key, Herring, Holcombe, and—by implication[8]—Bentley] associate the process of compromise or the final policy expression of compromise with the public interest. . . . Generally one would be safe in saying that in most cases their conception of the public interest refers to the actual result of the compromise process; the authors referred to in the preceding paragraphs are typical in this respect. [p. 623.]

We have already examined in considerably greater detail than does Sorauf in his article the public-interest theories of the above mentioned writers. So far as the point under consideration is concerned, confusion exists only to the extent that these Realists fail

---

8. The reference is to Fainsod, who was speaking (in the quotation used by Sorauf, p. 630, ftn.) of Bentley.

to draw the distinction between process and substance—the method and its results—which Sorauf recommends.[9] The question of where confusion lies depends upon whether Sorauf has created a straw man.

Is there really a difference, other than semantic, between a belief in compromise-as-method and a belief in compromise-as-result? How can one exist without the other? If one believes that policy formation is the product of interest conflict, and that the best way to resolve such conflict is to provide political machinery for accommodating and adjusting the demands of competing groups, acceptance of the method of compromise *necessarily implies* acceptance of the results produced by the method—at least temporarily and subject to attempts to change particular results by further recourse to the same or equivalent methods of decision-making.

c. Cassinelli.—C. W. Cassinelli, a political scientist who has commented upon Sorauf's article and who is himself obviously a defender of the Idealist faith, finds it easy to agree with Sorauf in rejecting the pretensions of the Rationalists: "the criticism of the 'public interest as commonly-held value,' " he says, "I consider excellent" [1958, p. 553]. Naturally. However, the only commonly held value between Sorauf and Cassinelli is their mutual antagonism to the concept of the public interest as commonly held value. Cassinelli attacks Sorauf's criticism of the "moral imperative" strand of Idealist thought, on the grounds that Sorauf's critique rests upon value judgments of his own. "In short," says Cassinelli, "the public interest is an ethical concept"; and "the problems involved in making value-judgments are perplexing in theory and disturbing in practice, but they cannot be avoided by accepting *the opinions of the public, even though these opinions be unanimously held*" [emphasis added; p. 555].

Cassinelli also considers Sorauf's method/results dichotomy to be spurious:

---

9. I have argued, in Chapter 1, that the public interest cannot be meaningfully *defined* in terms of substance; but that is a quite different matter than the present issue, which revolves around Sorauf's assertion that one can accept the process of interest accommodation while simultaneously repudiating the compromises which are the inevitable result of the process.

In adopting his own definition of the concept of the public interest (p. 638), Professor Sorauf has implicitly accepted the idea that the public interest is a commonly held value, at least with respect to the American public. Saying that the public is agreed upon a method, even though it may share no common policy-goals, is subject to all the objections that Professor Sorauf himself raised regarding the public interest as commonly held value. Moreover, as he points out later (pp. 635–6), interests in the sense of possessions are of the same basic nature, whether they are "selfish" or "altruistic"; the same remark applies to any distinction drawn between "substantive" interests and "procedural" interests. [p. 554.]

Of course, Cassinelli, like Sorauf, is in favor of democracy—but it seems to be the democracy of *The Republic* rather than that of the demes:

I consider it difficult to deny that the "process of group-accommodation" is an integral part of the political ethics we usually call "democracy." It is, however, only a *method,* and methods have value only insofar as their results are satisfactory. Moreover, group-accommodation is only part of the democratic method. . . .[10] The method can hardly be good in itself; it is desirable because it is a necessary condition for something else. Professor Sorauf, despite his earlier cogent criticism of the position, strongly suggests that he values the method of compromise and compromise alone. . . . But, as Professor John H. Hallowell has said, "compromise as a *self-sufficient* principle divorced from considerations of truth and justice is simply, in the last analysis, the ancient Thrasymachian doctrine that might makes right," and Professor Sorauf himself has previously labelled the idea an "unbecoming political Darwinism."

Sorauf had quoted with approval Lippmann's statement that the public interest "is in the workable rule which will define and predict the behavior of men so that they can make their adjustments" [1930, p. 105]. It is "to this search for the *modus vivendi,*" says Sorauf, that "American democracy is dedicated. This alone is its goal or purpose" [p. 638]. But for Cassinelli, "the democratic method is desirable because it among all methods goes

---

10. Only part, because Cassinelli [p. 556] does not think that the process of group accommodation applies to foreign affairs: "the process by which many of the most important policy-decisions are made has little if anything to do with accommodating groups; foreign policy is a relevant category and the Marshall Plan a good example." Cassinelli appears to believe that the Marshall Plan was hatched by a presidential stork; cf. the previously cited works by Dahl, Grassmuck, etc.

the farthest toward promoting liberty, equality, and fraternity among all the people." Cassinelli, therefore, accepts the "democratic method" *because of* the results that it produces; Sorauf espouses the method *irrespective of* the results it achieves in practice. Neither Cassinelli nor Sorauf, it seems to me, argues a consistent position. A thorough-going Idealist ought to reject the democratic method—at least, when this is defined in Bentlian terms as the struggle among interest groups—for precisely the reason suggested by Hallowell: there is no assurance that Virtue will triumph. The theorists of the group struggle—as several Bentlians, such as Bertram Gross, have explicitly avowed—assume that "everywhere there is one principle of justice, which is the interest of the stronger."[11] On the other hand, a consistent Due-Process Realist believes that the principal ethical consideration in the group struggle is the obligation of official mediators to maximize the opportunities for access and consideration of all relevant interests; of course he accepts, as part of the data of the empirical world, the compromises that reflect specific, albeit temporary, accommodations of group interests. (One is reminded of Margaret Fuller's supposed remark to Thomas Carlyle, "I accept the universe"; and his reputed comment, "By Gad, she'd better!")[12]

In a subsequent article [1958b], Cassinelli developed at greater length some of his reflections on the concept of the public interest. The burden of his essay, however, is an antipositivist, negative critique of Rationalist and Realist public-interest concepts, rather than an affirmative statement of the Idealist position which he admittedly [p. 49] favors. He discusses primarily three questions:

Is there a common interest possessed by the public?

Are public and private interests necessarily in conflict?

Is it the proper function of government to mediate between public and private interests?

His answer to each of these queries is a resounding "No!" But the adjustment by the government of conflict among *private* interests, thinks Cassinelli [p. 59], is a necessary condition of realizing the public interest. Such governmental interest-conflict media-

11. Plato, *The Republic,* Jowett ed. p. 19.
12. Miller [1957, p. 22].

tion, however, is justified neither on the grounds stated by Sorauf nor on those argued by various of the Realist theorists. According to Cassinelli, "these goals—the 'well-being' of the community, support of the government considered legitimate, and perhaps 'peace and prosperity'—are clearly not what democratic theorists have in mind as the highest ends of political association" [p. 58]. He adds [p. 59] that " 'law and order' cannot be the fundamental value of democratic political ethics"; a few pages earlier he had stated that "the desire to support and to defend any particular government is again not exactly what the democrat has in mind when he thinks about the ultimate ethical goal of political relationships."

What, then, do democrats and democratic theorists have in mind when they think of political absolutes? What is the highest ethical goal of political life? Nothing less, says Cassinelli, than the public interest! "The conception of the highest political good," he declares, is the public interest, which "ordinarily refers to the highest goal of political life" [p. 60]. But since Cassinelli defines the public interest only in terms of paraphrases of "highest political good" and "highest ethical goal," and since he nowhere undertakes to define affirmatively what he means to subsume under these supreme and ultimate ends, his concept of the public interest must be considered to be enigmatic. Perhaps it should be added, in fairness to Cassinelli, that he explicitly states that it was not his purpose, in this particular essay, to offer his own alternative conception of the public interest. However, the clear implication seems to be that, since the public interest is an essence to be attributed to, rather than "possessed by," the public, somebody other than the public must determine what are the interests *of* the public. Who is to make such a determination? How? And in terms of what criteria? Cassinelli does not say. Thus, his comments and reflections on the concept leave the public interest a mystery, enshrouded in the golden silence of unspoken—and perhaps unspeakable—words of ultimate wisdom.

   d. The Leys-Perry Report.—The remaining categorization of the concept has come from two well-known philosophers, who served as co-chairmen of the Committee to Advance Original Work in Philosophy. As the result of preliminary circulation of a working draft, the committee collected numerous comments and suggestions from a group of about seventy-five philosophers, lawyers, social scientists, and "practitioners." Following a critical discussion of "the theory of the public interest," as inferred from the literature, from the published remarks of other critics of the concept (such as Banfield, Sorauf, and myself), and from the correspondence with commentators upon the preliminary draft, authors Leys and Perry present the following summary of their findings, with the hope that this "will not close the inquiry but stimulate further investigation":

The "public interest" can have several radically different meanings, as follows:

1. Formal meaning: whatever is the object of duly authorized, governmental action.

   A. Simple conception: the intention of king or parliament.

   B. Pluralistic conception: the objectives that are sanctioned by any legal or political process, it being assumed that, as a matter of fact, decisions are made in various ways and in various places.

2. Substantive meaning: the object that *should* be sought in governmental action (or in non-governmental action that is a delegation of governmental power or accepted in lieu of governmental action.)

   A. Utilitarian or aggregationist conception: the maximization of particular interests.

   B. The decision which results when proper *procedures* are used.

   (i) Simple conceptions: due process of law, majority rule, etc.

   (ii) Pluralistic conceptions: observance of the procedural rules of whatever legal or political process happens to become the decision-maker for a given issue.

   C. A normative conception of public order. . . . It is difficult to give a fair characterization of this conception that will make sense to those who do not share it. [1959, p. 44.]

Leys and Perry disparage acceptance of "the formal meaning of public interest (#1)" as being in effect "an abandonment of any normative conception of the public interest." This, apparently, is a bad thing to do, like abandoning a bride at the altar or abandoning a foundling on a doorstep. There appears to be little to recommend a choice among the remaining alternatives, however. The authors conclude that: "As between the three normative conceptions of 'public interest' (2–A, 2–B, and 2–C), we suggest that a great deal of further reflection is needed" [p. 45]. This may be so; but it does not appear that the Leys-Perry formulation subsumes any ideas or proposals that are novel or not included among the views expressed by the various theorists whose concepts of the public interest we have examined in the preceding chapters.[13] Other than calling for further study of the problems of public-interest theory, the most that Leys and Perry seem to conclude is that sophisticated constructs and concepts are preferable to naive, simple-minded ones. Their discussion was intended, of course, to raise rather than to answer questions. Among the questions thus left unanswered is the one around which both their and our investigations have focused: what is the public interest?

Epilogue

OUR SURVEY OF THE FINDINGS of the critics shows that they have little to add to the results of our own investigation of public-interest theory. Some of them (e.g., Banfield, Sorauf, Leys and Perry) suggest differing perspectives from which the literature may be viewed and appraised. Such alternative formulations do not appear to lead to insights or to comprehension of public-interest theory significantly different from that produced by our own conceptual schema and summary. Any systematic typology

---

13. Possibly the appendices to the Leys-Perry report constitute an exception to the above generalization. I have made no attempt, for instance, to discuss in this work (as Leys and Perry do in their Appendix A) the outdated "affection" doctrine of the United States Supreme Court, which invoked the public interest as a constitutional justification under the Fourteenth Amendment for selective state regulation of private enterprise. In the hands of the Court, this so-called doctrine was never defined as a theoretical concept. It served no more than as a *post hoc* label which the Court attached, for half a century (roughly from 1877–1932), to those few exceptions to the general presumption of *laissez faire, laissez passez* that a majority of the justices were willing to accept. Thus, the affectation doctrine assisted the Court in rationalizing its approval of some kinds of state economic regulation which would have been awkward to justify on the basis of precedent and traditional norms. Such substantive identifications of the public interest have little relevance to contemporary theories of the public interest.

may have utility for analytical purposes, but no matter how the literature is classified and the data are compared, no systematic body of "public-interest theory" appears extant. American writers in the field of political science have evolved neither a unified nor a consistent theory to describe how the public interest *is* defined in governmental decision-making; they have not constructed theoretical models with the degree of precision and specificity necessary if such models are to be used as description of, or as a guide to, the actual behavior of real people. A theory of the public interest in governmental decision-making ought to describe a relationship between concepts of the public interest and official behavior in such terms that it might be possible to attempt to validate empirically hypotheses concerning the relationship. If extant theory does not lend itself to such uses, it is difficult to comprehend the justification for teaching students of political science that subservience to the public interest is a relevant norm of official responsibility.

Moreover, our investigation has failed to reveal a statement of public-interest theory that offers much promise either as a guide to public officials who are supposed to make decisions in the public interest, or to research scholars who might wish to investigate the extent to which governmental decisions are empirically made in the public interest. For either of the latter purposes, it would be necessary to have operational definitions of the public-interest concept; and neither my analysis nor that of other contemporary critics suggests that the public-interest theory prevalent in America today either is or is readily capable of being made operational.

Rationalist theory has limited relevance to the empirical world, since it speaks primarily of faithful execution of decisions that *somebody other than the actor* has made; it offers little guidance to the decision-maker who is expected to make policy in the face of the conflicting demands of an articulate and organized clientele. In fact, the more important the decision—and as a usual consequence, the more complex the decision-making milieu—the less guidance has Rationalist theory to offer. It might, for instance, indicate what would be responsible presidential behavior in signing commissions for the promotional lists of the armed forces; it most certainly will not be very helpful to the president in deciding whether and how to get a man to the moon. To get back down to earth, it will not even tell him when, and in terms of what criteria, he should exercise his veto power, since the Constitution clearly did not presume that the president would take his orders from Congress (or vice versa) in exercising his power to grant or to withhold his approval of enrolled bills—even if we assume, with the Rationalists, that constitutional intent is the fundamental consideration in such circumstances. The theoretical apparatus of the Rationalists, however elegant it otherwise may be, is limited precisely by their insistence that a science of political behavior cannot be concerned with political choice. The model constructed by the Rationalists is a sausage machine: the public will is poured into one end and out of the other end drops neat little segments of the public interest, each wrapped in its own natural casing.

Idealist theory, to the contrary, speaks precisely to the macroscopic type of decision with which the Rationalists cannot be concerned. But what does Idealism have to offer, other than moralistic exhortations to do good? It leaves the decision-maker to rely upon his own best lights, whether these are conceived of as a Platonic soul, a Calvinistic conscience, or as Catholic natural law. It may be that any of these provides the best standards available for guiding some decision-makers in some situations; but labeling as "the public interest" either such a process or the result that it produces adds nothing to what we would have—except from the point of view of the engineering of consent—if there were no such phrase as the public interest. With or without the label, we must rely upon the prior political socialization and the ethical preconditioning of the individual decision-maker for whatever kind or degree of responsibility that ensues in such circumstances.

Moreover, the concept of the *public* interest logically is irrelevant to decision-making in accordance with Idealist theory, in which ultimate obligations and responsibility are nonpolitical. It is neither to the public nor to hierarchical superiors nor to the affected clientele that the decision-maker looks for guidance; his responsibility lies in faithfulness to his personal perception of other abstractions, such as "justice," that are at least equally as devoid of a predictable content as "the public interest." Unless the Idealists are prepared to advocate the "brain-washing" of candidates for public employment to assure the establishment of a single party line among government officials, the practical utility of their theory would seem to be quite limited unless, in the alternative, they can explain how men with differing value orientations are to commune with the infinite and come up with common answers. Idealist theory really implies an officialdom of Supermen, which in turn evokes all of the difficulties to be encountered in breeding a race of official heroes—or, if it makes a difference, of heroic officials. None of the Idealist writers in recent years seem to have improved very much upon Plato's discussion of this subject, nor do they appear to have resolved the age-old dilemma: how to keep the tyrants benevolent.

Realists advise the decision-maker that his job is to resolve the conflicting claims of competing interest groups, and to keep the boat from rocking so far as possible. Except on the merely mechanical and purportedly descriptive level of naive Bentlianism, he should do this with as much consideration as he is capable of giving, or as he can be *made* capable of giving—by the structuring of the decision-making situation—to the probable consequences of his choice. The principal difficulty with the theory, even in its most sophisticated form, lies in its generality, for the Due-Process–Equilibrium Realists describe wondrous engines (including the human mind) into which are poured all sorts of miscellaneous ingredients which, after a decent period of agitation, are spewed forth from time to time, each bearing a union label reading: "Made in the Public Interest in the U.S.A."[14] But their hero is neither the Charlie Chaplin of *Modern Times* nor Prometheus unbound; he is the counterpart of the politician described by Herring in *The Politics of Democracy*.

The problem facing Realist theorists is to demonstrate how it is possible to bridge the hiatus between the ideal they posit and

---

14. Many Due-Process–Equilibrium Realists would insist that the identification of the public interest in accordance with their theory is a probability statement and not a label; but no matter. It looks exactly like a union label in any particular case.

the empirical world. It is true that the statements of at least the Administrative–Due-Process Realists do suggest the possibility of constructing more detailed models of specific decisional processes in particular agencies with identifiable functions to perform. Such models, whether as descriptions of existing agencies, or as blueprints for reorganized or new agencies, might lend themselves, at least in principle, to empirical verification. Assuming, for the sake of argument, that the paperwork can be done, it would still be necessary to construct and implement, upon an experimental basis, at least one model prefabricated political decision-making process; budget estimating might be a good place to begin. Assuming that this also could be done, ahead lie questions of continuous reorganization to cope with predictable problems of obsolescence, the development of more genuinely interchangeable human cogs, and—not least—the impatience of the American public after it becomes known to the world that the Russians have perfected a successfully functioning (and much bigger) organization of the same type several months before the American protomodel is announced. And that announcement, we might as well anticipate, will come at the same time that the American team of responsible budget analysts is about to produce its first under-balanced budget—which will be made, needless to say, in the public interest.

* * *

It may be somewhat difficult for some readers to accept the conclusion that there is no public-interest theory worthy of the name and that the concept itself is significant primarily as a datum of politics. As such, it may at times fulfill a "hair shirt" function, to borrow Sorauf's felicitous phrase; it may also be nothing more than a label attached indiscriminately to a miscellany of particular compromises of the moment. In either case, "the public interest" neither adds to nor detracts from the theory and methods presently available for analyzing political behavior.

I recognize also that there may be readers who will consider this study incomplete, since I have criticized the public-interest theories of other persons without making any attempt to "do something positive" by suggesting a public-interest concept of my own. The expectation that the iconoclast *ought* to pick up the pieces and build a new and better temple on the ruins of the old runs like a steel thread through the moral fiber of most Americans, including academicians. I would dispute the premise. I would also argue, in any event, that if the public-interest concept makes no operational sense, notwithstanding the efforts of a generation of capable scholars, then political scientists might better spend their time nurturing concepts that offer greater promise of becoming useful tools in the scientific study of political responsibility.

references

ADLER, MORTIMER. "Parties and the Common Good," *Review of Politics*, I (1939), 51–83.

ANDREWS, RUSSELL P. *Wilderness Sanctuary*. Rev. ed. ("Inter-University Case Series," No. 13.) University, Ala.: University of Alabama Press, 1954.

APPLEBY, PAUL. *Policy and Administration*. University, Ala.: University of Alabama Press, 1949.

——. *Morality and Administration in Democratic Government*. Baton Rouge: Louisiana State University Press, 1952.

ARNOW, KATHRYN SMUL. *The Consumers' Counsel and the National Bituminous Coal Commission, 1937–1938*. Rev. ed. Washington: *Committee* on Public Administration Cases, 1950.

BAILEY, STEPHEN K. *Congress Makes a Law*. New York: Columbia University Press, 1950.

BEARD, CHARLES A. *The Idea of National Interest*. New York: Macmillan Co., 1934a.

——. *The Open Door at Home: A Trial Philosophy of the National Interest*. New York: Macmillan Co., 1934b.

————. "Neglected Aspects of Political Science," *American Political Science Review*, XLII (1948), 211–22.

BENTLEY, ARTHUR F. *The Process of Government*, 1949 ed. Bloomington, Ind.: Principia Press, 1908.

BERGMANN, GUSTAV, and ZERBY, LEWIS. "The Formalism in Kelsen's Pure Theory of Law," *Ethics*, LV (1945), 110–30.

BERNS, WALTER. *Freedom, Virtue and the First Amendment*. Baton Rouge: Louisiana State University Press, 1957.

BERNSTEIN, MARVER H. *Regulating Business by Independent Commission*. Princeton: Princeton University Press, 1955.

BEUTEL, FREDERICK K. *Some Potentialities of Experimental Jurisprudence as a New Branch of Social Science*. Lincoln: University of Nebraska Press, 1957.

BINKLEY, WILFRED E. *President and Congress*. New York: Alfred Knopf, 1947.

BLOUGH, ROY M. *Price and the Public Interest*. New York: United States Steel Corporation, 1958.

BROWNLOW, LOUIS. *The President and the Presidency*. Chicago: Public Administration Service, 1949.

BURKE, EDMUND. *Works*, Vol. II. 7th ed. Boston: Little, Brown, 1881.

BURNS, JAMES M. *Congress on Trial*. New York: Harper Bros., 1949.

CAHILL, FRED V., JR. *Judicial Legislation: A Study in American Legal Theory*. New York: Ronald Press, 1952.

CARDOZO, BENJAMIN N. *The Nature of the Judicial Process*. New Haven: Yale University Press, 1921.

CASSINELLI, C. W. "Comments on Frank J. Sorauf's 'The Public Interest Reconsidered," *Journal of Politics*, XX (1958a), 553–56.

————. "Some Reflections on the Concept of the Public Interest," *Ethics*, LXIX (1958b), 48–61.

CHAMBERLAIN, JOSEPH P. *Legislative Processes: National and State*. New York: Appleton-Century, 1936.

CHILDS, HARWOOD L. *An Introduction to Public Opinion*. New York: Wiley, 1940.

CLEVELAND, HARLAN. "The Executive and the Public Interest," *Annals of the American Academy of Political and Social Science*, CCCVII (1956), 37–54.

COHEN, FELIX S. "Transcendental Nonsense and the Functional Approach," *Columbia Law Review*, XXXV (1935), 809–49.

COMMITTEE ON POLITICAL PARTIES OF THE AMERICAN POLITICAL SCIENCE ASSOCIATION. "Toward a More Responsible Two-Party System," *American Political Science Review*, XLIV, No. 3, Part 2, Supplement (September, 1950), 1–99. Also published separately by Rinehart and Co.

COOK, THOMAS I., and MOOS, MALCOLM. "The American Idea of International Interest," *American Political Science Review*, XLVII (1953), 28–44.

CORWIN, EDWARD S. *The President: Office and Powers, 1787–1948.* New York: New York University Press, 1948.

DAHL, ROBERT A. *Congress and Foreign Policy.* New York: Harcourt Brace, 1950.

——. "The Concept of Power," *Behavioral Science*, II (1957), 201–15.

——, and LINDBLOM, CHARLES E. *Politics Economics and Welfare.* New York: Harpers, 1953.

DAVIS, KENNETH CULP. "Some Reflections of a Law Professor about Instruction and Research in Public Administration," *American Political Science Review*, XLVII (1953), 728–52.

DE GRAZIA, ALFRED. "The Game Bag," *PROD*, I (May, 1958), 25–26.

DEWEY, JOHN. "Logical Method and Law," *Cornell Law Quarterly*, X (1924), 17–27.

——. *The Public and its Problems.* New York: Henry Holt, 1927.

DICKINSON, JOHN. "Social Order and Political Authority," *American Political Science Review*, XXIII (1929), 293–328, 593–632.

——. "Democratic Realities and Democratic Dogma," *American Political Science Review*, XXIV (1930), 283–309.

DISHMAN, ROBERT B. "The Public Interest in Emergency Labor Disputes," *American Political Science Review*, XLV (1951), 1100–14.

EASTON, DAVID. *The Political System.* New York: Alfred Knopf, 1953.

——. "Limits of the Equilibrium Model in Social Research," in Heinz Eulau, Samuel Eldersveld, and Morris Janowitz (eds.). *Political Behavior: A Reader in Theory and Research.* Glencoe, Ill.: The Free Press, 1956.

EBENSTEIN, WILLIAM. *The Pure Theory of Law.* Madison: University of Wisconsin Press, 1945.

EULAW, HEINZ; WAHLKE, JOHN C.; BUCHANAN, WILLIAM; and FERGUSON, LEROY C. "The Role of the Representative: Some Empirical Observations on the Theory of Edmund Burke," *American Political Science Review*, LIII (1959), 742–56.

FAINSOD, MERLE. "Some Reflections on the Nature of the Regulatory Process," in Carl J. Friedrich and Edward S. Mason (eds.). *Public Policy.* Vol. I. Cambridge: Harvard University Press, 1940.

FARRAND, MAX (ed). *The Records of the Federal Convention of 1787,* Vol. I. Rev. ed. New Haven: Yale University Press, 1937.

FARRIS, CHARLES D. "A Method of Determining Ideological Groupings in the Congress," *Journal of Politics*, XX (1958), 308–38.

FENNO, RICHARD F., JR. "President-Cabinet Relations: A Pattern and a Case Study," *American Political Science Review*, LII (1958), 388–405.

FINER, HERMAN. "Better Government Personnel," *Political Science Quarterly*, LI (1936), 569–99.

———. "Administrative Responsibility in Democratic Government," *Public Administration Review*, I (1941), 335–50.

FRANK, JEROME. *Law and the Modern Mind*. New York: Coward-McCann, 1930.

———. *Courts on Trial*. Princeton: Princeton University Press, 1949.

FREUND, ERNST. *Standards of American Legislation*. Chicago: University of Chicago Press, 1917.

FRIEDMANN, WOLFGANG. *Legal Theory*. 3d ed. London: Stevens, 1953.

FRIEDRICH, CARL J. "Public Policy and the Nature of Administrative Responsibility," in Carl J. Friedrich and Edward S. Mason (eds.). *Public Policy*, Vol. I, Cambridge: Harvard University Press, 1940.

———. *Constitutional Government and Democracy*. Rev. ed. Boston: Ginn & Co., 1950.

GALLOWAY, GEORGE B. *The Legislative Process in Congress*. New York: Thomas Y. Crowell, 1953.

GRAHAM, GEORGE A. *Morality in American Politics*. New York: Random House, 1952.

GRAICUNAS, V. A. "Relationship in Organization," in Luther Gulick and Lyndall Urwick (eds.). *Papers on the Science of Administration*. New York: Institute of Public Administration, 1937.

GRASSMUCK, GEORGE L. *Sectional Biases in Congress on Foreign Policy*. Baltimore: Johns Hopkins University Press, 1951.

GREER, SCOTT. "Individual Participation in Mass Society," in Roland Young (ed.). *Approaches to the Study of Politics*. Evanston: Northwestern University Press, 1958.

GRIFFITH, ERNEST S. "The Changing Pattern of Public Policy Formation," *American Political Science Review*, XXXVIII (1944), 445–59.

———. *Congress: Its Contemporary Role*. New York: New York University Press, 1951.

GROSS, BERTRAM. Book review of Bentley's *The Process of Government*, *American Political Science Review*, XLIV (1950), 742–48.

———. *The Legislative Struggle*. New York: McGraw-Hill, 1953.

GRUNDSTEIN, NATHAN D. "Law and the Morality of Administration," *George Washington Law Review*, XXI (1953a), 265–310.

———. "Bentham's Introduction to the Principles of Morals and Legislation," *Journal of Public Law*, II (1953b), 344–69.

GUETZKOW, HAROLD. "Building Models about Small Groups," in

Roland Young (ed.). *Approaches to the Study of Politics.* Evanston: Northwestern University Press, 1958.

GULICK, LUTHER, and URWICK, LYNDALL, (eds.). *Papers on the Science of Administration.* New York: Institute of Public Administration, 1937.

HAINES, CHARLES GROVE. "General Observations on the Effects of Personal, Political, and Economic Influences in the Decisions of Judges," *Illinois Law Review,* XVII (1922), 96–116.

HAMILTON, ALEXANDER, MADISON, JAMES, and JAY, JOHN. *The Federalist.* 1901 ed. 2 vols. Washington: M. Walter Dunne, Universal Classics.

HAND, LEARNED. "Is There a Common Will?" *Michigan Law Review,* XXVIII (1929), 46–52.

HART, JAMES. *The American Presidency in Action: 1789.* New York: Macmillan Co., 1948.

HAZLITT, HENRY. *A New Constitution Now.* New York: McGraw-Hill, 1942.

HECKSCHER, AUGUST. "Woodrow Wilson: An Appraisal and Recapitulation," in Earl Latham (ed.). *The Philosophy and Policies of Woodrow Wilson.* Chicago: University of Chicago Press, 1958.

HELMS, E. ALLEN. "The President and Party Politics," *Journal of Politics,* XI (1949), 42–64.

HERRING, E. PENDLETON. *Group Representation before Congress.* Baltimore: Johns Hopkins University Press, 1929.

———. *Public Administration and the Public Interest.* New York: McGraw-Hill, 1936.

———. *The Politics of Democracy.* New York: Norton, 1940a.

———. *Presidential Leadership.* New York: Rinehart, 1940b.

HOLCOMBE, ARTHUR N. *Our More Perfect Union.* Cambridge: Harvard University Press, 1950.

HOLMES, OLIVER WENDELL, JR. "Common Carriers and the Common Law," *American Law Review,* XIII (1879), 609–31.

———. "Privilege, Malice and Intent," *Harvard Law Review,* VIII (1894), 1–14.

———. "The Path of the Law," *Harvard Law Review,* X (1897), 451–78.

———. *Collected Legal Papers.* New York: Harcourt, Brace, 1920.

[HOOVER] Commission on Organization of the Executive Branch of the Government. *Task Force Report on Legal Services and Procedure.* Washington: Government Printing Office, 1955a.

———. *Legal Services and Procedure.* Washington: Government Printing Office, 1955b.

HUITT, RALPH K. "The Congressional Committee: A Case Study," *American Political Science Review,* XLVIII (1954), 340–65.

HUTCHESON, JOSEPH C., JR. "The Judgment Intuitive: The Function of the 'Hunch' in Judicial Decision," *Cornell Law Quarterly,* XIV (1929), 274–88.

HYMAN, SIDNEY. *The American President.* New York: Harper Bros., 1954.

HYNEMAN, CHARLES S. *Bureaucracy in a Democracy.* New York: Harper Bros., 1950.

IRISH, MARIAN D. "The Organization Man in the Presidency," *Journal of Politics,* XX (1958), 259–77.

JORDAN, ELIJAH. *Theory of Legislation: An Essay on the Dynamics of Public Mind.* Chicago: University of Chicago Press, 1930.

KELSEN, HANS. *General Theory of Law and State.* Cambridge: Harvard University Press, 1946.

KENDALL, WILLMOORE. "Prolegomena to any Future Work on Majority Rule," *Journal of Politics,* XII (1950), 694–713.

KEY, V. O., JR. *Politics, Parties, and Pressure Groups.* 3d. ed. New York: Crowell, 1952.

———. "The State of the Discipline," *American Political Science Review,* LII (1958), 961–71.

KOENIG, LOUIS W. "The Man and the Institution," *Annals of the American Academy of Political and Social Science,* CCCXCVII (1956), 10–14.

LANDIS, JAMES M. *The Administrative Process.* New Haven: Yale University Press, 1938.

LASKI, HAROLD J. "The Parliamentary and Presidential Systems," *Public Administration Review,* IV (1944), 347–59.

LASSWELL, HAROLD D. "Current Studies of the Decision Process: Automation versus Creativity," *Western Political Quarterly,* VIII (1955), 381–99.

LATHAM, EARL. *The Group Basis of Politics.* Ithaca: Cornell University Press, 1952a.

———. "The Group Basis of Politics: Notes for a Theory," *American Political Science Review,* XLVI (1952b), 376–97.

LEISERSON, AVERY. *Administrative Regulation.* Chicago: University of Chicago Press, 1942.

LEYS, WAYNE A. R. "Ethics and Administrative Discretion," *Public Administration Review,* III (1943), 10–23.

———. *Ethics for Policy Decisions.* New York: Prentice-Hall, 1952.

———. "Philosophy and the Public Interest," *PROD,* II (September, 1958), 12–13.

——— and PERRY, CHARNER, M. *Philosophy and the Public Interest.* Chicago: Committee to Advance Original Work in Philosophy, 1959.

LINK, ARTHUR S. "Portrait of the President," in Earl Latham (ed.).

The Philosophy and Policies of Woodrow Wilson. Chicago: University of Chicago Press, 1958.

LIPPMANN, WALTER. *The Phantom Public*. New York: Harcourt, Brace and Co., 1930.

———. *The Public Philosophy*. Boston: Little, Brown, 1955.

LLEWELLYN, KARL. "A Realistic Jurisprudence—The Next Step," *Columbia Law Review*, XXX (1930), 431–65.

———. "Some Realism about Realism," *Harvard Law Review*, XLIV (1931), 1222–64.

———. "The Constitution as an Institution," *Columbia Law Review*, XXXIV (1934), 1–40.

LONG, NORTON. "Power and Administration," *Public Administration Review*, IX (1949), 257–64.

———. "Bureaucracy and Constitutionalism," *American Political Science Review*, XLVI (1952), 808–18.

———. "Public Policy and Administration: The Goals of Rationality and Responsibility," *Public Administration Review*, XIV (1954), 22–31.

MAASS, ARTHUR. "In Accord with the Program of the President?" in Carl J. Friedrich and J. K. Galbraith (eds.). *Public Policy*, Vol. IV. Cambridge: Harvard University Press, 1953.

MacIVER, ROBERT M. *The Web of Government*. New York: Macmillan Co., 1947.

MACMAHON, ARTHUR. "Specialization and the Public Interest," in O. B. Conaway, Jr. (ed.). *Democracy in Federal Administration*. Washington: U.S. Dept. of Agriculture Graduate School, 1956.

———. "Woodrow Wilson: Political Leader and Administrator," in Earl Latham (ed.). *The Philosophy and Policies of Woodrow Wilson*. Chicago: University of Chicago Press, 1958.

MARCANTONIO, VITO. *I Vote My Conscience*. New York: Vito Marcantonio Memorial, 1956.

MARCH, JAMES C. "An Introduction to the Theory and Measurement of Influence," *American Political Science Review*, XLIX (1955), 431–51.

MASON, ALPHEUS T. "The Supreme Court: Instrument of Power or Revealed Truth?" *Boston University Law Review*, XXXIII (1953), 279–336.

———. *The Supreme Court from Taft to Warren*. Baton Rouge: Louisiana State University Press, 1958.

——— and BEANEY, WILLIAM M. *American Constitutional Law*. 2d. ed. New York: Prentice-Hall, 1959.

McCLOSKY, HERBERT. "The Fallacy of Absolute Majority Rule," *Journal of Politics*, XI (1949), 637–54.

McCONNELL, GRANT. *The Steel Seizure of 1952*. "Inter-University Case

Series," No. 52. University, Ala.: University of Alabama Press, 1960.

McGovern, William M., and Collier, David S. *Radicals and Conservatives*. Chicago: Regnery, 1957.

McMurray, Howard J. "The Responsible Majority—Some Reflections on Political Parties," *Western Political Quarterly*, XI (1958), 175–82.

Meyerson, Martin, and Banfield, Edward C. *Politics, Planning and the Public Interest*. Glencoe, Ill.: The Free Press, 1955.

Miller, Perry. "I Find No Intellect Comparable to My Own," *American Heritage*, VIII (February, 1957), 22–25, 96–99.

Monypenny, Phillip. "A Code of Ethics as a Means of Controlling Administrative Conduct," *Public Administration Review*, XIII (1953a), 184–87.

———. "A Code of Ethics for Public Administration," *George Washington Law Review*, XXI (1953b), 423–44.

Morgenthau, Hans J. *In Defense of the National Interest*. New York: Alfred Knopf, 1951.

———. "Another 'Great Debate': The National Interest of the United States," *American Political Science Review*, XLVI (1952), 961–88.

Morstein Marx, Fritz. "Administrative Ethics and the Rule of Law," *American Political Science Review*, XLIII (1949), 1119–44.

Muzzey, David S. *An American History*. Boston: Ginn Co., 1911.

Neustadt, Richard E. "Presidency and Legislation: The Growth of Central Clearance," *American Political Science Review*, XLVIII (1954), 641–71.

———. "Presidency and Legislation: Planning the President's Program," *American Political Science Review*, XLIX (1955), 980–1020.

Parkinson, C. Northcote. *Parkinson's Law and Other Studies in Administration*. Boston: Houghton Mifflin, 1957.

Patterson, Caleb Perry. *Presidential Government in the United States*. Chapel Hill: University of North Carolina Press, 1947.

Paul, Julius. "The Role of the Judge in Jerome Frank's Philosophy of Law," *Oklahoma Law Review*, X (1957), 143–66.

———. "Jerome Frank's Contributions to the Philosophy of American Legal Realism," *Vanderbilt Law Review*, XI (1958), 753–82.

Payne, W. Scott. *The Latin American Proceeding*. Washington: Committee on Public Administration Cases, 1949.

Pfiffner, John, and Presthus, Robert V. *Public Administration*. Rev. ed. New York: Ronald Press, 1953.

PLATO. *The Republic*. (*The Works of Plato*, trans. *Benjamin Jowett*, Vol. II.) New York: Tudor, n.d.

POUND, ROSCOE. "A Call for a Realist Jurisprudence," *Harvard Law Review*, XLIV (1931), 697–711.

———. *Social Control through Law*. New Haven: Yale University Press, 1942.

PRESIDENT'S COMMITTEE ON ADMINISTRATIVE MANAGEMENT. *Report with Special Studies*. Washington: Government Printing Office, 1937.

PRICE, DON K. "The Parliamentary and Presidential Systems," *Public Administration Review*, III (1943), 317–34.

———. "A Response to Mr. Laski," *Public Administration Review*, IV (1944), 360–63.

RANNEY, AUSTIN. "Toward a More Responsible Two-Party System: A Commentary," *American Political Science Review*, VLV (1951), 488–500.

RATNER, SIDNEY. "A. F. Bentley's Inquiries into the Behavioral Sciences and the Theory of Scientific Inquiry," in Richard W. Taylor (ed.). *Life, Language, Law*. Yellow Springs, Ohio: Antioch Press, 1957.

REDFORD, EMMETTE S. *Administration of National Economic Control*. New York: Macmillan Co., 1952.

———. "The Protection of the Public Interest with Special Reference to Administrative Regulation," *American Political Science Review*, XLVIII (1954), 1103–13.

———. *Ideal and Practice in Public Administration*. University, Ala.: University of Alabama Press, 1958.

RIGGS, FRED W. *Pressures on Congress*. New York: King's Crown Press, 1950.

RIKER, WILLIAM H. "The Senate and American Federalism," *American Political Science Review*, XLIX (1955), 452–69.

ROBINSON, JAMES A. "Newtonianism and the Constitution," *Midwest Journal of Political Science*, I (1957), 252–66.

———. "Decision Making in the House Rules Committee," *Administrative Science Quarterly*, III (1958), 73–86.

RODELL, FRED. *Woe Unto You, Lawyers!* New York: Reynal and Hitchcock, 1939.

ROOSEVELT, THEODORE. *An Autobiography*. New York: Charles Scribner's, 1913.

ROSSITER, CLINTON. *The American Presidency*. New York: Signet Key Books, 1956.

SANDBURG, CARL. *The People, Yes*. New York: Harcourt, Brace, 1936.

SCHATTSCHNEIDER, ELMER E. "Political Parties and the Public Interest," *Annals of the American Academy of Political and Social Science*, CCLXXX (1952), 18–26.

SCHUBERT, GLENDON. Book review of Cahill's *Judicial Legislation, American Political Science Review*, XLVI (1952), 1180–82.

———. "The Twenty-one Day Rule," *Political Science*, V (1953a), 16–29.

———. "The Steel Case: Presidential Responsibility and Judicial Irresponsibility, *Western Political Quarterly*, VI (1953b), 61–77.

———. *The Presidency in the Courts*. Minneapolis: University of Minnesota Press, 1957a.

———. "'The Public Interest' in Administrative Decision-Making: Theorem, Theosophy, or Theory?" *American Political Science Review*, LI (1957b), 346–68.

———. "The Theory of 'The Public Interest' in Judicial Decision-Making," *Midwest Journal of Political Science*, II (1958a), 1–25.

———. "The Theory of the Public Interest," *PROD*, I (May, 1958b), 34–36.

SHAPLEY, L. S., and SHUBIK, MARTIN. "A Method for Evaluating the Distribution of Power in a Committee System," *American Political Science Review*, XLVIII (1954), 787–92.

SHRIVER, HARRY C. (ed.). *Justice Oliver Wendell Holmes: His Book Notices and Uncollected Letters and Papers*. New York: Central Book Co., 1936.

SIMON, HERBERT A. *Administrative Behavior: A Study of Decision-Making Processes in Administrative Organization*. Rev. ed. New York: Macmillan Co., 1957.

———. SMITHBURG, DONALD, and THOMPSON, VICTOR. *Public Administration*. New York: Alfred Knopf, 1950.

SNYDER, RICHARD C., BRUCK, H. W., and SAPIN, BURTON. *Decision-Making as an Approach to the Study of International Politics*. (Organizational Behavior Section, "Foreign Policy Analysis Series," No. 3.) Princeton: Princeton University Press, 1954.

SORAUF, FRANK J. "The Public Interest Reconsidered," *Journal of Politics*, XIX (1957), 616–39.

STEIN, HAROLD (ed.). *Public Administration and Policy Development*. New York: Harcourt, Brace, 1952.

STONE, HARLAN F. *The Common Law in the United States*. Cambridge: Harvard University Press, 1937.

STONE, JULIUS. *The Province and Function of Law*. Cambridge: Harvard University Press, 1950.

STRAUSS, LEO. *Natural Right and History*. Chicago: University of Chicago Press, 1953.

TAFT, WILLIAM HOWARD. *Our Chief Magistrate and His Powers*. New York: Columbia University Press, 1916.

TAYLOR, RICHARD W. "Arthur F. Bentley's Political Science," *Western Political Quarterly*, V (1952), 214–30.

THACH, CHARLES C. *The Creation of the Presidency, 1775–1789.* Baltimore: Johns Hopkins University Press, 1923.

TRUMAN, DAVID B. *The Governmental Process.* New York: Alfred Knopf, 1951.

TURNER, JULIUS. "Responsible Parties: A Dissent from the Floor," *American Political Science Review*, XLV (1951), 143–52.

———. *Party and Constituency: Pressures on Congress.* Baltimore: Johns Hopkins University Press, 1952.

VOSE, CLEMENT E. "Litigation as a Form of Pressure Group Activity," *Annals of the American Academy of Political and Social Science*, CCCXIX (1958), 20–31.

———. *Caucasians Only: The Supreme Court, the NAACP, and the Restrictive Covenant Cases.* Berkeley and Los Angeles: University of California Press, 1959.

WALDO, DWIGHT. *The Administrative State.* New York: Ronald Press, 1948.

WALKER, HARVEY. *The Legislative Process.* New York: Ronald Press, 1948.

WANN, A. J. "The Development of Woodrow Wilson's Theory of the Presidency: Continuity and Change," in Earl Latham (ed.). *The Philosophy and Policies of Woodrow Wilson.* Chicago: University of Chicago Press, 1958.

WELDON, T. D. *The Vocabulary of Politics.* Great Britain: Penguin Books, The Pelican Philosophy Series, 1953.

WESTERFIELD, H. BRADFORD. *Foreign Policy and Party Politics: Pearl Harbor to Korea.* New Haven: Yale University Press, 1955.

WHITE, WILLIAM S. *Citadel: The Story of the U.S. Senate.* New York: Harper Bros., 1956.

WHYTE, WILLIAM H. *The Organization Man.* Garden City: Doubleday Anchor, 1956.

WILLOUGHBY, W. F. *The Principles of Legislative Organization and Administration.* Washington: Brookings Institution, 1934.

WILSON, WOODROW. *Congressional Government.* 15th ed. Boston: Houghton Mifflin, 1885.

———. *Constitutional Government in the United States.* New York: Columbia University Press, 1908.

WILTSE, CHARLES M. "The Representative Function of Bureaucracy," *American Political Science Review*, XXXV (1941), 510–16.

YOUNG, ROLAND. "Woodrow Wilson's *Congressional Government* Reconsidered," in Earl Latham (ed.). *The Philosophy and Policies of Woodrow Wilson.* Chicago: University of Chicago Press, 1958.

index

85
88